# AN ACTOR PREPARES

# AN ACTOR
# PREPARES

*by Constantin Stanislavski*

TRANSLATED BY
ELIZABETH REYNOLDS HAPGOOD
INTRODUCTION BY JOHN GIELGUD

THEATRE ARTS BOOKS

NEW YORK

*Twenty-fifth Printing, April 1972*

ISBN 0-87830-001-5

Theatre Arts Books are published
at 333 Sixth Avenue, New York 10014

PRINTED IN THE UNITED STATES OF AMERICA

# CONTENTS

# NOTE BY THE TRANSLATOR

FRIENDS of Mr. Stanislavski have long known that he wished to leave a record of the methods by which the Moscow Art Theatre was built up, in such a form that it could be of use to actors and producers after his death. The first time he mentioned this wish to me he spoke of the projected work as a grammar of acting. In his own *My Life in Art,* and in similar expressions by persons who studied under him, a wholly different contribution has been made, one much easier, and in his opinion of lesser importance. A manual, a handbook, a working text-book has been his dream, and a most difficult one to realize.

Since the modern theatre came into existence, something like three centuries ago, conventions have accumulated, outlived their usefulness, and become hardened, so that they stand in the way of fresh art and sincere emotion on the stage. For forty years the effort of the Moscow Art Company has been to get rid of what has become artificial, and therefore an impediment, and to prepare the actor to present the externals of life and their inner repercussions with convincing psychological truthfulness.

How was this long and difficult process to be put into a book? Mr. Stanislavski felt the need of a freedom of speech, especially about the faults that harass actors, that he would not have if he used the names of his actual players, from Moskvin and Kachalov down to the very beginners, and therefore he decided on a semi-fiction form. That he himself appears under the name of Tortsov can scarcely escape the astute reader, nor is it difficult to see that the enthusiastic student who keeps the record of the lessons is the Stanislavski of half a century ago who was feeling his way toward the methods best suited to mirror the modern world.

There is no claim made here to actual invention. The author is most ready to point out that a genius like Salvini or Duse may use without theory the right emotions and expressions that to the less inspired but intelligent student need to be taught. What Stanislavski has undertaken is not to discover a truth but to bring the truth in usable form within the reach of those actors and producers who are fairly well equipped by nature and who are willing to undergo the necessary discipline. The book does include, again and again, statements of general principles of art, but the great task set for himself by the author has been the embodiment of those principles in the simplest working examples, to be laboured over day after day and month after month. He has endeavoured to make the examples so simple, so near to the emotions that can be found as well in one country as in another, that they can be adapted to the needs of actors whether they happen to be born in Russia or Germany, in Italy, France, Poland, or America.

Of the importance of such a working record, in order that the greatest of modern acting companies shall shed its beams as far and as wide as may be, little need be said. What would we not give for detailed notes of how Molière rehearsed his own plays,—rehearsals of which echoes, true or outworn, remain in the Comédie Française? Or can the value be estimated that would inhere in a full picture of Shakespeare in the theatre, drilling his actors in *The Tempest, Romeo and Juliet,* or *King Lear?*

E. R. H.

# INTRODUCTION

## by John Gielgud

STANISLAVSKI'S now famous book is a contribution to the theatre and its students all over the world. The barrier of language is always a handicap in our ability to share and appreciate the fine work of the foreign theatre. Music, ballet, films even (with the help of translated titles)—these we can more easily enjoy. But one is apt to distrust one's judgment when one sees a play in a language one does not understand. It is easy to be too greatly impressed by the unfamiliar. After all, one says to oneself, the French, the Italians, the Russians are volatile expressive people— they convey so much with their eyes and hands and shoulders— their languages are more musical, more rhythmic than our own —they are trained in the grand style. Training—Ah, there it is— the eternal argument for and against dramatic schools and the necessary apprenticeship for our profession which can never, unfortunately, be sealed by a diploma. The skill of a player—in his early years at least—is so hard to assess in concrete terms.

But here, in this book, a fine actor and consummate director has found time to explain a thousand things that have always troubled actors and fascinated students, things that all of us players have discussed in our clumsy egotistical way at rehearsals and between performances all our lives, but that we have never been able to express in a simple, practical way in general constructive terms.

Stanislavski, an elderly man when he wrote this book, can look back on his life as an artist with a wise and tranquil vision. He is an authority. You know he has no axe to grind. He is not concerned with the commercial theatre as we know it in Western Europe—not for him the smash hit or sensational failure, the unions, the gossip, the publicity, the star system, the three-year run. He is an Olympian, a specialist in every department of the theatre, who cares so passionately for his art that he wishes to bequeath something from his great store of experience and knowledge to anyone who cares to read what he has set down. And, because he is an expert, writing of what he knows and loves, he is also a fascinating and lucid writer. The book is absorbing. One is enthralled by it—one cannot put it down.

In it there is much wonderful understanding and advice—both for those who practice acting and direction, and those who only study it. How to relax, to control the body. How to study a part, to work with imagination, to build a performance from within. How to work with other actors, the give and take, how to regard the audience so that one may control their reactions at certain times and allow them to take control at others. The style of playing in classical and realistic work, the art of concentration. All these matters are discussed and examined with masterly clearness and simplicity.

Stanislavski's theatre is a legend. Few are old enough to have seen it, and some of us may think, perhaps, that in perspective it has acquired too great a posthumous reputation. We are sometimes inclined to smile when our elders hold forth on the famous days that are no more—expatiating on the great Shakespearian productions of their youth, the theatre of Booth and Ada Rehan and Irving, of Ellen Terry, Sarah Bernhardt and Eleonora Duse—and the revolutionary struggles of the stage designer and director in the early nineteen-hundreds—Craig and Appia, Serge Diaghilev, Jacques Copeau, Max Reinhardt, Granville-Barker and Stanislavski.

But in this book, and in the author's earlier biography *My Life in Art,* we cannot help feeling how universal are the problems, the anxieties and difficulties of the theatre all over the world, in whatever language, for every succeeding generation. The theatre needs leaders, and in our own day, when leading figures, in the theatre as elsewhere, are no longer able, owing to world conditions, to dominate as autocrats, where syndicates govern and unions dictate, the counsel of a great artist who is also a great authority is doubly precious.

They say that Karsavina and Nijinski, at the height of their talents and success, went daily to their classes, under the great maestro Enrico Cecchetti, and were dressed down and disciplined with the same severity that was meted out to the youngest students of the Imperial Ballet School. Similarly, the great musical virtuosi of earlier generations would return each year to Paris or Vienna to study with their teachers. Only in the theatre does the successful star, whether young or middle-aged, work without steady disciplined supervision. A fine director may influence him, especially during rehearsals. An occasional criticism from a casual friend or a discerning critic may strike him as helpfully constructive. If he is an artist of integrity he may improve through his own watchfulness and concentration. Actors are, on the whole, conscientious creatures, but the strain of long runs without expert supervision is a danger to their emotional natures. Players trust their instinct, both in creating and sustaining a performance—but instinct can lead them astray when repetition has dulled the first creative invention. It is even easy to lose all spontaneity through an excess of conscientiousness. To whom shall the successful actor turn for true criticism and constructive advice as he encounters the perils and continual problems of his career? To whom can the student go when he embarks on the first perilous seas of stage experience?

In spite of their self-centredness, actors are uncertain in their hearts, though they may appear boundlessly confident before an audience. A tactless director whom they do not wholly admire, or whom they think prejudiced or personally hostile, can destroy their belief in themselves easily enough. Their knowledge is picked up haphazardly over many years, and they hardly dare to advise each other about acting because they feel that for every player the problem is a different one, a private secret to be jealously preserved. There are few set rules, except the most elementary—audibility, imagination, concentration. Actors fear lest they may become old fashioned and stilted on the one hand or slapdash and newfangled on the other. The basic craftsmanship—the five-finger exercises, the physical dexterity, the quickness of eye and hand and lips, these things are not easy to achieve. They are not practised or perfected in a daily routine as they are by executants of the sister arts, whether they are successful virtuosi or struggling beginners. Often players do not realise their own limitations or possibilities until they find themselves rehearsing a part which makes big demands upon them. Then they are not prepared—they lose their voices, find their costumes too heavy, their tongues become twisted in trying to sustain long speeches, they clip their words or find themselves out of breath. They do not excel in costume and modern dress to equal advantage—they are juveniles or character actors, but seldom both. Rarely are they equally at home in several different types of play. Stanislavski is aware of all these difficulties. He describes them vividly. He has tried to answer many questions. There are people who will say that his method is not practical for the commercial theatre. But this book is not a set textbook. It merely discusses difficulties, presents problems and suggests solutions.

Of course there are no practical directions in the book for the staging of the average commercial modern play. But the theory is what is important.

One can apply the Moscow Art theory, the art of living every moment of the part, to Shakespeare and the classics. But, you may say, apply it to *Hay Fever* and it easily becomes ridiculous. I am not so sure. I am pretty certain that the actor trained in the Stanislavski school would carry a tray in a farce comedy *better* than any actor trained in the normal Anglo-Saxon manner. Then too, while a Stanislavski version of *Hay Fever* might be quite different from Noel Coward's—entirely removed from his English conception of life in a riverside country cottage—it might still be able to amuse a Russian audience hugely (and intrigue an English audience as well). It might be a production which conveyed the spirit of the play wonderfully and made its own individual comment for Russian audiences who were amused by the situations though unfamiliar with English life. The Habima Theatre production of *Twelfth Night,* I remember, was altogether different in spirit from our traditional approach to Shakespeare's play. Yet it could hardly fail to delight audiences everywhere, as it did in London, because the acting and the direction were so extraordinarily creative and original.

I do not see any reason why Stanislavski's system should apply only to Russia. All schemes of training rest on the importance of finding young people who are really talented, and not lazy or stagestruck merely, and are prepared to go through a training course. The only danger is that unless a theatre school is able, from its own groups and with the help of a commercial management, to develop a *working* group of players, who can, after a year or so, act plays before paying audiences, it may not go very far.

Every young actor must wish, when he is very young, to be told the things that Stanislavski tells of in his book. And for the director, and the more experienced actor, too, Stanislavski's ability to distinguish between a cheap effect on the audience and the real effect of the artist must be immensely valuable. Another value of a studio like Stanislavski's is that it may lead young people into designing, directing, and other branches of the theatre, even if they have no talent for acting, but a real talent for other service to the theatre, as very often happens.

In Russia and on the Continent the theatre is taken seriously as an art. In Anglo-Saxon countries, it is, if you generalize, a business. The actor's looks, his sex appeal, his personality, count for far more in our theatre than in Stanislavski's. People drift into the acting profession for a dozen reasons besides real ability. There is not, at present, the same opportunity to build up a serious repertory theatre. There is no theatre for the classics in America—and it is deeply needed for the good of the theatre itself, as well as for the actors and for audiences—and without it an actor has very little chance to play the great parts. The actor, in these days, has often to make up his mind whether to be popular or to be a good actor. And often it is hard to gauge the difference between popularity and real talent. Alas, the modern commercial theatre is bound to be a bitter disappointment to those trained in Stanislavski's theories. But it is our theatre which is at fault and not the training.

Of course, a great personality, a really great 'star' actor, would be liable to disrupt Stanislavski's type of theatre. I should like to have asked Stanislavski how he could reconcile the supreme art of many of the great players of the past with the bad companies and the bad plays they often appeared in. Actors' taste in plays is seldom discerning. They are too fond of personal success, the limelight, the round of applause as they go off the stage. When they are offered a part they count their 'sides' instead of reading the play.

This book gives some of the reasons why such ambitions are unworthy, why a great artist should seek for truth and dignity and style in acting, why he must have a true appreciation of the quality of the play itself, and try to understand the intentions of his author and director, and help the efforts of his fellow players to work with him to interpret these intentions properly.

Many leading actors try to influence their companies by directing the plays in which they appear. Stanislavski himself did so, but often he played a supporting role rather than the leading part. In our day Laurence Olivier, Noel Coward, Maurice Evans, and myself have followed his example. Irving and Bernhardt directed, but always played the star part themselves. To combine two such important functions is exhausting and hazardous—but if it succeeds, it does often produce unusually successful results, and the presence of the director at every performance improves discipline and an adherence to the original mood of the rehearsals, which may otherwise deteriorate in a long run.

Are the Russian and the Continental theatres the only ones that produce great actors with true genius for direction also? Though the great actors of the last generation were often good directors, their attention was usually concentrated around themselves. They could not, or would not, have directed or acted in great productions of *The Cherry Orchard* or *Love For Love,* plays which were not written to show off individual stars.

Stanislavski's book is amazingly modern. We move very slowly in the theatre, almost imperceptibly changes come about. This book was published in New York in 1936. It must have been written over many years. How little the technique of production has changed in all that time! With the sole and honourable exception of Mr. Thornton Wilder's two plays, *Our Town* and *The Skin of Our Teeth,* we have seen little in England or America which creates any kind of revolution in the actor's craft or the director's problems. In other fields violent changes have set in—Technicolor, the talkies, television follow on one another's heels. But in the living theatre we lack writers, and above all, writers who can work with directors as Obey worked with St. Denis, as Heggen has worked with Logan, Williams with Kazan. If only there were companies of actors who would stay together under the same director, with authors working to provide them with plays and preparing them in a settled repertory theatre. No, say the managers, the authors demand full royalties on a continuous run—No, say the actors and directors, the temptation is too great. Times are hard. We need money. We must make films, do radio, keep ourselves free to put up our price as soon as we become popular. This was not Stanislavski's way—Popularity, success, those were not his slogans. He was a true artist in the deepest sense, and when you read his book, you feel how much more he had to give to the theatre than the mere trappings which so often delude its most ardent followers.

AN ACTOR PREPARES

# CHAPTER ONE

# The First Test

## I

WE WERE excited as we waited for our first lesson with the Director, Tortsov, today. But he came into our class only to make the unexpected announcement that in order to become better acquainted with us, he wished us to give a performance in which we should act bits from plays chosen by us. His purpose is to see us on the stage against the background of scenery, in make-up, in costume, behind footlights, with all the accessories. Only then, said he, will it be possible to judge our dramatic quality.

At first only a few favoured the proposed test. Among these were a stocky young fellow, Grisha Govorkov, who had already played in some small theatre; a tall, beautiful blonde, called Sonya Veliaminova; and a lively, noisy chap named Vanya Vyuntsov.

Gradually we all became accustomed to the idea of the coming try-out. The shining footlights grew more tempting and the performance soon seemed interesting, useful, even necessary.

In making our choices I, and two friends, Paul Shustov and Leo Pushchin, were at first modest. We thought of vaudeville or light comedy. But all around us we heard great names pronounced—Gogol, Ostrovski, Chekhov, and others. Imperceptibly we found that we had stepped ahead in our ambitions and would play something romantic, in costume, in verse.

I was tempted by the figure of Mozart; Leo by that of Salieri; Paul thought of Don Carlos. Then we began to discuss Shakespeare, and my own choice fell on Othello. When Paul agreed to play Iago. everything was decided. As we were leaving the theatre we were told that the first rehearsal was fixed for the next day.

When I reached home, late, I took down my copy of *Othello,* settled myself comfortably on the sofa, opened my book and began to read. Hardly had I read two pages when I was seized with a desire to act. In spite of myself, my hands, arms, legs, face, facial muscles and something inside of me all began to move. I declaimed the text. Suddenly I discovered a large ivory paper-cutter. I stuck it into my belt like a dagger. My fuzzy bath towel served as a white headcloth. Out of my sheets and blankets I made a kind of shirt and gown. My umbrella was pressed into service as a scimitar, but I had no shield. Here it occurred to me that in the dining-room which adjoined my room there was a big tray. With the shield in my hand I felt myself to be a genuine warrior. Yet my general aspect was modern and civilized, whereas Othello was African in origin and must have something suggestive of primitive life, perhaps a tiger, in him. In order to recall, suggest, and fix the walk of an animal, I began a whole new set of exercises.

Many of these moments I felt to be in a high degree successful. I had worked almost five hours without noticing the passage of time. To me this seemed to show that my inspiration was real.

2

I awoke much later than usual, rushed into my clothes and dashed to the theatre. As I went into the rehearsal room, where they were waiting for me, I was so embarrassed that instead of apology I made the careless remark, "I seem to be a little late." Rakhmanov, the Assistant Director, looked at me a long time reproachfully, and finally said:

"We have been sitting here waiting, our nerves on edge, angry, and 'it seems I am *a little* late.' We all came here full of enthusiasm for the work waiting to be done, and now, thanks to you, that mood has been destroyed. To arouse a desire to create is difficult; to kill that desire is extremely easy. If I interfere with my own work, it is my own affair, but what right have I to hold up the work of a whole group? The actor, no less than the soldier, must be subject to iron discipline."

For this first offence Rakhmanov said he would limit himself to a reprimand, and not enter it on the written record kept of students, but that I must apologize immediately to all, and make it a rule in the future to appear at rehearsals a quarter of an hour before they begin. Even after my apology Rakhmanov was unwilling to go on, because he said the first rehearsal is an event in an artist's life, and he should retain the best possible impression of it. Today's rehearsal was spoiled by my carelessness; let us hope that tomorrow's will be memorable.

\* \* \* \* \* \* \*

This evening I intended to go to bed early because I was afraid to work on my role. But my eye fell on a cake of chocolate. I melted it with some butter and obtained a brown mess. It was easy to smear it onto my face, and make myself into a Moor. As I sat in front of my mirror I admired at length the flash of my teeth. I learned how to show them off and how to turn my eyes until the white showed. In order to make the most of my make-up I had to put on my costume, and once I was dressed I wanted to act; but I didn't invent anything new; I merely repeated what I had done yesterday, and now it seems to have lost its point. However, I did think I had gained something in my idea of how Othello ought to look.

### 3

Today was our first rehearsal. I arrived long ahead of time. The Assistant Director suggested that we plan our own scenes and arrange the properties. Fortunately, Paul agreed to everything I proposed, as only the inner aspects of Iago interest him. For me the externals were of greatest importance. They must remind me of my own room. Without this setting I could not get back my inspiration. Yet no matter how I struggled to make myself believe I was in my own room all my efforts did not convince me. They merely interfered with my acting.

Paul already knew the whole of his role by heart, but I had to read my lines out of the book, or else to get by with approximations. To my astonishment the words did not help me. In fact they bothered me, so that I should have preferred to do without them entirely, or to cut the number in half. Not only the words, but also the thoughts, of the poet were foreign to me. Even the action as outlined tended to take away from me that freedom which I had felt in my own room.

Worse than that, I didn't recognize my own voice. Besides, neither the setting nor the plan which I had fixed during my work at home would harmonize with the playing of Paul. For example, how could I introduce, into a comparatively quiet scene, between Othello and Iago, those flashes with my teeth, rollings of my eyes, which were to get me into my part? Yet I could not break away from my fixed ideas of how to act the nature I conceived of as savage, nor even from the setting I had prepared. Perhaps the reason was that I had nothing to put in its place. I had read the text of the role by itself, I had played the character by itself, without relating the one to the other. The words interfered with the acting, and the acting with the words.

\*　　\*　　\*　　\*　　\*　　\*　　\*

When I worked at home today I still went over the old ground without finding anything new. Why do I keep on repeating the same scenes and methods? Why is my acting of yesterday so exactly like today's and tomorrow's? Has my imagination dried up, or have I no reserves of material? Why did my work in the beginning move along so swiftly, and then stop at one spot? As I was thinking things over, some people in the next room gathered for tea. In order not to attract attention to myself, I had to move my activities to a different part of my room, and to speak my lines as softly as possible, so as not to be overheard.

To my surprise, by these little changes, my mood was transformed. I had discovered a secret—not to remain too long at one point, forever repeating the too familiar.

## 4

At today's rehearsal, from the very start, I began to improvise. Instead of walking about, I sat on a chair, and played without gestures or movement, grimaces, or rolling eyes. What happened? Immediately I became confused, I forgot the text and my usual intonations. I stopped. There was nothing for it but to go back to my old method of acting, and even to the old business. I did not control my methods; rather they controlled me.

## 5

Today's rehearsal brought nothing new. However, I am becoming more accustomed to the place where we work, and to the play. At first my method of portraying the Moor could not be harmonized with the Iago of Paul at all. Today it seemed as though I actually succeeded in fitting our scenes together. At any rate, I felt the discrepancies less sharply.

## 6

Today our rehearsal was on the big stage. I counted on the effect of its atmosphere, and what happened? Instead of the brilliancy of the footlights, and the bustle of the wings filled with all sorts of scenery, I found myself in a place dimly lighted and deserted. The whole of the great stage lay open and bare. Only near the footlights there were a number of plain cane chairs, which were to outline our set. To the right there was a rack of lights. I had hardly stepped onto the stage when there loomed up in front of me the immense hole of the proscenium arch, and beyond it an endless expanse of dark mist. This was my first impression of the stage from behind.

"Begin!" someone called.

I was supposed to go into Othello's room, outlined by the cane chairs, and to take my place. I sat down in one of them, but it turned out to be the wrong chair. I could not even recognize the plan of our set. For a long time I could not fit myself into my surroundings, nor could I concentrate my attention on what was going on around me. I found it difficult even to look at Paul, who was standing right beside me. My glance passed by him and travelled out into the auditorium, or else backstage to the workrooms where people were walking around carrying things, hammering, arguing.

The astonishing thing was that I continued mechanically to speak and act. If it had not been for my long exercises at home, that had beaten into me certain methods, I must have stopped at the very first lines.

## 7

Today we had a second rehearsal on the stage. I arrived early, and decided to prepare myself right on the stage, which today was quite different from yesterday. Work was humming, as properties and scenery were being placed. It would have been useless, amid all this chaos, to try to find the quiet in which I was accustomed to get into my role at home. First of all it was necessary to adjust myself to my new surroundings. I went out to the front of the stage and stared into that awful hole beyond the footlights, trying to become accustomed to it, and to free myself from its pull; but the more I tried not to notice the place the more I thought about it. Just then a workman who was going by me dropped a package of nails. I started to help pick them up. As I did this I had the very pleasant sensation of feeling quite at home on the big stage. But the nails were soon picked up, and again I became oppressed by the size of the place.

I hurried down into the orchestra. Rehearsals of other scenes began, but I saw nothing. I was too full of excitement, waiting for my turn. There is a good side to this period of waiting.

It drives you into such a state that all you can do is to long for your turn, to get through with the thing that you are afraid of.

When our turn did come I went up onto the stage, where a sketchy set had been arranged out of bits taken from various productions. Some parts were wrong side up, and all the furniture was ill assorted. Nevertheless, the general appearance of the stage, now that it was lighted, was pleasant, and I felt at home in this room that had been prepared for Othello. By a great stretch of the imagination I could recognize a certain similarity to my own room. But the minute the curtain rose, and the auditorium appeared before me, I again felt myself possessed by its power. At the same time some new unexpected sensations surged inside of me. The set hems in the actor. It shuts off the backstage area. Above him are large dark spaces. At the sides are the wings that outline the room. This semi-isolation is pleasant, but a bad aspect is, that it projects the attention out into the public. Another new point was that my fears led me to feel an obligation to interest the audience. This feeling of obligation interfered with my throwing myself into what I was doing. I began to feel hurried, both in speech and in action. My favourite places flashed by like telegraph poles seen from a train. The slightest hesitation and a catastrophe would have been inevitable.

## 8

As I had to arrange for my make-up and costume for the dress rehearsal, I reached the theatre today even earlier than usual. A good dressing-room was given to me, as well as a gorgeous gown, which is really a museum piece, and is used by the Prince of Morocco in *The Merchant of Venice*. I sat down at the dressing table, on which were laid out various wigs, bits of hair, lacquer pots, grease paints, powder, brushes. I started to put on some dark brown colour with a brush, but it hardened so quickly that it left almost no trace. Then I tried a wash with the same result. I put the colour on my finger, and thence onto my face, but had no luck, except with the light blue, the very colour, it seemed to me, that was of no possible use in the make-up of Othello. I put some lacquer on my face, and tried to attach some hair. The lacquer pricked my skin and the hair stuck straight up from my face. I tried one wig after another. All, put on a face without make-up, were too obvious. Next I tried to wash off what little make-up I had on my face, but I had no idea how to do it.

About this time there came into my room a tall, very thin man with glasses, dressed in a long white smock. He leaned over and began to work on my face. First he cleaned off with vaseline all that I had put on, and then began again with fresh colours. When he saw that the colours were hard he dipped a brush into some oil. He also put oil onto my face. On that surface the brush could lay the colours smoothly. Then he covered my whole face with a sooty shade, proper to the complexion of a Moor. I rather missed the darker shade which the chocolate had contributed, because that had caused my eyes and teeth to shine.

When my make-up was finished and my costume put on I looked into the mirror and was delighted with the art of my make-up man, as well as with the whole impression. The angles of my arms and body disappeared in the flowing robes, and the gestures I had worked up went well with the costume. Paul and some others came into my dressing-room, and they congratulated me on my appearance. Their generous praise brought back my old confidence. But when I went out on the stage I was disturbed by the changes in the position of the furniture. In one place an armchair was unnaturally moved forward from the wall almost into the middle of the scene, and the table was too near the front. I seemed to be put on exhibition right in the most conspicuous place. Out of excitement I walked up and down and kept catching my dagger in the folds of my costume, and my knives on the corners of the furniture or scenery. But this did not keep me from an automatic delivery of my lines and an incessant activity on the stage. In spite of everything it seemed as though I should get through to the end of the scene, yet when I came to the culminating moment in my role the thought flashed into my mind: "Now I'll be stuck!" Whereupon I was seized with a panic, and stopped speaking. I do not know what guided me back to an automatic rendering of my part; but once more it saved me. I had only one thought in my mind, to finish as quickly as possible, to take off my make-up, and to get out of the theatre.

And here I am at home alone, where I am most unhappy. Fortunately Leo came around to see me. He had seen me out in the audience, and wanted to know what I thought of his performance, but I could not tell him because although I had watched his bit I did not notice anything, because of my own excitement in waiting for my turn.

He spoke familiarly about the play and the role of Othello. He was especially interesting in his explanation of the sorrow, the shock, the amazement of the Moor, that such vice could exist in the lovely form of Desdemona.

After he left, I tried to go over some parts of the role, with his interpretation, and I almost wept, I was so sorry for the Moor.

9

This is the day of the exhibition performance. I thought I could see ahead exactly what was going to happen. I was filled with a complete indifference until I reached my dressing room. But once inside, my heart began to pound and I felt almost nauseated.

On the stage what first disturbed me was the extraordinary solemnity, the quiet and order that reigned there. When I stepped away from the darkness of the wings to the full illumination of the footlights, headlights and spotlights, I felt blinded. The brightness was so intense that it seemed to form a curtain of light between me and the auditorium. I felt protected from the public, and for a moment I breathed freely, but soon my eyes became accustomed to the light, I could see into the darkness, and the fear and attraction of the public seemed stronger than ever. I was ready to turn myself inside out, to give them everything I had; yet inside of me I had never felt so empty. The effort to squeeze out more emotion than I had, the power-lessness to do the impossible, filled me with a fear that turned my face and my hands to stone. All my forces were spent on unnatural and fruitless efforts. My throat became constricted, my sounds all seemed to go to a high note. My hands, feet, gestures, and speech all became violent. I was ashamed of every word, of every gesture. I blushed, clenched my hands, and pressed myself against the back of the armchair. I was making a failure, and in my helplessness I was suddenly seized with rage. For several minutes I cut loose from everything about me. I flung out the famous line "Blood, Iago, blood!" I felt in these words all the injury to the soul of a trusting man. Leo's interpretation of Othello suddenly rose in my memory and aroused my emotion. Besides, it almost seemed as though for a moment the listeners strained forward, and that through the audience there ran a murmur.

The moment I felt this approval a sort of energy boiled up in me. I cannot remember how I finished the scene, because the footlights and the black hole disappeared from my conscious-ness, and I was free of all fear. I remember that Paul was at first astonished by the change in me; then he became infected by it, and acted with abandon. The curtain was rung down, out in the hall there was applause, and I was full of faith in myself.

With the airs of a visiting star, with assumed indifference, I went out into the audience during the intermission. I chose a place in the orchestra from which I could easily be seen by the Director and his Assistant and sat down, in the hope that they would call me over and make some pleasant comment. The footlights went up. The curtain was drawn, and instantly one of the students, Maria Maloletkova, flew down a flight of stairs. She fell to the floor, writhing, and cried: "Oh, help me!" in a way that chilled me to the heart. After that, she rose and spoke some lines, but so rapidly that it was impossible to understand them. Then in the middle of a word, as though she had for-gotten her part, she stopped, covered her face with her hands, and dashed off into the wings. After a little the curtain came down, but in my ears I still heard that cry. An entrance, one word, and the feeling goes across. The Director, it seemed to me, was electrified; but had I not done the same thing with that one phrase, "Blood, Iago, blood!" when the whole audience was in my power?

# CHAPTER TWO

# When Acting Is an Art

I

TODAY we were called together to hear the Director's criticism of our performance. He said:

"Above all look for what is fine in art and try to understand it. Therefore, we shall begin by discussing the constructive elements of the test. There are only two moments worth noting; the first, when Maria threw herself down the staircase with the despairing cry of 'Oh, help me!' and the second, more extended in time, when Kostya Nazvanov said 'Blood, Iago, blood!' In both instances, you who were playing, and we who were watching, gave ourselves up completely to what was happening on the stage. Such successful moments, by themselves, we can recognize as belonging to the art of living a part."

"And what is this art?" I asked.

"You experienced it yourself. Suppose you state what you felt."

"I neither know nor remember," said I, embarrassed by Tortsov's praise.

"What! You do not remember your own inner excitement? You do not remember that your hands, your eyes and your whole body tried to throw themselves forward to grasp something; you do not remember how you bit your lips and barely restrained your tears?"

"Now that you tell me about what happened, I seem to remember my actions," I confessed.

"But without me you could not have understood the ways in which your feelings found expression?"

"No, I admit I couldn't."

12

"You were acting with your subconscious, intuitively?" he concluded.

"Perhaps. I do not know. But is that good or bad?"

"Very good, if your intuition carries you along the right path, and very bad if it makes a mistake," explained Tortsov. "During the exhibition performance it did not mislead you, and what you gave us in those few successful moments was excellent."

"Is that really true?" I asked.

"Yes, because the very best that can happen is to have the actor completely carried away by the play. Then regardless of his own will he lives the part, not noticing *how* he feels, not thinking about *what* he does, and it all moves of its own accord, subconsciously and intuitively. Salvini said: 'The great actor should be full of feeling, and especially he should feel the thing he is portraying. He must feel an emotion not only once or twice while he is studying his part, but to a greater or lesser degree every time he plays it, no matter whether it is the first or the thousandth time.' Unfortunately this is not within our control. Our subconscious is inaccessible to our consciousness. We cannot enter into that realm. If for any reason we do penetrate into it, then the subconscious becomes conscious and dies.

"The result is a predicament; we are supposed to create under inspiration; only our subconscious gives us inspiration; yet we apparently can use this subconscious only through our consciousness, which kills it.

"Fortunately there is a way out. We find the solution in an oblique instead of a direct approach. In the soul of a human being there are certain elements which are subject to consciousness and will. These accessible parts are capable in turn of acting on psychic processes that are involuntary.

"To be sure, this calls for extremely complicated creative work. It is carried on in part under the control of our consciousness, but a much more significant proportion is subconscious and involuntary.

"To rouse your subconscious to creative work there is a

special technique. We must leave all that is in the fullest sense subconscious to nature, and address ourselves to what is within our reach. When the subconscious, when intuition, enters into our work we must know how not to interfere.

"One cannot always create subconsciously and with inspiration. No such genius exists in the world. Therefore our art teaches us first of all to create consciously and rightly, because that will best prepare the way for the blossoming of the subconscious, which is inspiration. The more you have of conscious creative moments in your role the more chance you will have of a flow of inspiration.

" 'You may play well or you may play badly; the important thing is that you should play truly,' wrote Shchepkin to his pupil Shumski.

"To play truly means to be right, logical, coherent, to think, strive, feel and act in unison with your role.

"If you take all these internal processes, and adapt them to the spiritual and physical life of the person you are representing, we call that living the part. This is of supreme significance in creative work. Aside from the fact that it opens up avenues for inspiration, living the part helps the artist to carry out one of his main objectives. His job is not to present merely the external life of his character. He must fit his own human qualities to the life of this other person, and pour into it all of his own soul. The fundamental aim of our art is the creation of this inner life of a human spirit, and its expression in an artistic form.

"That is why we begin by thinking about the inner side of a role, and how to create its spiritual life through the help of the internal process of living the part. You must live it by actually experiencing feelings that are analogous to it, each and every time you repeat the process of creating it."

"Why is the subconscious so dependent on the conscious?" said I.

"It seems entirely normal to me," was the reply. "The use of steam, electricity, wind, water and other involuntary forces in nature is dependent on the intelligence of an engineer. Our subconscious power cannot function without its own engineer—our conscious technique. It is only when an actor feels that his inner and outer life on the stage is flowing naturally and normally, in the circumstances that surround him, that the deeper sources of his subconscious gently open, and from them come feelings we cannot always analyse. For a shorter or longer space of time they take possession of us whenever some inner instinct bids them. Since we do not understand this governing power, and cannot study it, we actors call it simply nature.

"But if you break the laws of normal organic life, and cease to function rightly, then this highly sensitive subconscious becomes alarmed, and withdraws. To avoid this, plan your role consciously at first, then play it truthfully. At this point realism and even naturalism in the inner preparation of a part is essential, because it causes your subconscious to work and induces outbursts of inspiration."

"From what you have said I gather that to study our art we must assimilate a psychological technique of living a part, and that this will help us to accomplish our main object, which is to create the life of a human spirit," Paul Shustov said.

"That is correct but not complete," said Tortsov. "Our aim is not only to create the life of a human spirit, but also to 'express it in a beautiful, artistic form.' An actor is under the obligation to live his part inwardly, and then to give to his experience an external embodiment. I ask you to note especially that the dependence of the body on the soul is particularly important in our school of art. *In order to express a most delicate and largely subconscious life it is necessary to have control of an unusually responsive, excellently prepared vocal and physical apparatus.* This apparatus must be ready instantly and exactly to reproduce most delicate and all but intangible feelings with great sensitiveness and directness. *That is why an actor of our type is obliged to work so much more than others,* both on his inner equipment, which creates the life of the part, and also on his outer physical apparatus, which should reproduce the results of the creative work of his emotions with precision.

"Even the externalizing of a role is greatly influenced by the subconscious. In fact no artificial, theatrical technique can even compare with the marvels that nature brings forth.

"I have pointed out to you today, in general outlines, what we consider essential. Our experience has led to a firm belief that only our kind of art, soaked as it is in the living experiences of human beings, can artistically reproduce the impalpable shadings and depths of life. Only such art can completely absorb the spectator and make him both understand and also inwardly experience the happenings on the stage, enriching his inner life, and leaving impressions which will not fade with time.

"Moreover, and this is of primary importance, *the organic bases of the laws of nature on which our art is founded will protect you in the future from going down the wrong path.* Who knows under what directors, or in what theatres, you will work? Not everywhere, not with everyone, will you find creative work based on nature. In the vast majority of theatres the actors and producers are constantly violating nature in the most shameless manner. But if you are sure of the limits of true art, and of the organic laws of nature, you will not go astray, you will be able to understand your mistakes and correct them. That is why a study of the foundations of our art is the beginning of the work of every student actor."

"Yes, yes," I exclaimed, "I am so happy that I was able to take a step, if only a small one, in that direction."

"Not so fast," said Tortsov, "otherwise you will suffer the bitterest disillusion. Do not mix up living your part with what you showed us on the stage."

"Why, what did I show?"

"I have told you that in all that big scene from *Othello* there were only a few minutes in which you succeeded in living the part. I used them to illustrate to you, and to the other students, the foundations of our type of art. However, if we speak of the whole scene between Othello and Iago, we certainly cannot call it our type of art."

"What is it, then?"

"That is what we call forced acting," defined the Director.
"And what, really, is that?" said I, puzzled.

"When one acts as you did," he explained, "there are individual moments when you suddenly and unexpectedly rise to
great artistic heights and thrill your audience. In such moments
you are creating according to your inspiration, improvising, as
it were; but would you feel yourself capable enough, or strong
enough spiritually or physically, to play the five great acts of
*Othello* with the same lift with which you accidentally played
part of that one short scene?"

"I do not know," I said, conscientiously.

"I know, unquestionably, that such an undertaking would
be far beyond the strength not only of a genius with an extraordinary temperament, but even of a very Hercules," answered
Tortsov. "For our purposes you must have, in addition to the
help of nature, a well worked-out psychological technique, an
enormous talent, and great physical and nervous reserves. You
have not all these things, any more than do the personality actors
who do not admit technique. They, as you did, rely entirely on
inspiration. If this inspiration does not turn up then neither
you nor they have anything with which to fill in the blank
spaces. You have long stretches of nervous let-down in playing
your part, complete artistic impotence, and a naïve amateurish
sort of acting. At such times your playing is lifeless, stilted.
Consequently high moments alternate with over-acting."

2

Today we heard some more from Tortsov about our acting.
When he came to the classroom he turned to Paul and said
to him:

"You too gave us some interesting moments, but they were
rather typical of the 'art of representation.'

"Now since you successfully demonstrated this other way
of acting, Paul, why not recall for us how you created the role
of Iago?" suggested the Director.

"I went right at the role for its inner content, and studied that for a long time," said Paul. "At home it seemed to me that I really did live the part, and at some of the rehearsals there were certain places in the role that I seemed to feel. Therefore I do not know what the art of 'representation' has to do with it."

"In it the actor also lives his part," said Tortsov. "This partial identity with our method is what makes it possible to consider this other type also true art.

"Yet his objective is different. He lives his part as a preparation for perfecting an external form. Once that is determined to his satisfaction he reproduces that form through the aid of mechanically trained muscles. Therefore, in this other school, living your role is not the chief moment of creation as it is with us, but one of the preparatory stages for further artistic work."

"But Paul did use his own feelings at the exhibition performance!" I maintained.

Someone else agreed with me, and insisted that in Paul's acting, just as in mine, there had been a few scattered moments of truly living the part, mixed with a lot of incorrect acting.

"No," insisted Tortsov, *"in our art you must live the part every moment that you are playing it, and every time*. Each time it is recreated it must be lived afresh and incarnated afresh. This describes the few successful moments in Kostya's acting. But I did not notice freshness in improvisation, or in feeling his part, in Paul's playing. On the contrary, I was astonished in a number of places by the accuracy and artistic finish of a form and method of acting which is permanently fixed, and which is produced with a certain inner coldness. However, I did feel in those moments that the original, of which this was only the artificial copy, *had been* good and true. This echo of a former process of living the part made his acting, in certain moments, a true example of the art of representation."

"How could I have got hold of the art of mere reproduction?" Paul could not understand.

"Let us find out by your telling us more about how you prepared your Iago," suggested the Director.

"To be sure that my feelings were externally reflected I used a mirror."

"That is dangerous," remarked Tortsov. *"You must be very careful in the use of a mirror. It teaches an actor to watch the outside rather than the inside of his soul,* both in himself and in his part."

"Nevertheless, it did help me to see how my exterior reflected my sensations," Paul insisted.

"Your own sensations, or the sensations prepared for your part?"

"My own, but applicable to Iago," explained Paul.

"Consequently, while you were working with the mirror, what interested you was not so much your exterior, your general appearance, your gestures, but principally the way in which you externalized your inner sensations," probed Tortsov.

"Exactly!" exclaimed Paul.

"That is also typical," remarked the Director.

"I remember how pleased I was when I saw the correct reflection of what I felt," Paul continued to reminisce.

"You mean that you fixed these methods of expressing your feelings in a permanent form?" Tortsov asked.

"They became fixed by themselves through frequent repetition."

"Then in the end you worked out a definite external form for the interpretation of certain successful parts in your role, and you were able to achieve their external expression through technique?" asked Tortsov with interest.

"Evidently yes," admitted Paul.

"And you made use of this form each time that you repeated the role?" examined the Director.

"Evidently I did."

"Now tell me this: did this established form come to you each time through an inner process, or after it was once born did you repeat it mechanically, without the participation of any emotions?"

"It seemed to me that I lived it each time," declared Paul.

"No, that was not the impression that came to the spectators," said Tortsov. "Actors of the school we are discussing do what you did. At first they feel the part, but when once they have done so they do not go on feeling it anew, they merely remember and repeat the external movements, intonations, and expressions they worked out at first, making this repetition without emotion. Often they are extremely skilful in technique, and are able to get through a part with technique only, and no expenditure of nervous force. In fact, they often think it unwise to feel, after they have once decided on the pattern to follow. They think they are surer to give the right performance if they merely recall how they did it when they first got it right. This is applicable in some degree to the places we picked out in your playing of Iago. Try to remember what happened as you went on with your work."

Paul said that he was not satisfied with his work in other parts of the role, or with the appearance of Iago in his mirror, and he finally tried to copy an acquaintance whose appearance seemed to suggest a good example of wickedness and cunning.

"So you thought you could adapt him to your own uses?" Tortsov queried.

"Yes," Paul confessed.

"Well, then, what were you going to do with your own qualities?"

"To tell the truth, I was simply going to take on the external mannerisms of my acquaintance," admitted Paul frankly.

"That was a great mistake," Tortsov replied. "At that point you went over to sheer imitation, which has nothing to do with creativeness."

"What should I do?" asked Paul.

"You should first of all assimilate the model. This is complicated. You study it from the point of view of the epoch, the time, the country, condition of life, background, literature, psychology, the soul, way of living, social position, and external appearance; moreover, you study character, such as custom, manner, movements, voice, speech, intonations. All this work on your material will help you to permeate it with your own feelings. Without all this you will have no art.

"When, from this material, a living image of the role emerges, the artist of the school of representation transfers it to himself. This work is concretely described by one of the best representatives of this school, the famous French actor, Coquelin the elder: . . . 'The actor creates his model in his imagination, and then, just as does the painter, he takes every feature of it and transfers it, not onto canvas, but onto himself.' . . . He sees Tartuffe's costume and puts it on himself; he notices his gait and imitates it; he sees his physiognomy and adapts it to himself; he adapts his own face to it. He speaks with the same voice that he has heard Tartuffe use; he must make this person he has put together move, walk, gesticulate, listen and think like Tartuffe, in other words, hand over his soul to him. The portrait ready, it needs only to be framed; that is, put on the stage, and then the public will say either, 'That is Tartuffe,' or, 'The actor has not done a good job.' . . .'"

"But all that is frightfully difficult and complicated," said I with feeling.

"Yes, Coquelin himself admits it. He says: 'The actor does not live, he plays. He remains cold toward the object of his acting but his art must be perfection.' . . . And to be sure," added Tortsov, "the art of representation demands perfection if it is to remain an art.

"The confident answer by the school of representation is that 'art is not real life, nor is it even its reflection. Art is in itself a creator, it creates its own life, beautiful in its abstraction, beyond the limits of time, and space.' Of course we cannot agree to such a presumptuous defiance of that unique, perfect, and unattainable artist, our creative nature.

"Artists of the Coquelin school reason this way: The theatre is a convention, and the stage is too poor in resources to create the illusion of real life; therefore the theatre should not avoid conventions. . . . This type of art is less profound than beautiful, it is more immediately effective than truly powerful; in it the form is more interesting than its content. It acts more on your sense of sound and sight than on your soul. Consequently it is more likely to delight than to move you.

"You can receive great impressions through this art. But they will neither warm your soul nor penetrate deeply into it. Their effect is sharp but not lasting. Your astonishment rather than your faith is aroused. Only what can be accomplished through surprising theatrical beauty, or picturesque pathos, lies within the bounds of this art. But delicate and deep human feelings are not subject to such technique. They call for natural emotions *at the very moment* in which they appear before you in the flesh. *They call for the direct co-operation of nature itself.* Nevertheless, 'representing' the part, since it follows our process in part, must be acknowledged to be creative art."

## 3

At our lesson today, Grisha Govorkov said that he always feels very deeply what he does on the stage.

To this Tortsov replied:

"Everyone at every minute of his life must feel something. Only the dead have no sensations. It is important to know *what* you are feeling on the stage, because it often happens that even the most experienced actors work out at home and carry on to the stage something which is neither important nor essential for their parts. This happened to all of you. Some of the students showed off their voices, effective intonations, techniques of acting; others made the spectators laugh by their lively activity, ballet jumps, desperate over-acting; and preened themselves with beautiful gestures and poses; in short, what they brought to the stage was not what was needed for the roles they were portraying.

"As for you, Govorkov, you did not approach your role from

its inner content, you neither lived it nor represented it, but did something entirely different."

"What was it?" Grisha hastened to ask.

"Mechanical acting. To be sure, not bad of its kind, having rather elaborately worked out methods of presenting the role with conventional illustrations."

I shall omit the long discussion raised by Grisha, and jump directly to the explanation by Tortsov of the boundaries which divide true art from mechanical acting.

"There can be no true art without living. It begins where feeling comes into its own."

"And mechanical acting?" asked Grisha.

"That begins where creative art ends. In mechanical acting there is no call for a living process, and it appears only accidentally.

"You will understand this better when you come to recognize the origins and methods of mechanical acting, which we characterize as 'rubber stamps.' To reproduce feelings you must be able to identify them out of your own experience. But as mechanical actors do not experience feelings they cannot reproduce their external results.

"With the aid of his face, mimicry, voice, and gestures, the mechanical actor offers the public nothing but the dead mask of non-existent feeling. For this there has been worked out a large assortment of picturesque effects which pretend to portray all sorts of feelings through external means.

"Some of these established clichés have become traditional, and are passed down from generation to generation; as for instance spreading your hand over your heart to express love, or opening your mouth wide to give the idea of death. Others are taken ready-made, from talented contemporaries (such as rubbing the brow with the back of the hand, as Vera Komissarzhevskaya used to do in moments of tragedy). Still others are invented by actors for themselves.

"There are special ways of reciting a role, methods of diction and speech. (For instance, exaggeratedly high or low tones at critical moments in the role, done with specifically theatrical 'tremolo,' or with special declamatory vocal embellishments.) There are also methods of physical movement (mechanical actors do not walk, they 'progress' on the stage), for gestures and action, for plastic motion. There are methods for expressing all human feelings and passions (showing your teeth and rolling the whites of your eyes when you are jealous, or covering up the eyes and face with the hands instead of weeping; tearing your hair when in despair). There are ways of imitating all kinds of types of people, various classes in society (peasants spit on the floor, wipe their noses with the skirts of their coats, military men click their spurs, aristocrats play with their lorgnettes). Certain others characterize epochs (operatic gestures for the Middle Ages, mincing steps for the eighteenth century). These ready-made mechanical methods are easily acquired through constant exercise, so that they become second nature.

"Time and constant habit make even deformed and senseless things near and dear. As for instance, the time-honoured shoulder-shrugging of Opéra Comique, old ladies trying to look young, the doors that open and close by themselves as the hero of the play comes in or goes out. The ballet, opera, and especially the pseudo-classic tragedies are full of these conventions. By means of these forever-unchanging methods they expect to reproduce the most complicated and elevated experiences of heroes. For example: tearing one's heart out of one's bosom in moments of despair, shaking one's fists in revenge, or raising one's hands to heaven in prayer.

"According to the mechanical actor the object of theatrical speech and plastic movements—as exaggerated sweetness in lyric moments, dull monotone in reading epic poetry, hissing sounds to express hatred, false tears in the voice to represent grief—is to enhance voice, diction, and movements, to make actors more beautiful and give more power to their theatrical effectiveness.

"Unfortunately, there is far more bad taste in the world

than good. In the place of nobility a sort of showiness has been created, prettiness in place of beauty, theatrical effect in the place of expressiveness.

"The very worst fact is that *clichés will fill up every empty spot in a role, which is not already solid with living feeling.* Moreover, they often rush in ahead of feeling, and bar the road; that is why an actor must protect himself most conscientiously against such devices. And this is true even of gifted actors, capable of true creativeness.

"No matter how skilful an actor may be in his choice of stage conventions, because of their inherent mechanical quality he cannot move the spectators by them. He must have some supplementary means of arousing them, so he takes refuge in what we call theatrical emotions. These are a sort of artificial imitation of the periphery of physical feelings.

"If you clench your fists and stiffen the muscles of your body, or breathe spasmodically, you can bring yourself to a state of great physical intensity. This is often thought by the public to be an expression of a powerful temperament aroused by passion.

"Actors of a more nervous type can arouse theatrical emotions by artificially screwing up their nerves; this produces theatrical hysteria, an unhealthy ecstasy, which is usually just as lacking in inner content as is the artificial physical excitement."

4

At our lesson today the Director continued the discussion of our exhibition performance. Poor Vanya Vyuntsov came in for the worst of it. Tortsov did not recognize his acting as even mechanical.

"What was it, then?" said I.

"The most repulsive kind of over-acting," answered the Director.

"I at least did not have any of that?" I hazarded.

"You certainly did!" retorted Tortsov.

"When?" I exclaimed. "You yourself said that I played——!"

"I explained that your acting was made up of moments of true creativeness, taking turns with moments——"

"Of mechanical acting?" The question burst out of me.

"That can be developed only by long work, as in the case of Grisha, and you could never have had the time to create it. That is why you gave an exaggerated imitation of a savage, by means of the most amateurish kind of rubber stamps, in which there was no trace of technique. *Even mechanical acting cannot do without technique.*"

"But where did I get those rubber stamps, since this is the first time I have even been on the boards?" said I.

"Read *My Life in Art.* There is a story about two little girls who had never seen a theatre, or a performance, or even a rehearsal, and yet they played a tragedy with the most vicious and trivial clichés. Even you have many of them, fortunately."

"Why fortunately?" I asked.

"Because they are easier to fight than strongly rooted mechanical acting," said the Director.

"Beginners like you, if you have talent, can accidentally, and for a short space of time, fill a role very well, but you cannot reproduce it in a sustained artistic form, and therefore you always have recourse to exhibitionism. At first it is harmless enough, but you must never forget that it has in it the seeds of great danger. You must struggle with it from the very first moment so that it may not develop habits which will cripple you as an actor and side-track your native gifts.

"Take your own example. You are an intelligent person, yet why, at the exhibition performance, were you, with the exception of a few moments, absurd? Can you really believe that the Moors, who in their day were renowned for culture, were like wild animals, pacing up and down a cage? The savage that you portrayed, even in the quiet conversation with his ancient, roared at him, showed his teeth, and rolled his eyes. Where did you get any such approach to the role?"

I then gave a detailed account of nearly everything that I had written in my diary about my work on my role at home. For better visualization I put some chairs around according to their place in my room. At parts of my demonstration Tortsov laughed heartily.

"There, that shows you how the very worst kind of acting starts," said he, when I had finished. "When you were preparing for the exhibition performance you approached your role from the point of view of impressing the spectators. With what? With true organic feelings, that corresponded to those of the person you were portraying? *You did not have any. You did not even have a whole living image, which you could have, if only externally, copied. What was there left for you to do? To grab the first trait that happened to flash into your mind. Your mind is stored full of such things, ready for any occasion in life. Every impression, in some form or another, remains in our memories, and can be used when needed. In such hurried or general descriptions we care very little whether what we transmit corresponds to reality. We are satisfied with any general characteristic or illusion. To bring images to life, daily practice has produced for us stencils or external descriptive signs, which thanks to long usage have become intelligible to everyone.*

"That is what happened to you. You were tempted by the external appearance of a black man in general, and you hastily reproduced him without ever thinking about what Shakespeare wrote. You reached for an external characterization which seemed to you effective, vivid, and easy to reproduce. That is what always happens when an actor does not have at his disposal a wealth of live material taken from life. You could say to any one of us, 'Play for me immediately, without any preparation, a savage in general.' I am willing to wager that the majority would do just what you did; because tearing around, roaring, showing your teeth, rolling the whites of your eyes, has from time immemorial been intertwined in your imagination with a false idea of a savage. All these methods of portraying feelings in general exist in every one of us. And they are used without any relation to the why, wherefore, or circumstances in which a person has experienced them.

"*Whereas mechanical acting makes use of worked-out stencils to replace real feelings, over-acting takes the first general human conventions that come along and uses them without even sharpening or preparing them for the stage. What happened to you is understandable and excusable in a beginner. But be careful in the future, because amateurish over-acting grows into the worst kind of mechanical acting.*

"*First try to avoid all incorrect approaches to your work, and to that end study the basis of our school of acting; which is the basis of living your part. Second, do not repeat the senseless sort of work that you have just illustrated to us and which I have just criticized. Third, never allow yourself externally to portray anything that you have not inwardly experienced and which is not even interesting to you.*

"An artistic truth is hard to draw out, but it never palls. It becomes more pleasing, penetrates more deeply, all the time, until it embraces the whole being of an artist, and of his spectators as well. A role which is built of truth will grow, whereas one built on stereotype will shrivel.

"The conventions that you found soon wore out. They were not able to continue to excite you, as they had the first time, when you mistook them for inspiration.

"Then add to all this: the conditions of our theatre activities, the publicity attendant on the actors' performances, our dependence for success on the public, and the desire, that arises from those conditions, to use any means to make an impression. These professional stimuli very often take hold of an actor even when he is playing a well established role. They do not improve the quality of his acting, but on the contrary their influence is toward exhibitionism and the strengthening of stereotyped methods.

"In Grisha's case, he had really worked on his rubber stamps, with the result that they were more or less good; but yours were bad because you had not worked them up. That is why I called his work rather decent mechanical acting, and the unsuccessful part of your playing I considered *amateurish over-acting.*"

"Consequently, my acting was a mixture of the best and the worst there is in our profession?"

"No, not the very worst," said Tortsov. "What the others did was even worse. Your amateurishness is curable, but the mistakes of the others show a conscious principle which is far from easy to change or to root out of the artist."

"What is that?"

"The exploitation of art."

"What does that consist of?" asked one of the students.

"In what Sonya Veliaminova did."

"I!" The poor girl jumped out of her seat in surprise. "What did I do?"

"You showed us your little hands, your little feet, your whole person, because it could be seen better on the stage," answered the Director.

"How awful! And I never knew it!"

"That is what always happens with habits that are ingrained."

"Why did you praise me?"

"Because you had pretty hands and feet."

"Then what was bad about it?"

"The bad part was that you flirted with the audience and did not play Katherine. You see Shakespeare did not write the *Taming of the Shrew* in order that a student by the name of Sonya Veliaminova could show the audience her little foot from the stage or could flirt with her admirers. Shakespeare had a different end in view, one which remained foreign to you, and therefore unknown to us. Unfortunately, our art is frequently exploited for personal ends. You do it to show your beauty. Others do it to gain popularity or external success or to make a career. In our profession these are common phenomena and I hasten to restrain you from them.

"*Now remember firmly what I am going to tell you: the theatre on account of its publicity and spectacular side, attracts many people who merely want to capitalize their beauty or make careers. They take advantage of the ignorance of the public, its perverted taste, favouritism, intrigues, false success, and many other means which have no relation to creative art. These exploiters are the deadliest enemies of art. We have to use the sternest measures with them, and if they cannot be reformed they must be removed from the boards. Therefore,"* here he turned to Sonya again, *"you must make up your mind, once and for all, did you come here to serve art, and to make sacrifices for its sake, or to exploit your own personal ends?*

"However," Tortsov continued, turning to the rest of us, "it is only in theory that we can divide art into categories. Practically, all schools of acting are mixed together. It is unfortunately true that we frequently see great artists, because of human weakness, lowering themselves to mechanical acting, and mechanical actors rising for moments to heights of true art.

"Side by side we see moments of living a part, representing the part, mechanical acting, and exploitation. That is why it is so necessary for actors to recognize the boundaries of art."

It was quite clear to me, after listening to Tortsov's explanation, that the exhibition performance had done us more harm than good.

"No," he protested, when I told him my opinion. "The performance showed you what you must never do on the stage."

At the end of the discussion the Director announced that tomorrow, in addition to our work with him, we are to begin regular activities that have the purpose of developing our voices and bodies,—lessons in singing, gymnastics, dancing, and fencing. These classes will be held daily, because the development of the muscles of the human body requires systematic and thorough exercise, and a long time.

# CHAPTER THREE

## Action

### I

WHAT a day! It was our first lesson with the Director.

We gathered in the school, a small but perfectly equipped theatre. He came in, looked us all over carefully, and said: "Maria, please go up onto the stage."

The poor girl was terrified. She reminded me of a frightened puppy, the way she ran off to hide herself. At last we caught her and led her to the Director, who was laughing like a child. She covered her face with her hands, and repeated all her favourite exclamations: "Oh dear, I cannot do it! Oh dear, I am afraid!"

"Calm yourself," said he, looking her straight in the eye, "and let us do a little play. This is the plot." He was paying no attention to the young woman's agitation. "The curtain goes up, and you are sitting on the stage. You are alone. You sit and sit and sit. . . . At last the curtain comes down again. That is the whole play. Nothing simpler could be imagined, could it?"

Maria did not answer, so he took her by the arm and without a word led her onto the stage, while all the rest of us laughed.

The Director turned and said quietly: "My friends, you are in a schoolroom. And Maria is going through a most important moment in her artistic life. Try to learn when to laugh, and at what."

He took her out to the middle of the stage. We sat silent and waited for the curtain to rise. It went up slowly. She sat in the middle, near the front, her hands still covering her face. The solemn atmosphere and the long silence made themselves felt. She realized that something must be done.

First she removed one hand from her face, then the other, at the same time dropping her head so low that we could see nothing but the nape of her neck. Another pause. It was painful, but the Director waited in determined silence. Aware of the increasing tension, Maria looked out into the audience, but turned away instantly. Not knowing where to look, or what to do, she began to change, to sit first one way and then another, to take awkward positions, throw herself back and then straighten up, to bend over, pull hard at her very short skirt, look fixedly at something on the floor.

For a long time the Director was relentless, but at last he gave the sign for the curtain. I rushed up to him, because I wanted him to try me on the same exercise.

I was put in the middle of the stage. This was not a real performance; nevertheless I was full of self-contradictory impulses. Being on the stage, I was on exhibition, and yet an inner feeling demanded solitude. Part of me sought to entertain the onlookers, so that they would not become bored; another part told me to pay no attention to them. My legs, arms, head, and torso, although they did what I directed, added something superfluous of their own. You move your arm or leg quite simply, and suddenly you are all twisted, and look as though you were posing for a picture.

Strange! I had been on the stage only once, yet it was infinitely easier for me to sit on the stage affectedly than simply. I could not think what I ought to do. Afterward the others told me I looked in turn stupid, funny, embarrassed, guilty, apologetic. The Director merely waited. Then he tried the same exercise on the others.

"Now," said he, "let us go further. Later we shall return to these exercises, and learn how to sit on the stage."

"Isn't that what we have been doing?" we asked.

"Oh, no," he replied. "You were not simply sitting."

"What ought we to have done?"

Instead of giving his answer in words he rose quickly, walked up to the stage in a business-like way, and sat down heavily in an arm-chair to rest, as if he were at home. He neither did nor tried to do anything, yet his simple sitting posture was striking. We watched him, and wanted to know what was going on inside of him. He smiled. So did we. He looked thoughtful, and we were eager to know what was passing through his mind. He looked at something, and we felt we must see what it was that had attracted his attention.

In ordinary life one would not be specially interested in his manner of taking a seat, or remaining in it. But for some reason, when he is on the stage, one watches him closely, and perhaps has an actual pleasure in seeing him merely sit.

This did not happen when the others sat on the stage. We neither wanted to look at them nor to know what was going on inside them. Their helplessness and desire to please were ridiculous. Yet although the Director paid not the slightest attention to us, we were strongly drawn to him.

What is the secret? He told us himself.

Whatever happens on the stage must be for a *purpose*. Even keeping your seat must be for a purpose, a specific purpose, not merely the general purpose of being in sight of the audience. One must earn one's right to be sitting there. And it is not easy.

"Now let us repeat the experiment," he said, without leaving the stage. "Maria, come up here to me. I am going to act with you."

"You!" cried Maria, and she ran up onto the stage.

Again she was placed in the arm-chair, in the middle of the stage, and again she began to wait nervously, to move consciously, to pull her skirts.

The Director stood near her, and seemed to be looking for something very carefully in his notebook.

Meantime, gradually, Maria became more quiet, more concentrated, and finally was motionless, with her eyes fixed on him. She was afraid she might disturb him, and she merely waited for further orders. Her pose was life-like, natural. She almost seemed to be beautiful. The stage brought out her good features. Some time passed in just that way. Then the curtain fell.

"How do you feel?" the Director asked, as they returned to their places in the auditorium.

"I? Why? Did we act?"

"Of course."

"Oh! But I thought. . . . I was just sitting and waiting until you found your place in the book, and would tell me what to do. Why, I didn't act anything."

"That was the best part of it," said he. "You sat and waited, and did not act anything."

Then he turned to the rest of us. "Which struck you as more interesting?" he asked. "To sit on the stage and show off your small feet, as Sonya did, or your whole figure, like Grisha, or to sit for a specific purpose, even so simple a one as waiting for something to happen? It may not be of intrinsic interest in itself, but it is life, whereas showing yourself off takes you out of the realm of living art.

"On the stage, you must always be enacting something; action, motion, is the basis of the art followed by the actor."

"But," Grisha broke in, "you have just said that acting is necessary, and that showing off your feet or your figure, as I did, is not action. Why is it action to sit in a chair, as you did, without moving a finger? To me it looked like complete lack of action."

I interrupted boldly: "I do not know whether it was action or inaction, but all of us are agreed that his so-called lack of action was of far more interest than your action."

"You see," the Director said calmly, addressing Grisha, "the external immobility of a person sitting on the stage does not imply passiveness. You may sit without a motion and at the same time be in full action. Nor is that all. Frequently physical immobility is the direct result of inner intensity, and it is these inner activities that are far more important artistically. The essence of art is not in its external forms but in its spiritual content. So I will change the formula I gave you a moment ago, and put it like this:

"*On the stage it is necessary to act, either outwardly or inwardly.*"

2

"Let us give a new play," said the Director to Maria, as he came into the classroom today.

"Here is the gist of it: your mother has lost her job and her income; she has nothing to sell to pay for your tuition in dramatic school. In consequence you will be obliged to leave tomorrow. But a friend has come to your rescue. She has no cash to lend you, so she has brought you a brooch set in valuable stones. Her generous act has moved and excited you. Can you accept such a sacrifice? You cannot make up your mind. You try to refuse. Your friend sticks the pin into a curtain and walks out. You follow her into the corridor, where there is a long scene of persuasion, refusal, tears, gratitude. In the end you accept, your friend leaves, and you come back into the room to get the brooch. But—where is it? Can anyone have entered and taken it? In a rooming house that would be altogether possible. A careful, nerve-racking search ensues.

"Go up on the stage. I shall stick the pin in a fold of this curtain and you are to find it."

In a moment he announced that he was ready.

Maria dashed onto the stage as if she had been chased. She ran to the edge of the footlights and then back again, holding her head with both hands, and writhing with terror. Then she came forward again, and then again went away, this time in the opposite direction. Rushing out toward the front she seized the folds of the curtain and shook them desperately, finally burying her head in them. This act she intended to represent looking for the brooch. Not finding it, she turned quickly and dashed off the stage, alternately holding her head or beating her breast, apparently to represent the general tragedy of the situation.

Those of us who were sitting in the orchestra could scarcely keep from laughing.

It was not long before Maria came running down to us in a most triumphant manner. Her eyes shone, her cheeks flamed.

"How do you feel?" asked the Director.

"Oh, just wonderful! I can't tell you how wonderful. I'm so happy," she cried, hopping around on her seat. "I feel just as if I had made my début . . . really at home on the stage."

"That's fine," said he encouragingly, "but where is the brooch? Give it to me."

"Oh, yes," said she, "I forgot that."

"That is rather strange. You were looking hard for it, and you forgot it!"

We could scarcely look around before she was up on the stage again, and was going through the folds of the curtain.

"Do not forget this one thing," said the Director warningly, "if the brooch is found you are saved. You may continue to come to these classes. But if the pin is not found you will have to leave the school."

Immediately her face became intense. She glued her eyes on the curtain, and went over every fold of the material from top to bottom, painstakingly, systematically. This time her search was at a much slower pace, but we were all sure that she was not wasting a second of her time and that she was sincerely excited, although she made no effort to seem so.

"Oh, where is it? Oh, I've lost it."

This time the words were muttered in a low voice.

"It isn't there," she cried, with despair and consternation, when she had gone through every fold.

Her face was all worry and sadness. She stood motionless, as if her thoughts were far away. It was easy to feel how the loss of the pin had moved her.

We watched, and held our breath.

Finally the Director spoke.

"How do you feel now, after your second search?" he asked.

"How do I feel? I don't know." Her whole manner was languid, she shrugged her shoulders as she tried for some answer, and unconsciously her eyes were still on the floor of the stage. "I looked hard," she went on, after a moment.

"That's true. This time you really did look," said he. "But what did you do the first time?"

"Oh, the first time I was excited, I suffered."

"Which feeling was more agreeable, the first, when you rushed about and tore up the curtain, or the second, when you searched through it quietly?"

"Why, of course, the first time, when I was looking for the pin."

"No, do not try to make us believe that the first time you were looking for the pin," said he. "You did not even think of it. You merely sought to suffer, for the sake of suffering.

"But the second time you really did look. We all saw it; we understood, we believed, because your consternation and distraction actually existed.

"Your first search was bad. The second was good."

This verdict stunned her. "Oh," she said, "I nearly killed myself that first time."

"That doesn't count," said he. "It only interfered with a real search. On the stage do not run for the sake of running, or suffer for the sake of suffering. Don't act 'in general,' for the sake of action; always act with a purpose."

"And truthfully," said I.

"Yes," he agreed; "and now, get up on the stage and do it."

We went, but for a long time we did not know what to do. We felt we must make an impression, but I couldn't think of anything worth the attention of an audience. I started to be Othello, but soon stopped. Leo tried in turn an aristocrat, a general, and a peasant. Maria ran around holding her head and her heart to represent tragedy. Paul sat on a chair in a Hamlet-like pose and seemed to be representing either sorrow or disillusion. Sonya flirted around, and by her side Grisha declared his love in the most worn traditions of the stage. When I happened to look at Nicholas Umnovykh and Dasha Dymkova, who had as usual hidden themselves in a corner, I almost groaned to see their fixed stares and wooden attitudes, as they did a scene from Ibsen's *Brand*.

"Let's sum up what you have done," said the Director. "I shall begin with you," he said, indicating me. "And at the same time with you and you," he went on, pointing to Maria and Paul. "Sit right here, on these chairs, where I can see you better, and begin; you are to be jealous, you to suffer, you to grieve, just producing those moods for their own sakes."

We sat down, and immediately we felt the absurdity of our situation. As long as I was walking about, writhing like a savage, it was possible to imagine that there was some sense in what I was doing, but when I was put on a chair, with no external movements, the absurdity of my performance was clear.

"Well, what do you think?" asked the Director. "Can one sit on a chair, and for no reason at all be jealous? Or all stirred up? Or sad? Of course it is impossible. Fix this for all time in your memories: *On the stage there cannot be, under any circumstances, action which is directed immediately at the arousing of a feeling for its own sake.* To ignore this rule results only in the most disgusting artificiality. *When you are choosing some bit of action leave feeling and spiritual content alone.* Never seek to be jealous, or to make love, or to suffer, for its own sake. *All such feelings are the result of something that has gone before. Of the thing that goes before you should think as hard as you can. As for the result, it will produce itself.* The false acting of passions, or of types, or the mere use of conventional gestures,—these are all frequent faults in our profession. But you must keep away from these unrealities. You must not copy passions or copy types. You must live in the passions and in the types. Your acting of them must grow out of your living in them."

Vanya then suggested that we could act better if the stage was not so bare; if there were more properties about, furniture, fireplace, ash trays.

"Very well," agreed the Director, and ended the lesson at this point.

## 3

Our work for today was again scheduled for the School Stage, but when we arrived we found the entrance to the auditorium closed. However, another door was open that led directly onto the stage. As we entered we were astonished to find ourselves in a vestibule. Next to that was a cosy little living-room, in which were two doors, one opening into a dining-room and thence into a small bedroom, the other into a long corridor, on one side of which was a ballroom, brilliantly lighted. This whole apartment was partitioned off by scenery taken from productions in the repertory. The main curtain was down and barricaded with furniture.

Not feeling that we were on the boards we behaved as if we were at home. We began by examining the rooms, and then we settled down in groups and began to chat. It did not occur to any of us that the lesson had already begun. At last the Director reminded us that we had come together for work.

"What shall we do?" someone asked.

"The same thing as yesterday," was the reply.

But we continued to stand around.

"What is the matter?" he asked.

It was Paul who answered. "I don't know, really. Suddenly, for no reason at all, to act . . ." he stopped, as if at a loss.

"If it is uncomfortable to act for no reason at all, why then find a reason," said Tortsov. "I am not putting any restrictions on you. Only do not continue to stand there like sticks of wood."

"But," somebody ventured, "wouldn't that be acting for the sake of acting?"

"No," retorted the Director. "From now on there is to be acting only for some purpose. Now you have the surroundings you asked for yesterday; can't you suggest some inner motives

that will result in simple physical acts? For instance, if I ask
you, Vanya, to go and close that door, would you not do it?"

"Close the door? Of course." And Vanya went over, slammed
it and returned before we had a chance to look at him.

"That is not what is meant by closing a door," said the
Director. "By the word 'close' I imply a wish that the door shall
be shut, so that it will stay shut, to stop the draught, or so that
persons in the next room shall not hear what we are saying.
You merely banged the door, with no reason in your mind, and
in a way that might well make it swing open again, as in
fact it has done."

"It won't stay shut. Honestly it won't," said Vanya.

"If it is difficult, then it will require more time and care
to carry out my request," said the Director.

This time Vanya shut the door properly.

"Tell me something to do," I begged.

"Is it impossible for you to think of anything? There is a
fireplace and some wood. Go build a fire."

I did as I was told, laid the wood in the fireplace, but found
no matches, either in my pocket or on the mantelpiece. So I
came back and told Tortsov of my difficulty.

"What in the world do you want matches for?" asked he.

"To light the fire."

"The fireplace is made of paper. Did you intend to burn
down the theatre?"

"I was just going to pretend," I explained.

He held out an empty hand.

"To pretend to light a fire, pretended matches are sufficient.
As if the point were to strike a match!

"When you reach the point of playing Hamlet, threading a
way through his intricate psychology to the moment when he
kills the King, will it be important to you to have a life-size
sword in your hand? If you lack one, will you be unable to
finish the performance? You can kill the King without a sword,
and you can light the fire without a match. What needs to burn
is your imagination."

I went on pretending to light my fire. To lengthen the action I arranged that the make-believe matches should go out a number of times, although I tried hard to protect them with my hands. Also I tried to see the fire, to feel the heat, but failed, and soon began to be bored, so that I was compelled to think of something else to do. I began to move the furniture, then to count the objects in the room, but having no purpose behind these acts they were all mechanical.

"There is nothing surprising in that," explained the Director. "If an action has no inner foundation, it cannot hold your attention. It takes no time to push a few chairs about, but if you were compelled to arrange some chairs of different sorts for a particular purpose, as for guests at a dinner who must be seated according to rank, age, and personal harmony, you could spend a long time over them."

But my imagination had run dry.

As soon as he saw that the others had also run down, he gathered us together in the living-room. "Aren't you ashamed of yourselves? If I brought a dozen children in here and told them this is their new home, you would see their imagination sparkle; their games would be real games. Can't you be like them?"

"It is easy to say that," Paul complained. "But we aren't children. They naturally desire to play, and with us it must be forced."

"Of course," the Director answered, "if you either will not or cannot light a spark within yourselves, I have no more to say. Every person who is really an artist desires to create inside of himself another, deeper, more interesting life than the one that actually surrounds him."

Grisha broke in: "If the curtain were up, and the audience there, the desire would come."

"No," replied the Director with decision. "If you are really artists you will feel the desire without those accessories. Now be frank. Actually what was it that prevented your acting anything?"

I explained that I could light a fire, move furniture, open and shut doors, but these acts are not extended enough to hold my attention. I light the fire, or close the door, and that is the end of it. If one act led to another, and gave rise to a third, natural momentum and tension would be created.

"In short," he summed up, "what you think you need is not short, external, semi-mechanical acts, but some that have a broader perspective, are deeper, and more complicated?"

"No," I answered, "but give us something that, although simple, is interesting."

"Do you mean to say," said he, perplexed, "that all that depends on me? Surely the explanation must be sought in the inner motives, in the circumstances amid which, and for the sake of which, you are doing the act. Take that opening or shutting of a door. Nothing can be simpler, you might say, of less interest, or more mechanical.

"But suppose that in this apartment of Maria's, there used to live a man who became violently insane. They took him away to a psychopathic ward. If he escaped from there, and were behind that door, what would you do?"

Once the question was put in that form our whole inner aim, as the Director described it, was altered. We no longer thought about how to extend our activity, or worried about its external form. Our minds were centred on estimating the value or purpose of this or that act in view of the problem presented. Our eyes began to measure the distance to the door, and to look for safe approaches to it. They examined the surroundings for directions of escape, in case the madman should break through the door. Our instinct of self-preservation sensed danger, and suggested ways of dealing with it.

Either accidentally or on purpose, Vanya, who had been pressing against the door after it was shut, suddenly jumped away, and we all rushed after him, the girls screaming and running off into another room. In the end I found myself under a table, with a heavy bronze ash-receiver in my hand.

The job was not ended. The door was now closed, but not

locked. There was no key. Therefore the safest thing we could do was to barricade it with sofas, tables, and chairs, then call up the hospital and arrange to have them take the necessary steps to regain the custody of the madman.

The success of this improvisation put me in high spirits. I went over to the Director and begged him to give me another chance at lighting the fire.

Without a moment's hesitation he told me Maria had just inherited a fortune! That she has taken this apartment, and is celebrating her good luck by a housewarming, to which she has invited all her fellow-students. One of them, who is well acquainted with Kachalov, Moskvin, and Leonidov, has promised to bring them to the party. But the apartment is very chilly, the central heating has not yet been turned on, although it is very cold outside. Can some wood for an open fire be found?

Some sticks might be borrowed from a neighbor. A little fire is started, but it smokes badly, and must be put out. Meanwhile it has grown late. Another fire is started, but the wood is green, and will not burn. In another minute the guests will be here.

"Now," he continued, "let me see what you would do *if* my supposed facts were true."

When it was all over, the Director said: "Today I can say that you acted with a motive. You have learned that *all action in the theatre must have an inner justification, be logical, coherent, and real.* Second: *if* acts as a lever to lift us out of the world of actuality into the realm of imagination."

## 4

Today the Director proceeded to enumerate the various functions of *if*.

"This word has a peculiar quality, a kind of power which you sensed, and which produced in you an instantaneous, inner stimulus.

"Note too how easily and simply it came. That door, which was the starting point in our exercise, became a means of de-

fence, and your basic aim, the object of your concentrated attention, was desire for self-preservation.

"The supposition of danger is always exciting. It is a kind
of yeast that will ferment at any time. As for the door and the
fireplace, inanimate objects, they excite us only when they are
bound up with something else, of more importance to us.

"Take into consideration also that this inner stimulus was
brought about without force, and without deception. I did not
tell you that there was a madman behind the door. On the
contrary, by using the word *if* I frankly recognized the fact
that I was offering you only a supposition. All I wanted to
accomplish was to make you say what you would have done *if*
the supposition about the madman were a real fact, leaving you
to feel what anybody in the given circumstances must feel. You
in turn did not force yourselves, or make yourselves accept the
supposition as reality, but only as a supposition.

"What would have happened if, instead of this frank con-
fession, I had sworn to you that there was, really and truly, a
madman behind the door?"

"I should not have believed such an obvious deception," was
my reaction.

"With this special quality of *if*," explained the Director, "no-
body obliges you to believe or not believe anything. Everything
is clear, honest, and above-board. You are given a question, and
you are expected to answer it sincerely and definitely.

"Consequently, the secret of the effect of *if* lies first of all
in the fact that it does not use fear or force, or make the artist
do anything. On the contrary, it reassures him through its
honesty, and encourages him to have confidence in a supposed
situation. That is why, in your exercise, the stimulus was produced so naturally.

"This brings me to another quality. *It arouses an inner and
real activity,* and does this by natural means. Because you are
actors you did not give a simple answer to the question. You
felt you must answer the challenge to *action.*

"This important characteristic of *if* brings it close to one of the fundamentals of our school of acting—*activity in creativeness and art.*"

## 5

"Some of you are eager to put what I have been telling you into immediate practice," said the Director today. "That is quite right and I am glad to fall in with your wishes. Let us apply the use of *if* to a role.

"Suppose you were to play a dramatization of Chekhov's tale about an innocent farmer who unscrewed a nut off a railroad track to use as a sinker for his fishing line. For this he was tried and severely punished. This imaginary happening will sink into the consciousness of some, but for most people it will remain a 'funny story.' They will never even glimpse the tragedy of the legal and social conditions hidden behind the laughter. But the artist who is to act one of the parts in this scene cannot laugh. He must think through for himself and, most important, he must live through whatever it was that caused the author to write the story. How would you go about it?" The Director paused.

The students were silent and thoughtful for a time.

"In moments of doubt, when your thoughts, feelings, and imagination are silent, remember *if*. The author also began his work that way. He said to himself:

"'What would happen *if* a simple farmer, off on a fishing expedition, were to take a nut from a rail?' Now give yourselves the same problem and add: 'What would I do *if* the case came up to me to judge?'"

"I would convict the criminal," I answered, without hesitation.

"What of? On account of the sinker for his fishing line?"

"For the theft of a nut."

"Of course, one shouldn't steal," agreed Tortsov. "But can you punish a man severely for a crime of which he is entirely unconscious?"

"He must be made to realize that he might be the cause of wrecking a whole train, killing hundreds of people," I retorted.

"On account of one small nut? You will never get him to believe that," argued the Director.

"The man is only making believe. He understands the nature of his act," said I.

"If the man who plays the farmer has talent, he will prove to you by his acting that he is unconscious of any guilt," said the Director.

As the discussion went on he used every possible argument to justify the defendant, and in the end he succeeded in making me weaken a little. As soon as he noticed that he said:

"You felt that very same inner push which the judge himself probably experienced. If you played that part, analogous feelings would draw you close to the character.

"To achieve this kinship between the actor and the person he is portraying add some concrete detail which will fill out the play, giving it point and absorbing action. The circumstances which are predicated on *if* are taken from sources near to your own feelings, and they have a powerful influence on the inner life of an actor. Once you have established this contact between your life and your part, you will feel that inner push or stimulus. Add a whole series of contingencies based on your own experience in life, and you will see how easy it will be for you sincerely to believe in the possibility of what you are called upon to do on the stage.

"Work out an entire role in this fashion, and you will create a whole new life.

"The feelings aroused will express themselves in the acts of this imaginary person had he been placed in the circumstances made by the play."

"Are they conscious or unconscious?" I asked.

"Make the test yourself. Go over every detail in the process and decide what is conscious, what unconscious, in its origin. You will never unravel the puzzle, because you will not even remember some of the most important moments in it. These will arise, in whole or in part, of their own accord, and will pass by unnoticed, all in the realm of the subconscious.

"To convince yourself, ask an actor, after some great performance, how he felt while on the stage, and what he did there. He will not be able to answer because he was not aware of what he lived through, and does not remember many of the more significant moments. All you will get from him is that he felt comfortable on the stage, that he was in easy relationship to the other actors. Beyond that, he will be able to tell you nothing.

"You will astonish him by your description of his acting. He will gradually come to realize things about his performance of which he had been entirely unconscious.

"We may conclude from this that *if* is also a stimulus to the creative subconscious. Besides, it helps us to carry out another fundamental principle of our art: 'unconscious creativeness through conscious technique.'

"Up to this point I have explained the uses of *if* in connection with two of the main principles in our type of action. It is even more strongly bound up with a third. Our great poet Pushkin wrote about it in his unfinished article on the drama.

"Among other things he said:

" 'Sincerity of emotions, feelings that seem true in given circumstances—that is what we ask of a dramatist.'

"I add from myself that that is exactly what we ask of an actor.

"Think deeply about this saying, and later I shall give you a vivid example of how *if* helps us to carry it out."

"Sincerity of emotions, feelings that seem true in given circumstances," I repeated with all sorts of intonations.

"Stop," said the Director. "You make a banality of it without uncovering its essential meaning. When you cannot grasp a thought as a whole, break it up into its component parts, and study them one by one."

"Just what," asked Paul, "does the expression 'given circumstances' mean?"

"It means the story of the play, its facts, events, epoch, time and place of action, conditions of life, the actors' and regisseur's interpretation, the mise-en-scene, the production, the sets, the costumes, properties, lighting and sound effects,—all the circumstances that are given to an actor to take into account as he creates his role.

"*If* is the starting point, the given circumstances, the development. The one cannot exist without the other, if it is to possess a necessary stimulating quality. However, their functions differ somewhat: *if* gives the push to dormant imagination, whereas the *given circumstances* build the basis for *if* itself. And they both, together and separately, help to create an inner stimulus."

"And what," asked Vanya, with interest, "does 'sincerity of emotions' mean?"

"Just what it says—living human emotions, feelings which the actor himself has experienced."

"Well then," Vanya went on, "what are 'feelings that seem true'?"

"By true seeming we refer not to actual feelings themselves but to something nearly akin to them, to emotions reproduced indirectly, under the prompting of true inner feelings.

"In practice, this is approximately what you will have to do: first, you will have to imagine in your own way the 'given circumstances' offered by the play, the regisseur's production and your own artistic conception. All of this material will provide a general outline for the life of the character you are to enact, and the circumstances surrounding him. It is necessary that you really believe in the general possibilities of such a life, and then become so accustomed to it that you feel yourself close to it. If you are successful in this, you will find that 'sincere emotions,' or 'feelings that seem true' will spontaneously grow in you.

"However, when you use this third principle of acting, forget about your feelings, because they are largely of subconscious origin, and not subject to direct command. Direct all of your attention to the 'given circumstances.' They are always within reach."

Toward the end of the lesson he said: "I can now supplement what I said earlier about *if*. Its power depends not only on its own keenness, but also on the sharpness of outline of the given circumstances."

"But," broke in Grisha, "what is left for the actor since everything is prepared by others? Just trifles?"

"What do you mean, trifles?" said the Director indignantly. "Do you think that to believe in the imaginative fiction of another person, and bring it to life, is a trifle? Don't you know that to compose on a theme suggested by someone else, is much more difficult than to invent one yourself? We know of cases where a bad play has achieved world fame because of having been re-created by a great actor. We know that Shakespeare re-created stories by others. That is what we do to the work of the dramatist, we bring to life what is hidden under the words; we put our own thoughts into the author's lines, and we establish our own relationships to other characters in the play, and the conditions of their lives; we filter through ourselves all the materials that we receive from the author and the director; we work over them, supplementing them out of our own imagination. That material becomes part of us, spiritually, and even physically; our emotions are sincere, and as a final result we have truly productive activity—all of which is closely interwoven with the implications of the play.

"And that tremendous work you tell me is just trifles!

"No, indeed. That is creativeness and art."

With these words he ended the lesson.

6

Today, we did a series of exercises, consisting of setting ourselves problems in action, such as writing a letter, tidying up a room, looking for a lost object. These we framed in all sorts of exciting suppositions, and the object was to execute them under the circumstances we had created.

To such exercises the Director attributes so much significance that he worked long and enthusiastically on them.

After he had done an exercise with each one of us in turn he said:

"This is the beginning of the right road. You found it through your own experience. For the present there should be no other approach to a part or a play. To understand the importance of this right point of departure, compare what you have just done with what you did at the test performance. With the exception of a few scattered and accidental moments in the playing of Maria and Kostya, all of you began your work at the end instead of at the beginning. You were determined to arouse tremendous emotion in yourselves and your audience right at the start; to offer them some vivid images, and at the same time exhibit all your inner and outer gifts. This wrong approach naturally led to violence. To avoid such mistakes, remember, for all time, that when you begin to study each role you should first gather all the materials that have any bearing on it, and supplement them with more and more imagination, until you have achieved such a similarity to life that it is easy to believe in what you are doing. In the beginning forget about your feelings. When the inner conditions are prepared, and right, feelings will come to the surface of their own accord."

# CHAPTER FOUR

# Imagination

I

THE DIRECTOR asked us to come to his apartment today for our lesson. He seated us comfortably in his study, and began:

"You know now that our work on a play begins with the use of *if* as a lever to lift us out of everyday life onto the plane of imagination. The play, the parts in it, are the invention of the author's imagination, a whole series of *ifs* and given circumstances thought up by him. There is no such thing as actuality on the stage. Art is a product of the imagination, as the work of a dramatist should be. The aim of the actor should be to use his technique to turn the play into a theatrical reality. In this process imagination plays by far the greatest part."

He pointed to the walls of his study, which were covered with every conceivable design for theatre sets.

"Look," he said to us, "all these are the work of a favourite artist of mine, now dead. He was a strange person, who loved to make sets for plays which had not yet been written. Take for instance this design for the last act of a play Chekhov was planning to write just before his death: about an expedition lost in the icy North.

"Who would believe," said the Director, "that this was painted by a man who, in all his life, never stirred beyond the suburbs of Moscow? He made an arctic scene out of what he saw around him at home in winter, from stories and scientific publications, from photographs. Out of all that material his imagination painted a picture."

He then turned our attention to another wall, on which

were a series of landscapes, seen in varying moods. There, in each one, was the same row of attractive little houses near a pine grove—except that the time of year, the hour of the day, and the conditions of the weather were different. Farther along the wall was the same spot without houses, with only a clearing, a lake, and various kinds of trees. Evidently the artist enjoyed re-arranging nature and the attendant lives of human beings. In all his pictures he built and tore down houses and villages, changed the face of the locality, and moved mountains.

"And here are some sketches for a non-existent play about life between the planets,"—pointing out other drawings and water colours. "To paint such a picture the artist must have not only imagination, but fantasy as well."

"What is the difference between them?" asked one of the students.

"Imagination creates things that can be or can happen, whereas fantasy invents things that are not in existence, which never have been or will be. And yet, who knows, perhaps they will come to be. When fantasy created the Flying Carpet, who could have thought that one day we should be winging our way through space? Both fantasy and imagination are indispensable to a painter."

"And to an actor?" asked Paul.

"What do you think? Does the dramatist supply everything that the actors need to know about the play? Can you, in a hundred pages, give a full account of the life of the dramatis personae? For example, does the author give sufficient details of what has happened before the play begins? Does he let you know what will happen when it is ended, or what goes on behind the scenes? The dramatist is often a miser in commentary. In his text, all that you find may be 'the same and Peter'; or, 'exit Peter.' But one cannot appear out of the air, or disappear into it. We never believe in any action taken 'in general': 'he gets up,' 'he walks up and down in agitation,' 'he laughs,' 'he dies.' Even characteristics are given in laconic form, such as 'a young man of agreeable appearance, smokes a great deal.'

Hardly a sufficient basis for creating his entire external image, manners, way of walking.

"And what about the lines? Is it enough merely to learn them?

"Will what is given paint the character of the dramatis personae and give you all the shadings of their thoughts, feelings, impulses and acts?

"No, all this must be made fuller and deeper by the actor. In this creative process imagination leads the actor."

Our lesson was interrupted at this point by an unexpected call from a famous foreign tragic actor. He told us all about his triumphs, and after he left the Director said with a smile:

"Of course he romances, but an impressionable person of his sort really believes in his fabrications. We actors are so accustomed to embroider facts with details drawn from our own imaginations, that the habit is carried over into ordinary life. There, of course, the imagined details are as superfluous as they are necessary in the theatre.

"In talking about a genius you would not say that he lies; he sees realities with different eyes from ours. Is it just to blame him if his imagination makes him wear rose-coloured, blue, grey, or black glasses?

"I must admit that I myself have to lie quite frequently, when as an artist, or as a director, I am dealing with a part or a play that does not attract me. In such a case my creative faculties are paralysed. I must have some stimulant, so I begin to tell everyone how thrilled I am over my work. I am compelled to hunt for whatever there may be of interest and to boast about it. In this way my imagination is spurred on. If I were alone, I would not make this effort, but when working with others one must back up one's lies substantially. It often happens that one can use these lies as material for a role or production."

"If imagination plays such an important part in an actor's work," asked Paul rather shyly, "what can he do if he lacks it?"

"He must develop it," answered the Director, "or else leave

the theatre. Otherwise he will fall into the hands of directors who will make up for his lack by using their own imagina-tions, and he would become a pawn. Wouldn't it be better for him to build up an imagination of his own?"

"That, I am afraid," said I, "is very difficult."

"It all depends on what kind of an imagination you have," said the Director. "The kind that has initiative of its own can be developed without special effort, and will work steadily and untiringly, whether you are awake or asleep. Then there is the kind that lacks initiative, but is easily aroused and continues to work as soon as anything is suggested to it. The kind that does not respond to suggestions presents a more difficult problem. Here the actor takes in suggestions in a merely external, formal way. With such an equipment, development is fraught with difficulty, and there is very little hope of success unless the actor makes a great effort."

\*          \*          \*          \*          \*          \*          \*

Has my imagination initiative?

Is it suggestible? Will it develop by itself?

These questions give me no peace. Late in the evening, I closed myself in my room, settled myself comfortably on my sofa with pillows all around me, shut my eyes, and began to improvise. But my attention was distracted by round spots of colour that kept passing across my closed eyelids.

I put out my light, as I supposed it was causing these sen-sations.

What should I think about? My imagination showed me trees in a large pine forest, gently and rhythmically stirring in a soft breeze. I seemed to smell the fresh air.

Why . . . in all this serenity . . . can I hear a ticking clock? . . .

I had fallen asleep!

Why, of course, I realized, I should not imagine things with-out a purpose.

So I went up in an airplane, above the tree-tops, flying over

them, over the fields, rivers, cities, . . . tick, tick, goes the clock.
. . . Who is that snoring? Surely not I . . . did I drop off . . .
have I been asleep long . . . the clock strikes eight. . . .


2

I was so discomfited by the failure of my attempts to exercise
my imagination at home, that I told the Director about it at
our lesson today.

"You did not succeed because you made a series of mistakes,"
he explained. "In the first place, you forced your imagination,
instead of coaxing it. Then, you tried to think without having
any interesting subject. Your third mistake was that your
thoughts were passive. Activity in imagination is of utmost importance. First comes internal, and afterwards external action."

I pointed out that in a sense I had been active, since I was
flying over the forests at a high rate of speed.

"When you are reclining comfortably in an express train,
are you active?" asked the Director. "The engineer is working,
but the passenger is passive. Of course, if you are engaged in
some important business, conversation, or discussion, or are
writing a report, while on the train, then you would have some
basis for talking about action. Again, in your flight in the airplane, the pilot was working, but you were doing nothing. If
you had been at the controls, or taking topographical photographs, you might say you were active.

"Perhaps I can explain by describing my little niece's
favourite game.

" 'What are you doing?' the little girl asks.

" 'I am drinking tea,' I answer.

" 'But,' she says, 'if it were castor oil then how would you
drink it?'

"I am forced to recall the taste of castor oil, to show her
the disgust I feel, and when I succeed the child fills the room
with her laughter.

" 'Where are you sitting?'

" 'On a chair,' I reply.

" 'But if you were sitting on a hot stove, then what would you do?'

"I am obliged to think myself on a hot stove, and try to decide how I can save myself from being burned to death. When I succeed the child is sorry for me, and cries, 'I do not want to play any more.' If I go on, she ends by bursting into tears. Why don't you think up some such game as an exercise for arousing activity?"

Here I broke in to point out that this was elementary, and to ask how to develop the imagination in subtler ways.

"Don't be in a hurry," said the Director. "There will be plenty of time. Just now we need exercises bound up with the simple things that actually surround us.

"Take our class here as an example. This is an actual fact. Suppose the surroundings, the teacher, the students, remain as they are. Now with my magic *if* I shall put myself on the plane of make-believe, by changing one circumstance only: the hour of the day. I shall say, it is not three o'clock in the afternoon, but three o'clock in the night.

"Use your imagination to justify a lesson that lasts so late. Out of that simple circumstance there follows a whole series of consequences. At home your family will be anxious about you. As there is no telephone you cannot notify them. Another student will fail to appear at a party where he is expected. A third lives in the outskirts and has no idea how he will get home; the trains having stopped.

"All this brings external changes and inner ones as well, and gives a tone to what you do.

"Or try another angle.

"The time of day remains at three in the afternoon, but suppose the time of year has changed. Instead of winter it is spring, the air is wonderful, and it is hot out even in the shade.

"I see you are smiling already. After your lesson you will have time for a stroll. Decide what you intend to do; justify your decision with the necessary suppositions; and again you have the fundamentals of an exercise.

"This is merely one of countless examples of how you can use forces within you to change the material things about you. Do not try to get rid of these things. On the contrary, include them in your imaginary lives.

"That sort of transformation has a real place in our more intimate kind of exercises. We can use ordinary chairs to outline anything the imagination of an author or director can ask us to create; houses, city squares, ships, forests. It will do no harm if we find ourselves unable to believe that this chair is a particular object, because even without the belief we may have the feeling it arouses."

## 3

In opening the lesson today the Director said: "Up to this point our exercises for the development of the imagination have, to a greater or lesser degree, touched on material facts, like furniture, or on realities of life, like the seasons. Now I shall *transfer* our work to a different plane. We give up time, place, and action, as far as their external accompaniments are concerned, and you will do the whole thing directly with your mind. Now," he asked, turning to me, "where would you like to be, and at what time?"

"In my own room," I said, "at night."

"Good," said he. "If I were to be carried into those surroundings, it would be absolutely necessary for me first to make an approach to the house; to climb the outer steps; to ring the bell; to go through, in short, a whole series of acts leading up to my being in my room.

"Do you see a door-knob to grasp? Do you feel it turn? Does the door swing open? Now what is in front of you?"

"Straight before me is a closet, a bureau."

"What do you see on the left?"

"My sofa, and a table."

"Try walking up and down; living in the room. What are you thinking about?"

"I have found a letter, remember that it is not answered, and am embarrassed."

"Evidently you *are* in your room," the Director declared. "Now what are you going to do?"

"It depends on what time it is," said I.

"That," said he in a tone of approval, "is a sensible remark. Let us agree that it is eleven o'clock at night."

"The very best time," said I, "when everybody in the house is likely to be asleep."

"Just why," he asked, "do you particularly want this quiet?"

"To convince myself that I am a tragic actor."

"It is too bad you wish to use your time to such poor purpose; how do you plan to convince yourself?"

"I shall play, just for myself, some tragic role."

"What role? Othello?"

"Oh, no!" I exclaimed. "I can't play Othello in my own room. Every corner there has associations, and would only lead me to copy what I did before."

"Then, what are you going to play?" the Director demanded.

I did not answer, because I had not decided, so he asked: "What are you doing now?"

"I am looking around the room. Perhaps some object, some accidental thing, will suggest a creative theme."

"Well," he prodded, "have you thought of anything yet?"

I began to think aloud. "Back in my closet," I said, "there is a dark corner. One hook there is just right for a person to hang himself on. *If* I wanted to hang myself, how should I go about it?"

"Yes?" urged the Director.

"Of course, first of all, I should need to find some rope, or belt, a strap . . ."

"Now what are you doing?"

"I am going over my drawers, shelves, closets, to find a strap."

"Do you see anything?"

"Yes, I have the strap. But unfortunately the hook is too near the floor; my feet would touch."

"That is inconvenient," the Director agreed. "Look around for another hook."

"There is not another hook that would hold me."

"Then possibly you had better remain alive, and busy yourself with something more interesting, and less exciting."

"My imagination has dried up," said I.

"There is nothing surprising in that," said he. "Your plot was not logical. It would be most difficult to arrive at a logical conclusion to commit suicide because you were considering a change in your acting. It was only reasonable that your imagination should balk at being asked to work from a doubtful premise to a stupid conclusion.

"Nevertheless this exercise was a demonstration of a new way of using your imagination, in a place where everything was familiar to you. But what will you do when you are called upon to imagine an unfamiliar life?"

"Suppose you take a journey around the world. You must not think it out 'somehow,' or 'in general,' or 'approximately,' because all those terms do not belong in art. You must do it with all the details proper to such a large undertaking. Always remain in close contact with logic and coherence. This will help you to hold unsubstantial and slippery dreams close to steady solid facts.

"Now I want to explain to you how you can use the exercises we have been doing in various combinations. You can say to yourself: 'I will be a simple spectator, and watch what my imagination paints for me, while I take no part in this imaginary life.'

"Or if you decide to join in the activities of this imaginary life you will mentally picture your associates, and yourself with them, and again you will be a passive spectator.

In the end you will tire of being an observer, and wish to act. Then as an active participant in this imaginary life you will no longer see yourself, but only what surrounds you, and to this you will respond inwardly, because you are a real part of it."

4

Today the Director opened his remarks by telling us what we must always do when the author, the director, and the others who are working on a production, leave out things we need to know.

We must have, first of all, an unbroken series of supposed circumstances in the midst of which our exercise is played. Secondly we must have a solid line of inner visions bound up with those circumstances, so that they will be *illustrated* for us. *During every moment we are on the stage, during every moment of the development of the action of the play, we must be aware either of the external circumstances which surround us (the whole material setting of the production), or of an inner chain of circumstances which we ourselves have imagined in order to illustrate our parts.*

Out of these moments will be formed an unbroken series of images, something like a moving picture. As long as we are acting creatively, this film will unroll and be thrown on the screen of our inner vision, making vivid the circumstances among which we are moving. Moreover, these inner images create a corresponding mood, and arouse emotions, while holding us within the limits of the play.

"As to these inner images," the Director asked, "is it correct to say that we feel them to be inside of us? We possess the faculty to see things which are not there by making a mental picture of them. Take this chandelier. It exists outside of me. I look at it, and have the sensation that I am putting out, toward it, what you might call visual feelers. Now I close my eyes and see that chandelier again on the screen of my inner vision.

"The same process occurs when we are dealing with sounds.

We hear imaginary noises with an inner ear, and yet we feel the sources of these sounds, in the majority of cases, to be outside of us.

"You can test this in various ways such as giving a coherent account of your whole life in terms of images you remember. This may sound difficult but I think you will find that this work is actually not so complicated."

"Why is that?" asked several students at once.

"Because, although our feelings and emotional experiences are changeable and incapable of being grasped, what you have seen is much more substantial. Images are much more easily and firmly fixed in our visual memories, and can be recalled at will."

"The whole question then," said I, "is how to create a whole picture?"

"That question," said the Director, as he rose to leave, "we will discuss next time."

5

"Let us make an imaginary moving picture," said the Director as he came into class today.

"I am going to choose a passive theme because it will necessitate more work. At this point, I am not so much interested in the action itself as in the approach to it. That is why I suggest that you, Paul, are living the life of a tree."

"Good," said Paul with decision. "I am an age-old oak! However, even though I have said it, I don't really believe it."

"In that case," suggested the Director, "why don't you say to yourself: 'I am I; but *if* I were an old oak, set in certain surrounding conditions, what would I do?' and decide where you are, in a forest, in a meadow, on a mountain top; in whatever place affects you most."

Paul knit his brows, and finally decided that he was standing in an upland meadow near the Alps. To the left, there is a castle on a height.

"What do you see near you?" asked the Director.

"On myself I see a thick covering of leaves, which rustle."

"They do indeed," agreed the Director. "Up there the winds must often be strong."

"In my branches," continued Paul, "I see some birds' nests."

The Director then pushed him to describe every detail of his imaginary existence as an oak tree.

When Leo's turn came he made the most ordinary, uninspired choice. He said he was a cottage in a garden in the Park.

"What do you see?" asked the Director.

"The Park," was the answer.

"But you cannot see the whole Park at once. You must decide on some one definite spot. What is there right in front of you?"

"A fence."

"What kind of a fence?"

Leo was silent, so the Director went on: "What is this fence made of?"

"What material? . . . Cast iron."

"Describe it. What is the design?"

Leo drew his finger around on the table for a long time. It was evident that he had not thought out what he had said.

"I don't understand. You must describe it more clearly."

Obviously Leo was making no effort to arouse his own imagination. I wondered of what use such passive thinking could possibly be, so I asked the Director about it.

"In my method of putting a student's imagination to work," he explained, "there are certain points which should be noted. If his imagination is inactive I ask him some simple question. He will have to answer, since he has been addressed. If he responds thoughtlessly, I do not accept his answer. Then, in order to give a more satisfactory answer, he must either rouse his imagination or else approach the subject through his mind, by means of logical reasoning. Work on the imagination is often prepared and directed in this conscious, intellectual manner. The student then sees something, either in his memory or in his imagination: certain definite visual images are before him. For a brief moment, he lives in a dream. After that, another question, and the process is repeated. So with a third and fourth, until I have sustained and lengthened that brief moment into something approaching a whole picture. Perhaps, at first, this is not interesting. The valuable part about it is that the illusion has been woven together out of the student's own inner images. Once this is accomplished, he can repeat it once or twice or many times. The more often he recalls it, the more deeply it will be printed on his memory, and the more deeply he will live into it.

"However, we sometimes have to deal with sluggish imaginations, which will not respond to even the simplest questions. Then I have only one course open. I not only propound the question, I also suggest the answer. If the student can use that answer he goes on from there. If not, he changes it, and puts something else in its place. In either case he has been obliged to use his own inner vision. In the end something of an illusory existence is created, even if the material is only partially contributed by the student. The result may not be entirely satisfactory, but it does accomplish something.

"Before this attempt has been made, the student has either had no image in his mind's eye, or what he had was vague and confused. After the effort he can see something definite and even vivid. The ground has been prepared in which the teacher or the director can sow new seeds. This is the canvas on which the picture will be painted. Moreover, the student has learned the method by which he can take his imagination in hand and ply it with problems which his own mind will suggest. He will form the habit of deliberately wrestling with the passivity and inertia of his imagination, and that is a long step ahead."

6

Today we continued the same exercises in developing our imaginations.

"At our last lesson," said the Director to Paul, "you told me *who* you were, *where* you were, and what you saw, with your inner eye. Now describe to me what your inner ear hears as an imaginary old oak tree."

At first Paul could not hear anything.

"Don't you hear anything in the meadow around you?"

Then Paul said he could hear the sheep and the cows, the munching of grass, the tinkle of the cow-bells, the gossip of the women resting after their work in the fields.

"Now tell me *when* all this is happening in your imagination," said the Director with interest.

Paul chose the feudal period.

"Then, do you, as an aged oak, hear sounds that are particularly characteristic of that time?"

Paul reflected for a moment, and then said that he could hear a wandering minstrel on his way to a festival at the nearby castle.

"Why do you stand alone in a field?" the Director asked.

In response Paul gave the following explanation. The whole knoll on which the solitary old oak stands was formerly covered by a thick forest. But the baron of the nearby castle was constantly in danger of attack, and, fearing that this forest could hide the movements of his enemy's forces, he cut it down. Only this one powerful old oak was allowed to stand. It was to protect a spring, which, rising in its shade, provided the necessary water for the baron's flocks.

The Director then observed: "Generally speaking, this question—*for what reason?*—is extremely important. It obliges you to clarify the object of your meditations, it suggests the future, and it impels you to action. A tree, of course, cannot have an active goal, nevertheless, it can have some active significance, and can serve some purpose."

Here Paul intervened and suggested: "The oak is the highest point in the neighbourhood. Therefore it serves as a lookout, a protection against attack."

"Now," the Director then said, "that your imagination has gradually accumulated a sufficient number of given circumstances, let us compare notes with the beginning of this piece of work. At first all you could think of was that you were an oak standing in a meadow. Your mind's eye was full of generalities, clouded like a poorly developed negative. Now you can feel the earth under your roots. But you are deprived of the action necessary on the stage. Therefore there is one more step to be taken. You must find some single new circumstance that will move you emotionally and incite you to action."

Paul tried hard, but could think of nothing.

"In that case," said the Director, "let us try to solve the problem indirectly. First of all, tell me what you are most sensitive to in real life. What, more often than anything else, arouses your feelings—your fear or your joy? I am asking this quite apart from the theme of your imaginary life. When you know the inclinations of your own nature it is not difficult to adapt them to imaginary circumstances. Therefore, name some one trait, quality, interest, which is typical of you."

"I am very much excited by any kind of fight," said Paul after a moment of reflection.

"In that case a raid by the enemy is what we want. The forces of the hostile neighbouring duke are already swarming up the meadow in which you stand. The fight will start here at any moment now. You will be showered with arrows from the enemy crossbows, and some will be pointed with flaming pitch—steady now, and decide before it is too late, what you would do if this really happened to you?"

But Paul could only storm inside of himself without being able to do anything. Finally he broke out:

"What can a tree do to save itself when it is rooted in the earth and incapable of moving?"

"For me your excitement is sufficient," said the Director, with evident satisfaction. "This particular problem is insoluble, and you are not to blame if the theme has no action in it."

"Then why did you give it to him?" was asked.

"Just to prove to you that even a passive theme can produce an inner stimulus and challenge to action. This is an example of how all of our exercises for developing the imagination should teach you to prepare the material, the inner images, for your role."

## 7

At the beginning of our lesson today the Director made a few remarks about the value of imagination in freshening up and refurbishing something the actor has already prepared and used.

He showed us how to introduce a fresh supposition into our exercise with the madman behind the door which entirely changed its orientation.

"Adapt yourself to the new conditions, listen to what they suggest to you, and—act!"

We played with spirit and real excitement, and were complimented.

The end of the lesson was devoted to summing up what we had accomplished.

"Every invention of the actor's imagination must be thoroughly worked out and solidly built on a basis of facts. It must be able to answer all the questions (when, where, why, how) that he asks himself when he is driving his inventive faculties on to make a more and more definite picture of a make-believe existence. Sometimes he will not need to make all this conscious, intellectual effort. His imagination may work intuitively. But you have seen for yourselves that it cannot be counted on. To imagine 'in general,' without a well-defined and thoroughly founded theme is a sterile occupation.

"On the other hand, a conscious, reasoned approach to the imagination often produces a bloodless, counterfeit presentment of life. That will not do for the theatre. Our art demands that an actor's whole nature be actively involved, that he give himself up, both mind and body, to his part. *He must feel the challenge to action physically as well as intellectually* because the imagination, which has no substance or body, can reflexively affect our physical nature and make it act. This faculty is of the greatest importance in our emotion-technique.

"Therefore: *Every movement you make on the stage, every word you speak, is the result of the right life of your imagination.*

"If you speak any lines, or do anything, mechanically, without fully realizing who you are, where you came from, why, what you want, where you are going, and what you will do when you get there, you will be acting without imagination. That time, whether it be short or long, will be unreal, and you will be nothing more than a wound-up machine, an automaton.

"If I ask you a perfectly simple question now, 'Is it cold out today?' before you answer, even with a 'yes,' or 'it's not cold,' or 'I didn't notice,' you should, in your imagination, go back onto the street and remember how you walked or rode. You should test your sensations by remembering how the people you met were wrapped up, how they turned up their collars, how the snow crunched underfoot, and only then can you answer my question.

"If you adhere strictly to this rule in all your exercises, no matter to what part of our program they belong, you will find your imagination developing and growing in power."

# CHAPTER FIVE

## Concentration of Attention

### I

WE WERE working on exercises today when suddenly some of the chairs along one of the walls toppled over. At first we were puzzled and then we realized that somebody was raising the curtain. As long as we were in Maria's "drawing-room" we never had any sense of there being a right or wrong side to the room. Wherever we stood was right. But opening that fourth wall with its big black proscenium arch made you feel that you must constantly adjust yourself. You think of the people looking at you; you seek to be seen and heard by them and not by those who are in the room with you. Only a moment ago the Director and his assistant seemed a natural element here in the drawing-room, but now, transported into the orchestra, they became something quite different; we were all affected by the change. For my part I felt that until we learned how to overcome the effect of that black hole we should never go an inch forward in our work. Paul, however, was confident that we could do better with a new and exciting exercise. The Director's answer to this was:

"Very well. We can try it. Here is a tragedy, which I hope will take your minds off the audience.

"It takes place here in this apartment. Maria has married Kostya, who is treasurer of some public organization. They have a charming, new-born baby, that is being bathed by its mother in a room off the dining-room. The husband is going through some papers and counting money. It is not his money, but property in his care, just brought from the bank. A stack of packets of bank bills has been thrown on the table. In front of Kostya

68

stands Maria's younger brother, Vanya, a low type of moron, who watches him tear the coloured bindings off the packets, and throw them in the fire, where they blaze up and make a lovely glow.

"All the money is counted. As she judges her husband has finished his work Maria calls him in to admire the baby in his bath. The half-witted brother, in imitation of what he has seen, throws some papers into the fire, and whole packets, he finds, make the best blaze, so that in a frenzy of delight he throws in all—the public funds, just drawn from the bank by the treasurer! At this moment Kostya returns, and sees the last packet flaring up. Beside himself, he rushes to the fireplace and knocks down the moron, who falls with a groan, and, with a cry, pulls the last half-burned packet out of the fire.

"His frightened wife runs into the room and sees her brother stretched out on the floor. She tries to raise him, but cannot. Seeing blood on her hands she cries to her husband to bring some water, but he is in a daze and pays no heed, so she runs after it herself. From the other room a heart-rending scream is heard. The darling baby is dead—drowned in its bath.

"Is this enough of a tragedy to keep your minds off the audience?"

This new exercise stirred us with its melodrama and unexpectedness, and yet we accomplished nothing.

"Evidently," exclaimed the Director, "the magnet of the audience is more powerful than the tragedy happening right there on the stage. Since that is so, let us try it again, this time with the curtain down." He and his assistant came back out of the audience into our drawing-room, which once more became friendly and hospitable.

We began to act. The quiet parts, in the beginning of the exercise, we did well; but when we came to the dramatic places, it seemed to me that what I gave out was not at all adequate, and I wanted to do far more than I had feelings for.

This judgment of mine was confirmed when the Director

spoke. "In the beginning," he said, "you acted correctly, but at the end you were pretending to act. You were squeezing feelings out of yourself, so you cannot blame everything on the black hole. It is not the only thing in the way of your living properly on the stage, since with the curtain down the result is the same."

On the excuse of being bothered by any onlookers we were ostensibly left alone to act the exercise again. Actually we were watched through a hole in the scenery and were told that this time we had been both bad and self-assured. "The main fault," said the Director, "seems to lie in your lack of power to concentrate your attention, which is not yet prepared for creative work."

2

The lesson today took place on the school stage, but the curtain was up, and the chairs that stand against it were taken away. Our little living-room was now open to the whole auditorium, which took away all its atmosphere of intimacy and turned it into an ordinary theatrical set. Electric cables were hung on the wall, running in various directions, with bulbs on them, as if for an illumination. We were settled in a row, close to the footlights. Silence fell.

"Which of the girls has lost a heel off her shoe?" asked the Director suddenly.

The students busily examined each other's footgear and were completely absorbed when the Director interrupted.

"What," he asked us, "has just happened in the hall?"

We had no idea. "Do you mean to say you did not notice that my secretary has just brought in some papers for me to sign?" No one had seen him. "And with the curtain up too! The secret seems to be simple enough: *In order to get away from the auditorium you must be interested in something on the stage.*"

That impressed me at once, because I realized that from the very moment I concentrated on something behind the footlights, I cease to think about what was going on in front of them.

I remembered helping a man to pick up nails that had fallen on the stage, when I was rehearsing for my scenes from *Othello*. Then I was absorbed by the simple act of picking them up, and chatting with the man, and I entirely forgot the black hole beyond the footlights.

"Now you will realize that *an actor must have a point of attention, and this point of attention must not be in the auditorium.* The more attractive the object the more it will concentrate the attention. In real life there are always plenty of objects that fix our attention, but conditions in the theatre are different, and interfere with an actor's living normally, so that *an effort* to fix attention becomes necessary. It becomes requisite to learn anew to look at things, on the stage, *and to see them.* Instead of lecturing you further on this subject I will give you some examples.

"Let the points of light, which you will see in a moment, illustrate to you certain aspects of objects, familiar to you in ordinary life, and consequently needed on the stage as well."

There was complete darkness, both in the hall and on the stage. In a few seconds a light appeared, on the table near which we were sitting. In the surrounding gloom this light was noticeable and bright.

"This little lamp," explained the Director, "shining in the darkness, is an example of the Nearest Object. We make use of it in moments of greatest concentration, when it is necessary to gather in our whole attention, to keep it from dissipating itself on distant things."

After the lights were all turned on again, he continued:

"To concentrate on a point of light in surrounding darkness is comparatively easy. Let us repeat the exercise in the light."

He requested one of the students to examine the back of an armchair. I was to study the imitation enamel on a table top. To a third was given some piece of bric-a-brac, a fourth had a pencil, a fifth a piece of string, a sixth a match, and so on.

Paul started to untangle his piece of string, and I stopped him because I said the purpose of the exercise was concentration of attention and not action, that we should only examine the objects given us and think about them. As Paul disagreed with me, we took our difference of opinion to the Director, who said:

"Intensive observation of an object naturally arouses a desire to do something with it. To do something with it in turn intensifies your observation of it. This mutual inter-reaction establishes a stronger contact with the object of your attention."

When I turned back to study the enamel design on the table top I felt a desire to pick it out with some sharp instrument. This obliged me to look at the pattern more closely. Meantime Paul was enthusiastically rapt in the job of unknotting his string. And all the others were busy doing things or attentively observing their various objects.

Finally the Director said:

"I see that you are all able to concentrate on the nearest object in the light as well as in the dark."

After that he demonstrated, first without lights and then with them, objects at a moderate distance and objects at a far distance. We were to build some imaginary story around them and hold them in the centre of our attention as long as we could. This we were able to do when the main lights were turned off.

As soon as they were put on again he said:

"Now look around you very carefully and choose some one thing, either moderately near or farther off, and concentrate on it."

There were so many things all around us that at first my eyes kept running from one to the other. Finally I settled on a little statuette over on the mantelpiece. But I could not keep my eyes fixed on it for long. They were drawn away to other things about the room.

"Evidently before you can establish medium and far distant points of attention you will have to learn how to *look at and see things* on the stage," said the Director. "It is a difficult thing to do in front of people, and the dark proscenium arch.

"In ordinary life you walk and sit and talk and look, but on the stage you lose all these faculties. You feel the closeness of the public and you say to yourself, 'Why are they looking at me?' And you have to be taught all over again how to do all these things in public.

"Remember this: all of our acts, even the simplest, which are so familiar to us in everyday life, become strained when we appear behind the footlights before a public of a thousand people. That is why it is necessary to correct ourselves and learn again how to walk, move about, sit, or lie down. It is essential to re-educate ourselves to look and see, on the stage, to listen and to hear."

### 3

"Choose some one object," said the Director to us today, after we had been seated on the open stage. "Suppose you take that embroidered cloth over there, since it has a striking design."

We began to look at it very carefully, but he interrupted.

"That is not looking. It is staring."

We tried to relax our gaze, but we did not convince him that we were seeing what we were looking at.

"More attentively," he ordered.

We all bent forward.

"Still a lot of mechanical gazing," he insisted, "and little attention."

We knit our brows and seemed to me to be most attentive.

"To be attentive and to appear to be attentive are two different things," he said. "Make the test for yourselves, and see which way of looking is real, and which is imitative."

After a great deal of adjusting we finally settled down quietly, trying not to strain our eyes, and looked at the embroidered cloth.

Suddenly he burst out laughing, and turning to me he said:

"If only I could photograph you just as you are! You wouldn't believe that any human being could contort himself into such an absurd attitude. Why, your eyes are almost bursting from their sockets. Is it necessary for you to put so much effort into merely looking at something? Less, less! Much less effort! Relax! More——! Are you so drawn to this object that you have to bend forwards to it? Throw yourself back! A great deal more!"

He was able, finally, to reduce a little of my tenseness. The little he did accomplish made an enormous difference to me. No one can have any idea of this relief unless he has stood on the open stage, crippled with strained muscles.

"A chattering tongue or mechanically moving hands and feet cannot take the place of the comprehending eye. The eye of an actor which looks at and sees an object attracts the attention of the spectator, and by the same token points out to him what he should look at. Conversely, a blank eye lets the attention of the spectator wander away from the stage."

Here he went back to his demonstration with electric lights: "I have shown you a series of objects such as we all have in life. You have seen the objects in the way that an actor should feel them on the stage. Now I shall show you how they never should be looked at but nevertheless almost always are. I shall show you the objects with which an actor's attention is nearly always busied while he is on the boards."

All the lights went out again, and in the dark we saw little bulbs flashing all around. They dashed about the stage and then all through the audience. Suddenly they disappeared, and a strong light appeared above one of the seats in the orchestra.

"What is that?" asked a voice in the dark.

"That is the Severe Dramatic Critic," said the Director. "He comes in for a lot of attention at an opening."

The little lights began to flash again, then they stopped and again a strong light appeared, this time over the orchestra seat of the regisseur.

Scarcely had this gone out when a dim, weak, and tiny bulb

appeared on the stage. "That," said he ironically, "is the poor partner of an actor who pays little attention to her."

After this the little lights flashed all around again, and the big lights came on and off, sometimes simultaneously, sometimes separately,—an orgy of lights. It reminded me of the exhibition performance of *Othello,* when my attention was scattered all over the theatre, and when only accidentally, and at certain moments, was I able to concentrate on a nearby object.

"Is it now clear," the Director asked, "that an actor should choose the object of his attention on the stage, in the play, the role, and the setting? This is the difficult problem you must solve."

## 4

Today the Assistant Director, Rakhmanov, appeared and announced that he had been asked by the Director to take his place for a class in drill.

"Collect all of your attention," he said in a crisp, confident tone. "Your exercise will be as follows. I shall select an object for each of you to look at. You will notice its form, lines, colours, detail, characteristics. All this must be done while I count thirty. Then the lights will go out, so that you cannot see the object, and I shall call upon you to describe it. In the dark you will tell me everything that your visual memory has retained. I shall check up with the lights on, and compare what you have told me with the actual object. Listen closely. I am beginning. Maria—the mirror."

"O good gracious! Is this the one?"

"No unnecessary questions. There is one mirror in the room, and only one. An actor should be a good guesser.

"Leo—the picture, Grisha—the chandelier, Sonya—the scrapbook."

"The leather one?" she asked, in her honeyed voice.

"I have already pointed it out. I do not repeat. An actor should catch things on the fly. Kostya—the rug."

"There are a number of them," I said.

"In case of uncertainty, decide for yourself. You may be wrong, but do not hesitate. An actor must have presence of mind. Do not stop to enquire. Vanya—the vase. Nicholas—the window, Dasha—the pillow, Vassili—the piano. One, two, three, four, five . . ." He counted slowly up to thirty. "Lights out." He called on me first.

"You told me to look at a rug, and I could not decide at once, so I lost some time——"

"Be shorter, and stick to the point."

"The rug is Persian. The general background is reddish brown. A big border frames the edges——" I went on describing it until the Assistant Director called out "Lights."

"You remembered it all wrong. You didn't carry the impression. You scattered it. Leo!"

"I could not make out the subject of the painting, because it is so far away, and I am short-sighted. All I saw was a yellow tone on a red background."

"Lights. There is neither red nor yellow in the painting. Grisha."

"The chandelier is gilt. A cheap product. With glass pendants."

"Lights on. The chandelier is a museum piece, a real piece of Empire. You were asleep at the switch.

"Lights out. Kostya, describe your rug again."

"I'm sorry, I didn't know that I would be required to do it again."

"Never sit there for one instant doing nothing. I warn you all now that I shall examine you twice, or more times, until I get an exact idea of your impressions. Leo!"

He made a startled exclamation and said: "I wasn't noticing."

In the end we were forced to study our objects down to the last detail, and to describe them. In my case, I was called on five times before I succeeded. This work at high pressure lasted half an hour. Our eyes were tired and our attention strained. It would have been impossible to continue any longer with such intensity. So the lesson was divided into two parts, of a half hour each. After the first part we took a lesson in dancing. Then we went back and did exactly what we did before, except that the time of observation was cut down from thirty seconds to twenty. The Assistant Director remarked that the allowance for observation would eventually be reduced to two seconds.

## 5

The Director continued his demonstration with electric lights today.

"Up to now," he said, "we have been dealing with objects in the form of *points* of light. Now I am going to show you a *circle of attention*. It will consist of a whole section, large or small in dimension, and will include a series of independent points of objects. The eye may pass from one to another of these points, but it must not go beyond the indicated limit of the circle of attention."

First there was complete darkness. A moment later a large lamp was lighted on the table near which I was seated. The shade on the lamp threw the circle of the rays down on my head and hands, and made a bright light on the centre of the table, where there was a number of small things. These shone and reflected all sorts of different colours. The rest of the stage and the hall were swallowed up in darkness.

"This lighted space on the table," said the Director, "illustrates a Small Circle of Attention. You yourself, or rather your head and hands, on which the light falls, are the centre of this circle."

The effect on me was like magic. All the little knick-knacks on the table drew my attention without any forcing or any instruction on my part. In a circle of light, in the midst of darkness, you have the sensation of being entirely alone. I felt even more at home in this circle of light than in my own room.

In such a small space as in this circle you can use your concentrated attention to examine various objects in their most intricate details, and also to carry on more complicated activities, such as defining shades of feeling and thought. Evidently the Director realized my state of mind, for he came right up to the edge of the stage and said: "Make a note immediately of your mood; it is what we call Solitude in Public. You are in public because we are all here. It is solitude because you are divided from us by the small circle of attention. During a performance, before an audience of thousands, you can always enclose yourself in this circle like a snail in its shell."

After a pause he announced that he would now show us a Medium Circle; everything became dark; the spotlight then illumined a fairly large area, with a group of several pieces of furniture, a table, some chairs with students sitting on them, one corner of the piano, the fireplace with a big arm-chair in front of it. I found myself in the centre of the medium light circle. Of course we could not take in everything at once, but had to examine the area bit by bit, object by object, each thing within the circle making an independent point.

The greatest drawback was that the larger area of lighting produced reflected half-tones that fell on things beyond the circle, so that the wall of darkness did not seem impenetrable.

"Now you have the Large Circle," he went on. The whole living-room was flooded with light. The other rooms were dark, but soon lamps were turned on in them also, and the Director pointed out: "That is the very Largest Circle. Its dimensions depend on the length of your eyesight. Here in this room I have extended the circle as far as is possible. But if we were standing on the seashore or on a plain, the circle would be limited only by the horizon. On the stage such distant perspectives are furnished by the painting on the back-drop.

"Now let us try to repeat the exercises you have just done, except that this time we shall have all the lights on."

We all sat down on the stage, around the large table, with the large lamp. I was just where I had been a few moments before, and felt for the first time the sensation of being alone in public.

Now we were supposed to renew this feeling in full light with only a mental outline to make the circle of attention.

When we were unsuccessful in our attempts the Director explained to us why.

"When you have a spot of light surrounded by darkness," he said, "all the objects inside of it draw your attention because everything outside of it being invisible, there is no attraction there. The outlines of such a circle are so sharp and the encircling shadow so solid that you have no desire to go beyond its limits.

"When the lights are on you have an entirely different problem. As there is no obvious outline to your circle you are obliged to construct one mentally and not allow yourself to look beyond it. Your attention must now replace the light, holding you within certain limits, and this in spite of the drawing power of all sorts of objects now visible outside of it. Therefore since the conditions, with and without the spotlight, are opposite, the method of maintaining the circle must change."

He then outlined the given area by a series of objects in the room.

For instance, the round table outlined one circle, the smallest; in another part of the stage a rug, somewhat larger than the table on it, made a Medium Circle; and the largest rug in the room defined a Large Circle.

"Now let us take the whole apartment, the Largest Circle," said the Director.

Here everything that had helped me up to now to concentrate, failed, and—I felt powerless.

To encourage us he said:

"Time and practice will teach you how to use the method I just suggested to you. Don't forget it and meantime I will show you another technical device which will help to direct your attention. As the circle grows larger the area of your attention must stretch. This area, however, can continue to grow only up to the point where you can still hold it all within the limits of your attention, inside an imaginary line. *As soon as your border begins to waver, you must withdraw quickly to a smaller circle* which can be contained by your visual attention.

"At this point you will often get into trouble. Your attention will slip and become dissipated in space. *You must collect it again and redirect it as soon as possible to one single point or object,* such as, for instance, that lamp. It will not seem as bright as it did when there was darkness all around it, nevertheless it will still have the power to hold your attention.

"When you have established that point, surround it with a small circle with the lamp at its centre. Then enlarge it to a medium circle which will include several smaller ones. These will not be reinforced each by a central point. If you must have such a point, choose a new object and surround it with another small circle. Apply the same method to a medium circle."

But each time the area of our attention was stretched to a certain point we lost control of it. As each experiment failed the Director made new attempts.

After a time he went on to another phase of the same idea.

"Have you noticed," he said, "that up to now you have always been in the *centre* of the circle? Yet you may sometimes find yourself outside. For example——"

Everything became dark; then a ceiling light, in the next room, was lighted, throwing a spot on the white tablecloth and the dishes.

"Now you are beyond the limits of the small circle of your attention. Your role is a passive one; one of observation. As the circle of light is extended, and the illuminated area in the dining-room grows, your circle also becomes larger and larger, and the area of your observation increases in the same ratio. Also you can use the same method of choosing points of attention in these circles that lie beyond you."

6

When I exclaimed today that I wished I need never be separated from the small circle, the Director replied:

"You can carry it with you wherever you go, on the stage or off. Get up on the stage and walk around. Change your seat. Behave as you would if you were at home."

I got up and took several steps in the direction of the fireplace. Everything became entirely dark; then from somewhere appeared a spotlight, that moved along with me. In spite of moving about I felt at home and comfortable in the centre of a small circle. I paced up and down the room, the spotlight following me. I walked to the window and it came also. I sat down at the piano, still with the light. That convinced me that the small circle of attention that moves about with you is the most essential and practical thing I have yet learned.

To illustrate its use the Director told us a Hindu tale, about a Maharajah who, about to choose a minister, announced that he would take only the man who could walk around on top of the city walls, holding a dish full to the brim with milk, without spilling a drop. A number of candidates, yelled at, frightened, or in other ways distracted, spilled the milk. "Those," said the Maharajah, "are no ministers."

Then came another, whom no scream, no threat, and no form of distraction could cause to take his eyes from the rim of the bowl.

"Fire!" said the commander of the troops.

They fired, but with no result.

"There is a real Minister," said the Maharajah.

"Didn't you hear the cries?" he was asked.

"No."

"Didn't you see the attempts to frighten you?"

"No."

"Did you hear the shots?"

"No. I was watching the milk."

As another illustration of the moving circle, this time in concrete form, we were each handed a wooden hoop. Some of these hoops were larger, some smaller, according to the size of the circle to be created. As you walk about with your hoop, you get the picture of the moving centre of attention which you have to learn to carry around with you. I found it easier to adapt the suggestion about making a circle out of a series of objects. I could say to myself: from the tip of my left elbow across my body to my right elbow, including my legs that come forward as I walk, will be my circle of attention. I found I could easily carry this circle around with me, enclose myself in it, and in it find solitude in public. Even on the way home, in the confusion of the street, in the bright sunlight, I found it much easier to draw such a line around myself and stay in it, than it was in the theatre with dimmed footlights, and with a hoop.

## 7

"Up to now we have been dealing with what we call external attention," said the Director today. "This is directed to material objects which lie outside of ourselves."

He went on to explain what is meant by "inner attention" which centres on things we see, hear, touch, and feel in imaginary circumstances. He reminded us of what he said earlier about imagination, and how we felt that the source of a given image was internal and yet was mentally carried over to a point outside of ourselves. To the fact that we see such images with inner vision he added that the same was true of our sense of hearing, smelling, touch and taste.

"The objects of your 'inner attention' are scattered through the whole range of your five senses," he said.

"An actor on the stage lives inside or outside of himself. He lives a real or an imaginary life. This abstract life contributes an unending source of material for our inner concentration of attention. The difficulty in using it lies in the fact that it is fragile. Material things around us on the stage call for a well-trained attention, but imaginary objects demand an even far more disciplined power of concentration.

"What I said on the subject of external attention, at earlier lessons, applies in equal degree to inner attention.

"The inner attention is of particular importance to an actor because so much of his life takes place in the realm of imaginary circumstances.

"Outside of work in the theatre, this training must be carried over into your daily lives. *For this purpose you can use the exercises we developed for the imagination, as they are equally effective for concentrating attention.*

"When you have gone to bed at night, and put out your light, train yourself to go over your whole day, and try to put in every possible concrete detail. If you are recalling a meal, don't just remember the food, but visualize the dishes on which it was served, and their general arrangement. Bring back all the thoughts and inner emotions which were touched by your conversation at the meal. At other times refresh your earlier memories.

"Make an effort to review in detail the apartments, rooms, and various places where you have happened to take a walk, or drunk tea, and visualize individual objects connected with these activities. Try also to recall, as vividly as possible, your friends and also strangers, and even others who have passed away. That is the only way to develop a strong, sharp, solid power of inner and outer attention. To accomplish this requires prolonged and systematic work.

"Conscientious, daily work means that you must have a strong will, determination and endurance."

8

At our lesson today the Director said:

"We have been experimenting with outer and inner attention, and making use of objects in a mechanical, photographic, formal way.

"We have had to do with arbitrary attention, intellectual in its origin. This is necessary for actors but not very frequently. It is particularly useful in collecting attention which has strayed. The simple looking at an object helps to fix it. But it cannot hold you for long. To grasp your object firmly when you are acting you need another type of attention, which causes an emotional reaction. You must have something which will *interest you* in the object of your attention, and serve to set in motion your whole creative apparatus.

"It is, of course, not necessary to endow every object with an imaginary life, but you should be sensitive to its influence on you."

As an example of the distinction between attention based on intellect, and that based on feeling, he said:

"Look at this antique chandelier. It dates back to the days of the Emperor. How many branches has it? What is its form, its design?

"You have been using your external, intellectual attention in examining that chandelier. Now I want you to tell me this: do you like it? If so, what is it that especially attracts you? What can it be used for? You can say to yourself: this chandelier may have been in the house of some Field Marshal when he received Napoleon. It may even have hung in the French Emperor's own room when he signed the historic act concerning the regulations of the Théâtre Français in Paris.

"In this case your object has remained unchanged. But now you know that imagined circumstances can transform the object itself and heighten the reaction of your emotions to it."

## 9

Vassili said today that it seemed to him not only difficult but impossible to be thinking at one and the same time about your role, technical methods, the audience, the words of your part, your cues, and several points of attention as well.

"You feel powerless in the face of such a task," said the Director, "and yet any simple juggler in a circus would have no hesitation in handling far more complicated things, risking his life as he does it.

"The reason why he can do this is that attention is built in many layers and they do not interfere with one another. Fortunately, habit makes a large part of your attention automatic. The most difficult time is in the early stages of learning.

"Of course, if you have thought up to now that an actor relies merely on inspiration you will have to change your mind. Talent without work is nothing more than raw unfinished material."

There followed a discussion with Grisha about the fourth wall, the question being how to visualize an object on it without looking at the audience. The Director's answer to this was:

"Let us suppose that you are looking at this non-existent fourth wall. It is very near. How should your eyes focus? Almost at the same angle as if you were looking at the tip of your nose. That is the only way in which you can fix your attention on an imaginary object on that fourth wall.

"And yet what do most actors do? Pretending to look at this imaginary wall they focus their eyes on someone in the orchestra. Their angle of vision is quite different from what it must be to see a nearby object. Do you think that the actor himself, the person opposite to whom he is playing, or the spectator, gets any real satisfaction from such a physiological error? Can he successfully fool either his own nature or ours by doing something so abnormal?

"Suppose your part calls for looking over to the horizon on the ocean, where the sail of a vessel is still visible. Do you remember how your eyes will be focussed to see it? They will be looking in almost parallel lines. To get them into that position, when you are standing on the stage, you must mentally remove the wall at the far end of the auditorium and find, far beyond it, an imaginary point on which you can fix your attention. Here again an actor will usually let his eyes focus as though he were looking at some one in the orchestra.

"When, by aid of the required technique, you learn how to put an object in its right place, when you understand the relation of vision to distance, then it will be safe for you to look toward the auditorium, letting your vision go beyond the spectators or stop this side of them. For the present, turn your face to the right or to the left, above or sideways. Do not be afraid that your eyes will not be seen. Moreover, when you feel the natural necessity to do so, you will find that yours will of their own accord turn toward an object beyond the footlights. When this happens it will be done naturally, instinctively, and rightly. Unless you feel this subconscious need, avoid looking at that nonexisting fourth wall, or into the distance, until you have mastered the technique with which it can be done."

10

At our lesson today the Director said:

"An actor should be observant not only on the stage, but also in real life. He should concentrate with all his being on whatever attracts his attention. He should look at an object, not as any absent-minded passerby, but with penetration. Otherwise his whole creative method will prove lopsided and bear no relation to life.

"There are people gifted by nature with powers of observation. Without effort they form a sharp impression of whatever is going on around them, in themselves, and in others. Also they know how to cull out of these observations whatever is most significant, typical, or colourful. When you hear such people talk you are struck by the amount that an unobservant person misses.

"Other people are unable to develop this power of observation even sufficiently to preserve their own simplest interests. How much less able, then, are they to do it for the sake of studying life itself.

"Average people have no conception of how to observe the facial expression, the look of the eye, the tone of the voice, in order to comprehend the state of mind of the persons with whom they talk. They can neither actively grasp the complex truths of life nor listen in a way to understand what they hear. If they could do this, life, for them, would be better and easier, and their creative work immeasurably richer, finer, and deeper. But you cannot put into a person what he does not possess; he can only try to develop whatever power he may have. In the field of attention this development calls for a tremendous amount of work, time, desire to succeed, and systematic practice.

"How can we teach unobservant people to notice what nature and life are trying to show them? First of all they must be taught to look at, to listen to, and to hear what is beautiful. Such habits elevate their minds and arouse feelings which will leave deep traces in their emotion memories. Nothing in life is more beautiful than nature, and it should be the object of constant observation. To begin with, take a little flower, or a petal from it, or a spider web, or a design made by frost on the window pane. Try to express in words what it is in these things that gives pleasure. Such an effort causes you to observe the object more closely, more effectively, in order to appreciate it and define its qualities. And do not shun the darker side of nature. Look for it in marshes, in the slime of the sea, amid plagues of insects, and remember that hidden behind these phenomena there is beauty, just as in loveliness there is unloveliness. What is truly beautiful has nothing to fear from disfigurement. Indeed, disfigurement often emphasizes and sets off beauty in higher relief.

"Search out both beauty and its opposite, and define them, learn to know and to see them. Otherwise your conception of beauty will be incomplete, saccharine, prettified, sentimental.

"Next turn to what the human race has produced in art, literature, music.

"At the bottom of every process of obtaining creative material for our work is emotion. Feeling, however, does not replace an immense amount of work on the part of our intellects. Perhaps you are afraid that the little touches which your mind may add on its own account will spoil your material drawn from life? Never fear that. Often these original additions enhance it greatly if your belief in them is sincere.

"Let me tell you about an old woman I once saw trundling a baby carriage along a boulevard. In it was a cage with a canary. Probably the woman had placed all her bundles in the carriage to get them home more easily. But I wanted to see things in a different light, so I decided that the poor old woman had lost all of her children and grand-children and the only living creature left in her life was—this canary. So she was taking him out for a ride on the boulevard, just as she had done, not long before, her grandson, now lost. All this is more interesting and suited to the theatre than the actual truth. Why should I not tuck that impression into the storehouse of my memory? I am not a census taker, who is responsible for collecting exact facts. I am an artist who must have material that will stir my emotions.

"After you have learned how to observe life around you and draw on it for your work you will turn to the study of the most necessary, important, and living emotional material on which your main creativeness is based. I mean those impressions which you get from direct, personal intercourse with other human beings. This material is difficult to obtain because in large part it is intangible, indefinable, and only inwardly perceivable. To be sure, many invisible, spiritual experiences are reflected in our facial expression, in our eyes, voice, speech, gestures, but even so it is no easy thing to sense another's inmost being, because people do not often open the doors of their souls and allow others to see them as they really are.

"When the inner world of someone you have under observation becomes clear to you through his acts, thoughts, and impulses, follow his actions closely and study the conditions in which he finds himself. Why did he do this or that? What did he have in his mind?

"Very often we cannot come through definite data to know the inner life of the person we are studying, and can only reach toward it by means of intuitive feeling. Here we are dealing with the most delicate type of concentration of attention, and with powers of observation that are subconscious in their origin. Our ordinary type of attention is not sufficiently far-reaching to carry out the process of penetrating another person's soul.

"If I were to assure you that your technique could achieve so much I should be deceiving you. As you progress you will learn more and more ways in which to stimulate your subconscious selves, and to draw them into your creative process, but it must be admitted that we cannot reduce this study of the inner life of other human beings to a scientific technique."

# CHAPTER SIX

## Relaxation of Muscles

### I

WHEN the Director came into the classroom he called on Maria, Vanya, and me to play the scene where the money is burned.

We went on the stage and started.

In the beginning things went well. But when we reached the tragic part I felt that something inside of me faltered, then, to give myself some support from outside, I pressed with all my strength against some object under my hand. Suddenly something cracked; at the same time I felt a sharp pain; some warm liquid wet my hand.

I am not sure when I fainted. I remember some confusion of sounds. After that increasing weakness, dizziness, and then unconsciousness.

My unfortunate accident (I had grazed an artery and lost so much blood that I was in bed for some days) led the Director to make a change of plan, and take up ahead of schedule part of our physical training. A summary of his remarks was given me by Paul.

Tortsov said: "It will be necessary to interrupt the strictly systematic development of our program, and to explain to you, somewhat ahead of the usual order, an important step which we call 'Freeing our Muscles.' The natural point at which I should tell you about this is when we come to the external side of our training. But Kostya's situation leads to our discussing this question now.

"*You cannot, at the very beginning of our work, have any conception of the evil that results from muscular spasms and physical contraction.* When such a condition occurs in the vocal organs a person with otherwise naturally good tones becomes hoarse or even loses his voice. If such contraction attacks the legs, an actor walks like a paralytic; if it is in his hands, they grow numb and move like sticks. The same sort of spasms occur in the spine, the neck and the shoulders. In each case they cripple the actor and prevent him from playing. It is worst of all, however, when this condition affects his face, twisting his features, paralysing them, or making his expression turn to stone. The eyes protrude, the taut muscles give an unpleasant look to the face, expressing quite the contrary of what is going on inside the actor, and bearing no relation to his emotions. The spasms can attack the diaphragm and other organs connected with breathing and interfere with proper respiration and cause shortness of breath. This muscular tautness affects other parts of the body also and cannot but have a deleterious effect on the emotions the actor is experiencing, his expression of them, and his general state of feeling.

"To convince you of how physical tenseness paralyses our actions, and is bound up with our inner life, let us make an experiment. Over there is a grand piano. Try to lift it."

The students, in turn, made tremendous efforts and succeeded in raising only one corner of the heavy instrument.

"While you are holding the piano up, multiply quickly thirty-seven times nine," said the Director to one of the students. "You can't do it? Well, then, use your visual memory to recall all the stores along the street from the corner to the theatre. . . . Can't do that either? Then sing me the Cavatina from *Faust.* No luck? Well, try to remember the taste of a dish of kidney stew, or the feel of silk plush, or the smell of something burning."

To carry out his orders the student let down the corner of the piano, which he had been holding up with great effort, rested for a moment, recalled the questions put to him, let them sink into his consciousness, and then began to respond to them, calling up each required sensation. After that he renewed his muscular effort, and with difficulty lifted one corner of the piano.

"So you see," said Tortsov, "that in order to answer my questions you had to let down the weight, relax your muscles, and only then could you devote yourself to the operation of your five senses.

"Doesn't this prove that muscular tautness interferes with inner emotional experience? As long as you have this physical tenseness you cannot even think about delicate shadings of feeling or the spiritual life of your part. Consequently, before you attempt to create anything it is necessary for you to get your muscles in proper condition, so that they do not impede your actions.

"Here is the convincing case of Kostya's accident. Let us hope that his misfortune will serve as an effective lesson to him, and to you all, in what you must not do on the stage."

"But is it possible to rid yourself of this tenseness?" someone asked.

The Director recalled the actor described in *My Life in Art,* who suffered from a particularly strong tendency to muscular spasms. With the aid of acquired habits and constant checking up, he was able to reach the point where, as soon as he set foot on the stage, his muscles began to soften. The same thing happened at critical moments in creating his part—his muscles of their own accord tried to shake off all tensity.

"It is not only a strong general muscular spasm that interferes with proper functioning. Even the slightest pressure at a given point may arrest the creative faculty. Let me give you an example. A certain actress, with a wonderful temperament, was able to use it only at rare and accidental intervals. Ordinarily her emotions were replaced by plain effort. She was worked over from the point of view of loosening up her muscles, but with only partial success. Quite accidentally, in the dramatic parts of her role, her right eyebrow would contract, ever so slightly. So I suggested that when she came to these difficult transitions in her part she should try to get rid of all tenseness in her face and completely free it. When she was able to accomplish this, all the rest of the muscles in her body relaxed spontaneously. She was transformed. Her body became light, her face became mobile and expressed her inner emotions vividly. Her feelings had gained a free outlet to the surface.

"Just think: the pressure of one muscle, at a single point, had been able to throw out her whole organism, both spiritually and physically!"

### 2

Nicholas, who came to see me today, asserts that the Director said it is impossible completely to free the body from all unnecessary tenseness. Aside from being impossible, it is also superfluous. And yet Paul, from the same remarks of Tortsov, concluded that to relax our muscles is absolutely incumbent on us, both when we are on the stage, and in ordinary life.

How can these contradictions be reconciled?

As Paul came after Nicholas, I give his explanation:

"As a human being, an actor is inevitably subject to muscular tensity. This will set in whenever he appears in public. He can rid himself of the pressure in his back, and it will go to his shoulder. Let him chase it away from there and it will appear in his diaphragm. Constantly in some place or other there will be pressure.

"Among the nervous people of our generation this muscular tensity is inescapable. To destroy it completely is impossible, but we must struggle with it incessantly. Our method consists of developing a sort of control; an observer, as it were. This observer must, under all circumstances, see that at no point shall there be an extra amount of contraction. This process of self-observation and removal of unnecessary tenseness should be developed to the point where it becomes a subconscious, mechanical habit. Nor is that sufficient. It must be a normal habit and a natural necessity, not only during the quieter parts of your role, but especially at times of the greatest nervous and physical lift."

"What do you mean?" I exclaimed. "That one should not be tense in moments of excitement?"

"Not only should you not be tense," explained Paul, "but you should make all the greater effort to relax."

He went on to quote the Director as saying that actors usually strain themselves in the exciting moments. Therefore, at times of great stress it is especially necessary to achieve a complete freeing of the muscles. In fact, in the high moments of a part the tendency to relax should become more normal than the tendency to contraction.

"Is that really feasible?" I asked.

"The Director asserts that it is," Paul said. "He does add that although it is not possible to get rid of all tenseness at an exciting point yet one can learn constantly to relax. Let the tenseness come, he says, if you cannot avoid it. But immediately let your control step in and remove it."

Until this control becomes a mechanical habit, it will be necessary to give a lot of thought to it, and that will detract from our creative work. Later, this relaxing of the muscles should become a normal phenomenon. This habit should be developed daily, constantly, systematically, both during our exercises at school and at home. It should proceed while we are going to bed or getting up, dining, walking, working, resting, in moments of joy and of sorrow. The "controller" of our muscles must be made part of our physical make-up, our second nature. Only then will it cease to interfere when we are doing creative work. If we relax our muscles only during special hours set aside for that purpose, we cannot get results, because such exercises are not custom-forming, they cannot become unconscious, mechanical habits.

When I showed doubt at the possibility of doing what Paul had just explained to me, he gave the Director's own experiences as an example. It seems that in his early years of artistic activity, muscular tenseness developed in him almost to the point of cramp—and yet, since he has developed a mechanical control, he feels the need of relaxing at times of intense nerve excitement rather than the need to stiffen his muscles.

## 3

Today I was also called on by Rakhmanov, the Assistant Director, who is a very agreeable person. He brought me greetings from Tortsov, and said he had been sent to instruct me in some exercises.

The Director had said: "Kostya can't be busy while he is lying there in bed, so let him try out some appropriate way of spending his time."

The exercise consists of lying on my back on a flat, hard surface, such as the floor, and making a note of various groups of muscles throughout my body that are unnecessarily tense.

"I feel a contraction in my shoulder, neck, shoulder-blade, around my waist——"

The places noted should then be immediately relaxed, and others searched out. I tried to do this simple exercise in front of Rakhmanov, only instead of on the floor I lay on a soft bed. After I had relaxed the tense muscles and left only such as seemed necessary to bear the weight of my body I named the following places:

"Both shoulder blades and base of the spinal cord." But Rakhmanov objected. "You should do as small children and animals do," he said firmly.

It seems that if you lay an infant, or a cat, on some sand, to rest or to sleep, and then carefully lift him up, you will find the imprint of his whole body on the soft surface. But if you make the very same experiment with a person of our nervous generation, all you will find on the sand are the marks of his shoulder blades and rump—whereas all the rest of his body, thanks to chronic muscle tension, will never touch the sand at all.

In order to make a sculptural imprint on a soft surface, when we lie down we must rid our bodies of every muscular contraction. That will give the body a better chance to rest.

In lying this way, you can in half an hour or an hour, refresh yourself more than by a whole night of lying in a constrained position. No wonder that caravan drivers use this method. They cannot remain long in the desert, so the time they can give to rest is limited. Instead of a long rest the same result is brought about by completely freeing their bodies from muscular tension.

The Assistant Director makes constant use of this method during his short periods of rest between his day and evening occupations. After ten minutes of this kind of rest he feels completely refreshed. Without this breathing spell he could not possibly do all the work that falls to him.

As soon as Rakhmanov had gone I found our cat and laid him on one of the soft pillows on my sofa. He left a complete imprint of his body. I decided to learn from him how to rest.

The Director says: "An actor, like an infant, must learn everything from the beginning, to look, to walk, to talk, and so on. . . . We all know how to do these things in ordinary life. But unfortunately, the vast majority of us do them badly. One reason for this is that any defects show up much more noticeably in the full glare of the footlights, and another is that the stage has a bad influence on the general state of the actor." Obviously these words of Tortsov apply also to lying down. That is why I now lie on the sofa with the cat. I watch him sleep and try to imitate the way he does it. But it is no easy matter to lie so that not one muscle is tense and so that all the parts of your body touch the surface. I can't say that it is difficult to note this or that contracted muscle. And it's no particular trick to loosen it up. But the trouble is that you no sooner get rid of one tight muscle than another appears, and a third, and so on. The more you notice them, the more there are of them. For a while I succeeded in getting rid of tenseness in the region of my back and neck. I can't say that this resulted in any feeling of renewed vigour but it did make clear to me how much superfluous, harmful tenseness we are subject to without realizing it. When you think of the treacherously contracting eyebrow of that actress you begin seriously to fear physical tenseness.

My main difficulty seems to be that I become confused among a variety of muscular sensations. This multiplies by ten the number of points of tenseness and also increases the intensity of each. I end up by not knowing where my hands or head are.

How tired I am from today's exercises!

You don't get any rest from the kind of lying down in which I have been indulging.

### 4

Today Leo stopped by and told me about the drill at school. Rakhmanov, following the Director's orders, had the students lie motionless, then take a variety of poses, both horizontal and vertical, sitting up straight, half sitting, standing, half standing, kneeling, crouching, alone, in groups, with chairs, with a table or other furniture. In each position they had to make a note of the tense muscles and name them. Obviously some muscles would be tense in each of the poses. But only those directly involved should be allowed to remain contracted, and not any others in the vicinity. Also one must remember that there are various types of tenseness. A muscle which is necessary to holding a given position may be contracted but only so much as is necessary to the pose.

All these exercises called for intensified checking up by the "controller." It is not as simple as it sounds. First of all, it requires a well-trained power of attention, capable of quick adjustment and able to distinguish among various physical sensations. It is not easy, in a complicated pose, to know which muscles must contract, and which should not.

As soon as Leo left, I turned to the cat. It makes no difference what position I invent for him, whether he is put down head first, or made to lie on his side or back. He hangs by each of his paws in succession and all four at once. Each time it is easy to see that he bends like a spring for a second, and then, with extraordinary ease, arranges his muscles, loosening up those he does not need, and holding tense the ones he is using. What amazing adaptability!

During my session with the cat, who should appear but Grisha. He was not at all the same person who always argues with the Director, and he was very interesting in his account of the classes. In talking about muscle relaxation, and of the necessary tenseness to hold a pose, Tortsov told a story out of his own life: in Rome, in a private house, he had the opportunity of watching an exhibition to test equilibrium, on the part of an American lady who was interested in the restoration of antique sculpture. In gathering up broken pieces and putting them together she tried to reconstitute the original pose of the statue. For this work she was obliged to make a thorough study of weight in the human body, and to find out, through experiments with her own body, where the centre of gravity lies in any given pose. She acquired a remarkable flair for the quick discovery in herself of those centres which establish equilibrium. On the occasion described, she was pushed, and flung about, caused to stumble, put in what seemed to be untenable positions, but in each case she proved herself able to maintain her balance. Moreover this lady, with two fingers, was able to upset a rather portly gentleman. This also she had learned through study of centres of weight. She could find the places that threatened the equilibrium of her opponent and overthrow him, without any effort, by pushing him in those spots.

Tortsov did not learn the secret of her art. But he understood, from watching her, the importance of centres of gravity. He saw to what degree of agility, litheness, and adaptability the human body can be trained, and that in this work the muscles do what is required by a sense of equilibrium.

5

Today Leo came in to report on the progress of the drill at school. It seems that some substantial additions to the program were made. The Director insisted that each pose, whether lying down or standing up, or any other, should be subject not only to the control of self-observation, but should also be based on some imaginative idea, and enhanced by "given circumstances." When this is done it ceases to be a mere pose. It becomes action. Suppose I raise my hand above my head and say to myself:

"*If* I were standing this way and over me on a high branch hung a peach, what should I do to pick it?"

You have only to believe in this fiction and immediately a lifeless pose becomes a real, lively act with an actual objective: to pick the peach. If you just feel the truthfulness of this act, your intention and subconsciousness will come to your aid. Then superfluous tension will disappear, the necessary muscles will come into action, and all this will happen without the interference of any conscious technique.

There should never be any posing on the stage that has no basis. There is no place for theatrical conventionality in true creative art, or in any serious art. If it is necessary to use a conventional pose you must give it a foundation, so that it can serve an inner purpose.

Leo then went on to tell about certain exercises which were done today, and these he proceeded to demonstrate. It was funny to see his fat figure stretched out on my divan in the first pose he happened to fall into. Half of his body hung over the edge, his face was near the floor, and one arm was stretched out in front of him. You felt that he was ill at ease and that he did not know which muscles to flex and which to relax.

Suddenly he exclaimed: "There goes a huge fly. Watch me swat him!"

At that moment he stretched himself towards an imaginary point to crush the insect and immediately all the parts of his body, all of his muscles, took their rightful positions and worked as they should. His pose had a reason, it was credible.

Nature operates a live organism better than our much advertised technique!

The exercises which the Director used today had the purpose of making the students conscious of the fact that on the stage, in every pose or position of the body, there are three moments:

*First: superfluous tenseness which comes necessarily with each new pose taken and with the excitement of doing it in public.*

*Second: the mechanical relaxation of that superfluous tension, under the direction of the "controller."*

*Third: justification of the pose if it in itself does not convince the actor.*

After Leo left it was the cat's turn to help me try out these exercises and get at their meaning.

To put him into a receptive mood I laid the cat on the bed beside me and stroked him. But instead of remaining there he jumped across me down onto the floor, and stole softly toward the corner where he apparently sensed a prey.

I followed his every curve with closest attention. To do this I had to bend myself around and that was difficult because of my bandaged hand, I made use of my new "controller" of muscles to test my own movements. At first things went well, only those muscles were flexed that needed to be. That was because I had a live objective. But the minute I transferred my attention from the cat to myself, everything changed. My concentration evaporated, I felt muscle pressure in all sorts of places, and the muscles which I had to use to hold my pose were tense almost to the point of spasm. Contiguous muscles also were unnecessarily involved.

"Now I'll repeat that same pose," said I to myself. And I did. But as my real objective was gone the pose was lifeless. In checking up on the work of my muscles I found that the more conscious I was in my attitude toward them the more extra tenseness was introduced and the more difficult it became to disentangle the superfluous from the necessary use of them.

At this point I interested myself in a dark spot on the floor. I reached down to feel it, to find out what it was. It turned out to be a defect in the wood. In making the movement all my muscles operated naturally and properly—which led me to the conclusion that a *live objective and real action* (it can be real or imaginary as long as it is properly founded on given circumstances in which the actor can truly believe) *naturally and unconsciously put nature to work. And it is only nature itself that can fully control our muscles, tense them properly or relax them.*

## 6

According to Paul, the Director went on today from fixed poses to gestures.

The lesson took place in a large room. The students were lined up, as if for inspection. Tortsov ordered them to raise their right hands. This they did as one man.

Their arms were slowly raised like the bars at a grade crossing. As they did it Rakhmanov felt their muscles and made comments: "Not right, relax your neck and back. Your whole arm is tense"—and so on.

It would seem that the task given was a simple one. And yet not one of the students could execute it rightly. They were required to do a so-called "isolated act," to use only the group of muscles involved in movements of the shoulder, and no others, none in the neck, back, especially not any in the region of the waist. These often throw the whole body off in the opposite direction from the raised arm, to compensate for the movement.

These contiguous muscles that contract remind one of broken keys in a piano, which when you strike one push down several, blurring the sound of the note you want. It is not astonishing, therefore, that our actions are not clear-cut. They must be clear, like notes on an instrument. Otherwise the pattern of movements in a role is messy, and both its inner and outer rendering are bound to be indefinite and inartistic. The more delicate the feeling, the more it requires precision, clarity and plastic quality in its physical expression.

Paul went on to say: "The impression that remains with me from today's lesson is that the Director took us all apart, like so much machinery, unscrewed, sorted out every little bone, oiled, reassembled and screwed us all together again. Since that process I feel myself decidedly more supple, agile, and expressive."

"What else happened?" I asked.

"He insisted that when we use an 'isolated' group of muscles, be they shoulder, arm, leg, back muscles, all other parts of the body must remain free and without any tension. For example: in raising one's arm by the aid of shoulder muscles and contracting such as are necessary to the movement, one must let the rest of the arm, the elbow, the wrist, the fingers, all these joints hang completely limp."

"Could you succeed in doing this?" I asked.

"No," admitted Paul. "But we did get an idea of how it will feel when we shall have worked up to that point."

"Is it really so difficult?" I asked, puzzled.

"At first, it looks easy. And yet not one of us was able to do the exercise properly. Apparently there is no escape from completely transforming ourselves if we are to be adapted to the demands of our art. Defects that pass in ordinary life become noticeable in the glare of the footlights and they make a definite impression on the public."

The reason is easy to find: life on the stage is shown in small compass, as in the lens of a camera. People look at it with opera glasses, the way they examine a miniature with a magnifying glass. Consequently no detail escapes the public, not the slightest. If these stiff arms are half-way passable in ordinary life, on the stage they are simply intolerable. They give a wooden quality to the human body, make it look like a mannikin. The resulting impression is that the actor's soul is likely to be as wooden as his arms. If you add to this a stiff back, which bends only at the waist and at right angles, you have a complete picture of a stick. What emotions can such a stick reflect?

Apparently, according to Paul, they didn't succeed at all, in today's lesson, in doing this one simple thing, raising an arm with only the necessary shoulder muscles. They were just as unsuccessful in doing similar exercises with the elbow, wrist, and the various joints of the hand. Each time the whole hand became involved. And worst of all they did the exercises of moving all the parts of the arm in turn, from shoulder to finger tips and back again. That was only natural. Since they did not succeed in part they could not succeed in the whole exercise, which was so much more difficult.

As a matter of fact Tortsov did not demonstrate these exercises with the idea that we could do them at once. He was outlining work which his assistant will do with us in his *drill and discipline* course. He also showed exercises to do with the neck, at all angles, with the back, the waist, legs and so on.

Later Leo came in. He was good enough to do the exercises that Paul had described, especially the bending and unbending of the back, joint by joint, beginning with the top one, at the base of the head, and working down. Even that is not so simple. I was only able to sense three places in which I bent my back, and yet we have twenty-four vertebrae.

After Paul and Leo had gone the cat came in. I continued my observation of him in varied and unusual, indescribable poses. When he raises his paw, or unsheathes his claws I have the feeling that he is using groups of muscles that are especially adapted to that movement. I am not made that way. I cannot even move my fourth finger by itself. Both the third and fifth move with it.

A development and degree of finish in the cultivation of muscle technique as it exists in some animals is unattainable for us. No technique can achieve any such perfection in muscle control. When this cat pounces on my finger, he instantaneously passes from complete repose to lightning motion, which is hard to follow. Yet what economy of energy! How carefully it is apportioned! When preparing to make a movement, to spring, he does not waste any force in superfluous contractions. He saves up all his strength, to throw it at a given moment to the point where he will need it. That is why his movements are so clear-cut, well-defined and powerful.

To test myself, I began to go through the tiger-like motions I had used in playing Othello. By the time I had taken one step all my muscles tightened up and I was forcibly reminded of just how I felt at the test performance, and realized what my main mistake had been at that time. A numb creature, whose whole body is in the throes of muscular spasms, cannot possibly feel any freedom on the stage, nor can he have any proper life. If it is difficult to do simple multiplication while holding up one end of a piano, how much less possible must it be to express the delicate emotions of a complicated role. What a good lesson the Director gave us in that test performance, when we did all the wrong things with complete assurance.

It was a wise and convincing way of proving his point.

# CHAPTER SEVEN

## Units and Objectives

### I

WHEN we came into the theatre auditorium today, we were faced with a large placard, on which were these words: UNITS AND OBJECTIVES.

The Director congratulated us on arriving at a new and important stage in our work, explaining what he meant by units, telling us how a play and a part are divided into their elements. Everything he said was, as always, clear and interesting. However, before I write about that, I want to put down what happened after the lesson was over, because it helped me to appreciate more fully what he had said.

I was invited, for the first time, to dine at the home of Paul's uncle, the famous actor, Shustov. He asked what we were doing at school. Paul told him we had just reached the study of "units and objectives." Of course he and his children are familiar with our technical expressions.

"Children!" said he laughingly, as the maid set a large turkey in front of him, "Imagine that this is not a turkey but a five act play, *The Inspector General.* Can you do away with it in a mouthful? No; you cannot make a single mouthful either of a whole turkey or a five act play. Therefore you must carve it, first, into large pieces, like this . . ." (cutting off the legs, wings, and soft parts of the roast and laying them on an empty plate).

"There you have the first big divisions. But you cannot swallow even such chunks. Therefore you must cut them into smaller pieces, like this . . ." and he disjointed the bird still further.

"Now pass your plate," said Mr. Shustov to the eldest child. "There's a big piece for you. That's the first scene."

To which the boy, as he passed his plate, quoted the opening lines of *The Inspector General,* in a somewhat unsteady bass voice: "Gentlemen, I have called you together, to give you a highly unpleasant piece of news."

"Eugene," said Mr. Shustov to his second son, "here is the scene with the Postmaster. And now, Igor and Theodore, here is the scene between Bobchinski and Dobchinski. You two girls can do the piece between the Mayor's wife and daughter."

"Swallow it," he ordered, and they threw themselves on their food, shoving enormous chunks into their mouths, and nearly choking themselves to death. Whereupon Mr. Shustov warned them to cut their pieces finer and finer still, if necessary.

"What tough, dry meat," he exclaimed suddenly to his wife.

"Give it taste," said one of the children, "by adding 'an invention of the imagination.'"

"Or," said another, passing him the gravy, "with a sauce made of magic *ifs.* Allow the author to present his 'given circumstances.'"

"And here," added one of the daughters, giving him some horse radish, "is something from the regisseur."

"More spice, from the actor himself," put in one of the boys, sprinkling pepper on the meat.

"Some mustard, from a left wing artist?" said the youngest girl.

Uncle Shustov cut up his meat in the sauce made of the children's offerings.

"This is good," he said. "Even this shoe leather almost seems to be meat. That's what you must do with the bits of your part, soak them more and more in the sauce of 'given circumstances.' The drier the part the more sauce you need."

\*      \*      \*      \*      \*      \*      \*

I left the Shustovs' with my head full of ideas about units. As soon as my attention was drawn in this direction I began to look for ways of carrying out this new idea.

As I bade them goodnight, I said to myself: one bit. Going

downstairs I was puzzled: should I count each step a unit? The Shustovs live on the third floor,—sixty steps—sixty units. On that basis, every step along the sidewalk would have to count. I decided that the whole act of going downstairs was one bit, and walking home, another.

How about opening the street-door; should that be one unit or several? I decided in favor of several. Therefore, I went downstairs—two units; I took hold of the door knob—three; I turned it—four; I opened the door—five; I crossed the threshold —six; I shut the door—seven; I released the knob—eight; I went home—nine.

I jostled someone—no, that was an accident, not a unit. I stopped in front of a bookshop. What about that? Should the reading of each individual title count, or should the general survey be lumped under one heading? I made up my mind to call it one. Which made my total ten.

By the time I was home, undressed, and reaching for the soap to wash my hands I was counting two hundred and seven. I washed my hands—two hundred and eight; I laid down the soap—two hundred and nine; I rinsed the bowl—two hundred and ten. Finally I got into bed and pulled up the covers—two hundred and sixteen.

But now what? My head was full of thoughts. Was each a unit? If you had to go through a five act tragedy, like *Othello,* on this basis, you would roll up a score of several thousand units. You would get all tangled up, so there must be some way of limiting them. But how?

## 2

Today I spoke to the Director about this. His answer was: "A certain pilot was asked how he could ever remember, over a long stretch, all the minute details of a coast with its turns, shallows and reefs. He replied: 'I am not concerned with them; *I stick to the channel.'*

"So an actor must proceed, not by a multitude of details, but by those important units which, like signals, mark his channel and keep him in the right creative line. If you had to stage your departure from the Shustovs' you would have to say to yourself: first of all, what am I doing? Your answer—*going home*—gives you the key to your main objective.

"Along the way, however, there were stops. You stood still at one point and did something else. Therefore *looking in the shop window* is an independent unit. Then as you proceeded you returned to your first unit.

"Finally you reached your room and undressed. This was another bit. When you *lay down* and *began to think* you began still another unit.

"We have cut your total of units from over two hundred down to four. These mark your *channel*.

"Together they create one large objective—*going home.*

"Suppose you are staging the first bit. You are going home, you just walk and walk and do nothing else. Or the second bit, standing in front of the shop window; you just stand and stand. For the third you wash yourself, and for the fourth you lie and lie. If you do that your acting will be boring, monotonous. Your director will insist on a more detailed development of each bit. This will oblige you to break each unit up into finer details and reproduce them clearly and minutely.

"If these finer divisions are still too monotonous you will have to break them up still further until your walk down the street reflects the details typical of such an act: meeting friends, a greeting, observation of what is going on around you, jostling passers-by and so on."

The Director then discussed the things Paul's uncle had talked about. We exchanged knowing smiles as we remembered the turkey.

"The largest pieces you reduce to medium size, then to small, and then to fine, only to reverse the process eventually and re-assemble the whole.

"Always remember," he warned, "that the division is temporary. The part and the play must not remain in fragments. A broken statue, or a slashed canvas, is not a work of art, no matter how beautiful its parts may be. It is only in the preparation of a role that we use small units. During its actual creation they fuse into large units. The larger and fewer the divisions, the less you have to deal with, the easier it is for you to handle the whole role.

"Actors conquer these larger divisions easily if they are thoroughly filled out. Strung along through a play, they take the place of buoys to mark the channel. This channel points the true course of creativeness and makes it possible to avoid the shallows and reefs.

"Unfortunately many actors dispense with this channel. They are incapable of dissecting a play and analysing it. Therefore they find themselves forced to handle a multitude of superficial, unrelated details, so many that they become confused and lose *all sense of the larger whole*.

"Do not take such actors for your model. *Do not break up a play more than is necessary, do not use details to guide you. Create a channel outlined by large divisions, which have been thoroughly worked out and filled down to the last detail.*

"The technique of division is comparatively simple. You ask yourself: '*What is the core of the play—the thing without which it cannot exist?*' *Then you go over the main points without entering into detail*. Let us say that we are studying Gogol's *Inspector General*. What is essential to it?"

"The Inspector General," said Vanya.

"Or rather the episode with Khlestakov," corrected Paul.

"Agreed," said the Director, "but that is not sufficient. There must be an appropriate background for this tragi-comical occurrence pictured by Gogol. This is furnished by scoundrels of the type of the Mayor, the superintendents of various public institutions, the pair of gossips, etc. Therefore we are obliged to conclude that the play could not exist without both Khlestakov *and* the naïve inhabitants of the town.

"What else is necessary to the play?" he continued.

"*Stupid romanticism* and the *provincial flirts,* like the Mayor's wife who precipitated the engagement of her daughter and upset the whole town," suggested someone.

"The postmaster's curiosity and Ossip's sanity," other students threw in. "The bribery, the letter, the arrival of the real Inspector."

"You have divided the play into its main organic episodes— its largest units. Now draw from each of these units its essential content and you will have the inner outline of the whole play. Each large unit is in turn divided into the medium and small parts which, together, compose it. In shaping these divisions it is often necessary to combine several small units.

"You now have a general notion of how to divide a play into its component units, and how to mark out a channel to guide you through it," said Tortsov in conclusion.

## 3

"The division of a play into units, to study its structure, has one purpose," explained the Director today. "There is another, far more important, inner reason. At the heart of every unit lies a *creative objective*.

"Each objective is an organic part of the unit or, conversely, it creates the unit which surrounds it.

"It is just as impossible to inject extraneous objectives into a play as it is to put in units which are not related to it, because the objectives must form a logical and coherent stream. Given this direct, organic bond, all that has been said about *units* applies equally to *objectives*."

"Does that mean," I asked, "that they are also divided up into major and minor steps?"

"Yes, indeed," said he.

"What about the channel?" I asked.

"The objective will be the light that shows the right way," explained the Director.

"The mistake most actors make is that they think about the result instead of about the action that must prepare it. By avoid-

ing action and aiming straight at the result you get a forced product which can lead to nothing but ham acting.

"Try to avoid straining after the result. Act with truth, full-
ness and integrity of purpose. You can develop this type of
action by choosing lively objectives. Set yourself some such problem now and execute it," he suggested.

While Maria and I were thinking it over Paul came to us
with the following proposal:

Suppose we are both in love with Maria and have proposed
to her. What would we do?

First we laid out a general scheme and then divided it into
various units and objectives, each of which, in turn, gave rise
to action. When our activity died down, we threw in fresh suppositions, and had new problems to solve. Under the influence of
this constant pressure we were so wrapped up in what we were
doing that we did not notice when the curtain was raised and
the bare stage appeared.

The Director suggested that we continue our work out there,
which we did, and when we had finished he said:

"Do you recall one of our first lessons when I asked you to
go out onto the bare stage and act? You did not know what
to do but floundered around helplessly with external forms and
passions? But today, in spite of the bare stage, you felt quite
free and moved around easily. What helped you do this?"

"Inner, active objectives," both Paul and I said.

"Yes," he agreed, "because they direct an actor along the
right path and restrain him from false acting. It is the objective
that gives him faith in his right to come onto the stage and
stay there.

"Unfortunately, today's experiment was not altogether convincing. The objectives some of you set were chosen for their
own sakes and not because of their inner spring of action. That
results in tricks and showing off. Others took purely external
objectives related to exhibitionism. As for Grisha, his purpose
was, as usual, to let his technique shine. That is just being spectacular, it cannot result in any real stimulus to action. Leo's

objective was good enough but was too exclusively intellectual and literary.

"We find innumerable objectives on the stage and not all of them are either necessary or good; in fact, many are harmful. An actor must learn to recognize quality, to avoid the useless, and to choose essentially right objectives."

"How can we know them?" I asked.

"I should define right objectives as follows," said he:

"1) They must be on our side of the footlights. They must be directed toward the other actors, and not toward the spectators.

"2) They should be personal yet analogous to those of the character you are portraying.

"3) They must be creative and artistic because their function should be to fulfill the main purpose of our art: to create the life of a human soul and render it in artistic form.

"4) They should be real, live, and human, not dead, conventional, or theatrical.

"5) They should be truthful so that you yourself, the actors playing with you, and your audience can believe in them.

"6) They should have the quality of attracting and moving you.

"7) They must be clear cut and typical of the role you are playing. They must tolerate no vagueness. They must be distinctly woven into the fabric of your part.

"8) They should have value and content, to correspond to the inner body of your part. They must not be shallow, or skim along the surface.

"9) They should be active, to push your role ahead and not let it stagnate.

"Let me warn you against a dangerous form of objective, purely motor, which is prevalent in the theatre and leads to mechanical performance.

"We admit three types of objectives; the external or physical, the inner or psychological, and the rudimentary psychological type."

Vanya expressed dismay at these big words and the Director explained his meaning by an example.

"Suppose you come into the room," he began, "and greet me, nod your head, shake my hand. That is an ordinary *mechanical* objective. It has nothing to do with psychology."

"Is that wrong?" broke in Vanya.

The Director hastened to disabuse him.

"Of course you may say how do you do, but you may not love, suffer, hate or carry out any living, human objective in a purely mechanical way, without experiencing any feeling.

"A different case," he continued, "is holding out your hand and trying to express sentiments of love, respect, gratitude through your grasp and the look in your eye. That is how we execute an *ordinary objective* and yet there is a psychological element in it, so we, in our jargon, define it as a rudimentary type.

"Now here is a third way. Yesterday you and I had a quarrel. I insulted you publicly. Today, when we meet, I want to go up to you and offer my hand, indicating by this gesture that I wish to apologize, admit that I was wrong and beg you to forget the incident. To stretch out my hand to my enemy of yesterday is not a simple problem. I will have to think it over carefully, go through and overcome many emotions before I can do it. That is what we call a *psychological* objective.

"Another important point about an objective is that besides being believable, it should have attraction for the actor, make him wish to carry it out. This magnetism is a challenge to his creative will.

"Objectives which contain these necessary qualities we call creative. It is difficult to cull them out. Rehearsals are taken up, in the main, with the task of finding the right objectives, getting control of them and living with them."

The Director turned to Nicholas. "What is your objective in that favourite scene of yours from *Brand*?" he asked.

"To save humanity," Nicholas replied.

"A large purpose!" exclaimed the Director half laughingly. "It is impossible to grasp it all at once. Don't you think you had better take some simple physical objective?"

"But is a physical objective—interesting?" asked Nicholas with a shy smile.

"Interesting to whom?" said the Director.

"To the public."

"Forget about the public. Think about yourself," he advised. "If you are interested, the public will follow you."

"But I am not interested in it either," pleaded Nicholas. "I should prefer something psychological."

"You will have time enough for that. It is too early to become involved in psychology. For the time being, limit yourself to what is simple and physical. In every physical objective there is some psychology and vice versa. You cannot separate them. For instance: the psychology of a man about to commit suicide is extremely complicated. It is difficult for him to make up his mind to go over to the table, take the key from his pocket, open the drawer, take out the revolver, load it and put a bullet through his head. Those are all physical acts yet how much psychology they contain! Perhaps it would be even truer to say that they are all complicated psychological acts, yet how much of the physical there is in them!

"Now take an example of the simplest sort of bodily action: you go up to another person and slap him. Yet, if you are to do this with sincerity, think of the intricate psychological sensations you must bring to fruition before you act! Take advantage of the fact that the division between them is vague. Do not try to draw too fine a line between physical and spiritual nature. Go by your instincts, always leaning a little toward the physical.

"Let us agree that, for the present, we will limit ourselves to physical objectives. They are easier, more readily available and more possible of execution. In doing this you reduce the risk of falling into false acting."

## 4

The important question today was: how to draw an objective from a unit of work. The method is simple. It consists of finding the most appropriate name for the unit, one which characterizes its inner essence.

"Why all these christenings?" asked Grisha, ironically.

The Director replied: "Have you any conception of what a really good name for a unit represents? It stands for its essential quality. To obtain it you must subject the unit to a process of crystallization. For that crystal you find a name.

*"The right name, which crystallizes the essence of a unit, discovers its fundamental objective.*

"To demonstrate this to you in a practical way," said he, "let us take the first two units of the scene with the baby's clothes, from *Brand*.

"Agnes, the wife of Pastor Brand, has lost her only son. In her grief she is going over his clothing, toys, and other precious relics. Each object is bathed in tears. Her heart is bursting with memories. The tragedy was brought about by the fact that they live in a damp, unhealthy locality. When their child fell ill, the mother implored the husband to leave the parish. But Brand, a fanatic, would not sacrifice his duty as pastor for the salvation of his family. This decision took the life of their son.

"The gist of the second unit is: Brand comes in. He, too, is suffering, on account of Agnes. Yet his conception of duty forces him to be severe, and to persuade his wife to give the sacred relics of her little son to a poor gypsy woman, on the ground that they hinder her from giving herself entirely to the Lord, and from carrying out the basic principle of their lives, service to one's neighbour.

"Now sum up these two bits. Find the name for each that corresponds to its essential quality."

"We see a loving mother, talking to a child's belongings as though to the child himself. The death of a beloved person is the fundamental motive of the unit," I said decisively.

"Try to get away from the mother's grief and to make a coherent survey of the major and minor parts of this scene," said the Director. "That is the way to get at its inner meaning. When your feelings and consciousness have mastered it, search for a word which will embrace the innermost meaning of the whole unit. This word will spell your objective."

"I can't see that there is any difficulty about that," said Grisha. "Surely the name of the first objective is—*a mother's love,* and that of the second—*the fanatic's duty.*"

"In the first place," corrected the Director, "you are trying to name the unit and not the objective. Those are two quite different things. Secondly, *you should not try to express the meaning of your objective in terms of a noun.* That can be used for a unit but the objective must always employ a *verb.*"

We expressed surprise, and the Director said:

"I shall help you find the answer. But first execute the objectives, just described by the nouns—1) A Mother's Love, and 2) The Fanatic's Duty."

Vanya and Sonya undertook this. He put on an angry expression, making his eyes start from their sockets, and stiffening his backbone rigidly. He walked across the floor with great firmness, stamping his heels. He spoke in a harsh voice, he bristled, hoping to make an impression of power, decision, as the expression of duty. Sonya made a great effort in the opposite direction, to express tenderness and love "in general."

"Don't you find," asked the Director after watching them, "that the nouns you used as names for your objectives tend to make you play the picture of a strong man and the image of a passion—a mother's love?

"You show what power and love are but you are not yourselves power and love. This is because a noun calls forth an intellectual concept of a state of mind, a form, a phenomenon, but can only define what is presented by an image, without indicating motion or action. *Every objective must carry in itself the germ of action.*"

Grisha started to argue that nouns can be illustrated, described, portrayed, which is action.

"Yes," admitted the Director, "that is action, but it is not true, full integrated action. What you describe is theatrical and representational, and as such is not art in our sense."

Then he went on to explain:

"If, instead of a *noun* we use a *verb,* let us see what happens. Just add 'I wish' or 'I wish to do—so and so.'

"Take the word 'power' as an example. Put 'I wish' in front of it and you have 'I wish power.' But that is too general. If you introduce something more definitely active, state a question so that it requires an answer, it will push you to some fruitful activity to carry out that purpose. Consequently you say: 'wish to do so and so, to obtain power.' Or you can put it this way: 'What must I wish to do to obtain power?' When you answer that you will know what action you must take."

"I wish to be powerful," suggested Vanya.

"The verb 'to be' is static. It does not contain the active germ necessary to an objective."

"I wish to obtain power," ventured Sonya.

"That is closer to action," said the Director. "Unfortunately it is too general and cannot be executed at once. Try sitting on this chair and wishing for power, *in general.* You must have something more concrete, real, nearer, more possible to do. As you see, not any verb will do, not any word can give an impetus to full action."

"I wish to obtain power in order to bring happiness to all humanity," suggested someone.

"That is a lovely phrase," remarked the Director. "But it is hard to believe in the possibility of its realization."

"I wish to obtain power to enjoy life, to be gay, to be distinguished, to indulge my desires, to satisfy my ambition," Grisha said.

"That is more realistic and easier to carry out but to do it you must take a series of preparatory steps. You cannot reach such an ultimate goal at once. You will approach it gradually. Go over those steps and enumerate them."

"I wish to appear successful and wise in business, to create confidence. I wish to earn the affection of the public to be accounted powerful. I wish to distinguish myself, to rise ir rank, to cause myself to be noticed."

The Director went back to the scene from *Brand* and had each of us do a similar exercise. He suggested:

"Suppose all the men put themselves in the position of Brand They will appreciate more readily the psychology of a crusader for an idea. Let the women take the part of Agnes. The delicacy of feminine and maternal love is closer to them.

"One, two, three! Let the tournament between the men and the women begin!"

"I wish to obtain power over Agnes in order to persuade her to make a sacrifice, to save her, to direct her in the right path." These words were hardly out of my mouth before the women came forward with:

"I wish to remember my dead child."

"I wish to be near him, to communicate with him."

"I wish to care for, to caress, to tend him."

"I wish to bring him back! I wish to follow him! I wish to feel him near me! I wish to see him with his toys! I wish to call him back from the grave! I wish to bring back the past! I wish to forget the present, to drown my sorrow."

Louder than anyone I heard Maria cry: "I wish to be so close to him that we can never be separated!"

"In that case," the men broke in, "we shall fight! I wish to make Agnes love me! I wish to draw her to me! I wish to make her feel that I understand her suffering! I wish to paint for her the great joy that will come from a duty performed. I wish her to understand man's larger destiny."

"Then," came from the women, "I wish to move my husband through my grief! I wish him to see my tears."

And Maria cried: "I wish to take hold of my child more firmly than ever and never let him go!"

The men retorted: "I wish to instill in her a sense of responsibility toward humanity! I wish to threaten her with punishment and separation! I wish to express despair at the impossibility of our understanding each other!"

All during this exchange the *verbs* provoked thoughts and feelings which were, in turn, inner challenges to action.

"Every one of the objectives you have chosen, is, in a way, true, and calls for some degree of action," said the Director. "Those of you who are of a lively temperament, might find little to appeal to your emotions in 'I wish to remember my dead child.' You would prefer 'I wish to take hold of him and never let go.' Of what? Of the things, memories, thoughts of the dead child. Others would be unmoved by that. So it is important that an objective have the power to attract and to excite the actor.

"It seems to me that you have given the answer to your own question why it is necessary to use a *verb* instead of a noun in choosing an objective.

"That is all for the present about *units and objectives*. You will learn more about psychological technique later, when you have a play and parts which we can actually divide into units and objectives."

# CHAPTER EIGHT

# Faith and a Sense of Truth

## I

"FAITH AND A SENSE OF TRUTH" was inscribed on a large placard on the wall at school today.

Before our work began we were up on the stage, engaged in one of our periodic searches for Maria's lost purse. Suddenly we heard the voice of the Director who, without our knowing it, had been watching us from the orchestra.

"What an excellent frame, for anything you want to present, is provided by the stage and the footlights," said he. "You were entirely sincere in what you were doing. There was a sense of truthfulness about it all, and a feeling of believing in all physical objectives which you set yourselves. They were well defined and clear, and your attention was sharply concentrated. All these necessary elements were operating properly and harmoniously to create—can we say art? No! That was not art. It was actuality. Therefore repeat what you have just been doing."

We put the purse back where it had been and we began to hunt it. Only this time we did not have to search because the object had already been found once. As a result we accomplished nothing.

"No. I saw neither objectives, activity nor truth in what you did," was Tortsov's criticism. "And why? If what you were doing the first time was actual fact, why were you not able to repeat it? One might suppose that to do that much you would not need to be an actor, but just an ordinary human being."

We tried to explain to Tortsov that the first time it was *necessary* to find the lost purse, whereas the second time we knew there was no need for it. As a result we had reality at first and a false imitation of it the second time.

"Well then, go ahead and play the scene with truth instead of falseness," he suggested.

We objected, and said it was not as simple as all that. We insisted that we should prepare, rehearse, live the scene. . . .

"*Live* it?" the Director exclaimed. "But you just did *live* it!"

Step by step, with the aid of questions and explanation, Tortsov led us to the conclusion that there are two kinds of truth and sense of belief in what you are doing. *First, there is the one that is created automatically and on the plane of actual fact* (as in the case of our search for Maloletkova's purse when Tortsov first watched us) and second, there is the *scenic type*, which is *equally truthful but which originates on the plane of imaginative and artistic fiction.*

"To achieve this latter sense of truth, and to reproduce it in the scene of searching for the purse, you must use a lever to lift you on to the plane of imaginary life," the Director explained. "There you will prepare a fiction, analogous to what you have just done in reality. Properly envisaged 'given circumstances' will help you to feel and to create a scenic truth in which you can believe while you are on the stage. Consequently, *in ordinary life, truth is what really exists, what a person really knows. Whereas on the stage it consists of something that is not actually in existence but which could happen.*"

"Excuse me," argued Grisha, "but I don't see how there can be any question of truth in the theatre since everything about it is fictitious, beginning with the very plays of Shakespeare and ending with the papier maché dagger with which Othello stabs himself."

"Do not worry too much about that dagger being made of cardboard instead of steel," said Tortsov, in a conciliatory tone. "You have a perfect right to call it an impostor. But if you go beyond that, and brand all art as a lie, and all life in the theatre as unworthy of faith, then you will have to change your point of view. What counts in the theatre is not the material out of which Othello's dagger is made, be it steel or cardboard, but the inner feeling of the actor who can justify his suicide. What is important is how the actor, a human being, *would have acted* if the circumstances and conditions which surrounded Othello were real and the dagger with which he stabbed himself were metal.

"Of significance to us is: *the reality of the inner life of a human spirit in a part and a belief in that reality. We are not concerned with the actual naturalistic existence of what surrounds us on the stage, the reality of the material world!* This is of use to us only in so far as it supplies a general background for our feelings.

"What we mean by *truth* in the theatre is the scenic truth which an actor must make use of in his moments of creativeness. Try always to begin by working from the inside, both on the factual and imaginary parts of a play and its setting. Put life into all the imagined circumstances and actions until you have completely satisfied your *sense of truth,* and until you have awakened a *sense of faith* in the reality of your sensations. This process is what we call *justification* of a part."

As I wished to be absolutely sure of his meaning, I asked Tortsov to sum up in a few words what he had said. His answer was:

"*Truth on the stage is whatever we can believe in with sincerity, whether in ourselves or in our colleagues.* Truth cannot be separated from *belief,* nor *belief* from truth. They cannot exist without each other and without both of them it is impossible to live your part, or to create anything. Everything that happens on the stage must be convincing to the actor himself, to his associates and to the spectators. It must inspire belief in the possibility, in real life, of emotions analogous to those being experienced on the stage by the actor. Each and every moment must be saturated with a belief in the truthfulness of the emotion felt, and in the action carried out, by the actor."

2

The Director began our lesson today by saying: "I have explained to you, in general terms, the part that *truth* plays in the creative process. Let us now talk about its opposite.

"A sense of truth contains within itself a sense of what is untrue as well. You must have both. But it will be in varying proportions. Some have, let us say, 75 per cent sense of truth, and only 25 per cent of sense of falseness; or these proportions reversed; or 50 per cent of each. Are you surprised that I differentiate and contrast these two senses? This is why I do it," he added, and then, turning to Nicholas, he said:

"There are actors who, like you, are so strict with themselves in adhering to truth that they often carry that attitude, without being conscious of it, to extremes that amount to falseness. You should not exaggerate your preference for truth and your abhorrence of lies, because it tends to make you overplay truth for its own sake, and that, in itself, is the worst of lies. Therefore try to be cool and impartial. You need truth, in the theatre, to the extent to which you can believe in it.

"You can even get some use from falseness if you are reasonable in your approach to it. It sets the pitch for you and shows you what you should not do. Under such conditions a slight error can be used by an actor to determine the line beyond which he may not transgress.

"This method of checking up on yourself is absolutely essential whenever you are engaged in creative activity. Because of the presence of a large audience an actor feels bound, whether he wishes to or not, to give out an unnecessary amount of effort and motions that are supposed to represent feelings. Yet no matter what he does, as long as he stands before the footlights, it seems to him that it is not enough. Consequently we see an excess of acting amounting to as much as 90 per cent. That is why, during my rehearsals, you will often hear me say, 'Cut out 90 per cent.'

"If you only knew how important is the *process of self-study!*

It should continue ceaselessly, without the actor even being aware of it, and it should test every step he takes. When you point out to him the palpable absurdity of some false action he has taken he is more than willing to cut it. But what can he do if his own feelings are not able to convince him? Who will guarantee that, having rid himself of one lie, another will not immediately take its place? No, the approach must be different. A grain of truth must be planted under the falsehood, eventually to supplant it, as a child's second set of teeth pushes out the first."

Here the Director was called away, on some business connected with the theatre, so the students were turned over to the assistant for a period of drill.

When Tortsov returned a short time later, he told us about an artist who possessed an extraordinarily fine sense of truth in criticizing the work of other actors. Yet when he himself acts, he completely loses that sense. "It is difficult to believe," said he, "that it is the same person who at one moment shows such a keen sense of discrimination between what is true and what is false in the acting of his colleagues, and at the next will go on the stage and himself perpetrate worse mistakes.

"In his case his sensitiveness to truth and falseness as a spectator and as an actor are entirely divorced. This phenomenon is widespread."

## 3

We thought up a new game today: we decided to check falseness in each other's actions both on the stage and in ordinary life.

It so happened that we were delayed in a corridor because the school stage was not ready. While we were standing around Maria suddenly raised a hue and cry because she had lost her key. We all precipitated ourselves into the search for it.

Grisha began to criticize her.

"You are leaning over," said he, "and I don't believe there is basis for it. You are doing it for us, not to find the key."

His carpings were duplicated by remarks of Leo, Vassili, Paul and by some of mine, and soon the whole search was at a standstill.

"You silly children! How dare you!" the Director cried out.

His appearance, catching us unaware in the middle of our game, left us in dismay.

"Now you sit down on the benches along the wall, and you two," said he brusquely to Maria and Sonya, "walk up and down the hall.

"No, not like that. Can you imagine anyone walking that way? Put your heels in and turn your toes out! Why don't you bend your knees? Why don't you put more swing into your hips? Pay attention! Look out for your centres of balance. Don't you know how to walk? Why do you stagger? Look where you're going!"

The longer they went on the more he scolded them. The more he scolded the less control they had over themselves. He finally reduced them to a state where they could not tell their heads from their heels, and came to a standstill in the middle of the hall.

When I looked at the Director I was amazed to find that he was smothering his laughter behind a handkerchief.

Then it dawned on us what he had been doing.

"Are you convinced now," he asked the two girls, "that a nagging critic can drive an actor mad and reduce him to a state of helplessness? Search for falseness only so far as it helps you to find truth. Don't forget that the carping critic can create more falsehood on the stage than anyone else because the actor whom he is criticizing involuntarily ceases to pursue his right course and exaggerates truth itself to the point of its becoming false.

"What you should develop is a sane, calm, wise, and understanding critic, who is the artist's best friend. He will not nag you over trifles, but will have his eye on the substance of your work.

"Another word of counsel about watching the creative work

of others. Begin to exercise your sense of truth by looking, first of all, for the good points. In studying another's work limit yourself to the role of a mirror and say honestly whether or not you believe in what you have seen and heard, and point out particularly the moments that were most convincing to you.

"If the theatre-going public were as strict about truthfulness on the stage as you were here today in real life we poor actors would never dare show our faces."

"But isn't the audience severe?" someone asked.

"No, indeed. They are not carping, as you were. On the contrary, an audience wishes, above all, to believe everything that happens on the stage."

4

"We have had enough of theory," said the Director when he began work today. "Let us put some of it into practice." Whereupon he called on me and on Vanya to go up on the stage and play the exercise of burning the money. "You do not get hold of this exercise because, in the first place, you are anxious to believe all of the terrible things I put into the plot. But do not try to do it all at once; proceed bit by bit, helping yourselves along by small truths. Found your actions on the simplest possible physical bases.

"I shall give you neither real nor property money. Working with air will compel you to bring back more details, and build a better sequence. If every little auxiliary act is executed truthfully, then the whole action will unfold rightly."

I began to count the non-existent bank notes.

"I don't believe it," said Tortsov, stopping me as I was just reaching for the money.

"What don't you believe?"

"You did not even look at the thing you were touching."

I had looked over to the make-believe piles of bills, seen nothing; merely stretched out my arm and brought it back.

"If only for the sake of appearances you might press your fingers together so that the packet won't fall from them. Don't throw it down. Put it down. And who would undo a package that way? First find the end of the string. No, not like that. It cannot be done so suddenly. The ends are tucked in carefully, so that they do not come loose. It is not easy to untangle them. That's right," said he approvingly at last. "Now count the hundreds first, there are usually ten of them to a packet. Oh, dear! How quickly you did all that! Not even the most expert cashier could have counted those crumpled, dirty old banknotes at such a rate!

"*Now do you see to what extent of realistic detail you must go in order to convince our physical natures of the truth of what you are doing on the stage?*"

He then proceeded to direct my physical actions, movement after movement, second by second, until coherent sequence was achieved.

While I was counting the make-believe money I recalled the exact method and order in which this is done in real life. Then all the logical details suggested to me by the Director developed an entirely different attitude on my part toward the air I was handling as money. It is one thing to move your fingers around in the empty air. It is quite another to handle dirty, crumpled notes which you see distinctly in your mind's eye.

The moment I was convinced of the truth of my physical actions, I felt perfectly at ease on the stage.

Then, too, I found little additional improvisations cropping out. I rolled up the string carefully and laid it beside the pile of notes on the table. That little bit encouraged me, and it led to many more. For example, before I undertook to count the packets I tapped them for some time on the table in order to make neat piles.

"That is what we mean by completely, fully justified physical action. It is what an artist can place his whole organic faith in," Tortsov summed up, and with that he intended to conclude the work of the day. But Grisha wished to argue.

"How can you call activity based on thin air *physical* or *organic*?"

Paul agreed. He maintained that actions concerned with material, and those concerned with imaginary objects, were necessarily of two differing types.

"Take the drinking of water," said he. "It develops a whole process of really physical and organic activity: the taking of the liquid into the mouth, the sensation of taste, letting the water flow back on the tongue and then swallowing it."

"Exactly," interrupted the Director, "all these fine details must be repeated even when you have no water, because otherwise you will never swallow."

"But how can you repeat them," insisted Grisha, "when you have nothing in your mouth?"

"Swallow your saliva, or air! Does it make any difference?" asked Tortsov. "You will maintain that it is not the same thing as swallowing water or wine. Agreed. There is a difference. Even so there is a sufficient amount of physical truth in what we do, for our purposes."

## 5

"Today we shall go on to the second part of the exercise we did yesterday, and work on it in the same way as we did in the first," said the Director at the beginning of our lesson.

"This is a much more complicated problem."

"I dare say we shall not be able to solve it," I remarked as I joined Maria and Vanya to go up onto the stage.

"No harm will be done," said Tortsov, comfortingly. "I did not give you this exercise because I thought you could play it. It was rather because by taking something beyond your powers you would be able better to understand what your shortcomings are, and what you need to work on. For the present, attempt only what is within your reach. Create for me the sequence of external, physical action. Let me feel the truth in it.

"To start with, are you able to leave your work for a while

and, in response to your wife's call, go into the other room and watch her give the baby his bath?"

"That's not difficult," said I, getting up and going toward the next room.

"Oh, no, indeed," said the Director as he stopped me. "It seems to me that it is the very thing you cannot properly do. Moreover, you say that to come onto the stage, into a room, and to go out again, is an easy thing to do. If so it is only because you have just admitted a mass of incoherence and lack of logical sequence into your action.

"Check up for yourself how many small, almost imperceptible, but essential physical movements and truths you have just omitted. As an example: before leaving the room you were not occupied with matters of small consequence. You were doing work of great importance: sorting community accounts, and checking funds. How could you drop that so suddenly and rush out of the room as though you thought the ceiling was about to fall? Nothing terrible has occurred. It was only your wife calling. Moreover, would you, in real life, have dreamed of going in to see a new-born baby with a lighted cigarette in your mouth? And is it likely that the baby's mother would even think of letting a man with a cigarette into the room where she is bathing him? Therefore you must, first of all, find a place to put your cigarette, leave it here in this room, and then you may go. Each one of these little auxiliary acts is easy to do by itself."

I did as he said, laid down my cigarette in the living-room, and went off the stage into the wings to wait for my next entrance.

"There now," said the Director, "you have executed each little act in detail and built them all together into one large action: that of going into the next room."

After that my return into the living-room was subjected to innumerable corrections. This time, however, it was because I lacked simplicity and tended to string out every little thing. Such over-emphasis is also false.

Finally we approached the most interesting and dramatic part. As I came into the room and started toward my work, I saw that Vanya had burned the money to amuse himself, taking a stupid half-witted pleasure in what he had done.

Sensing a tragic possibility I rushed forward, and, giving free rein to my temperament, wallowed in overacting.

"Stop! You have taken the wrong turning," cried Tortsov. "While the trail is still hot, go over what you have just done."

All that it was necessary for me to do was simply to run to the fireplace and snatch out a burning packet of money. To do it, however, I had to plan my path and push my moron brother-in-law aside. The Director was not satisfied that such a wild thrust could result in death and a catastrophe.

I was puzzled to know how to produce and to justify such a harsh act.

"Do you see this slip of paper?" he asked. "I am going to set fire to it and throw it into this large ash-tray. You go over there and as soon as you see the flame, run and try to save some of the paper from burning."

As soon as he lighted the paper I rushed forward with such violence that I nearly broke Vanya's arm on the way.

"Now can you see whether there is any resemblance between what you have just done, and your performance before? Just now we might actually have had a catastrophe. But before it was mere exaggeration.

"You must not conclude that I recommend breaking arms and mutilating one another on the stage. What I do wish you to realize is that you overlooked a most important circumstance: which is that money burns instantaneously. Consequently, if you are to save it you must act instantaneously. This you did not do. Naturally there was no truth in your actions."

After a short pause he said: "Now let us go on."

"Do you mean that we are to do nothing more in this part?" I exclaimed.

"What more do you wish to do?" asked Tortsov. "You saved all that you could and the rest was burnt up."

"But the killing?"

"There was no murder," he said.

"Do you mean there was no one killed?" I asked.

"Well, of course, there was. But for the person whose part you were playing, no murder exists. You are so depressed by the loss of the money that you are not even aware that you knocked the half-witted brother down. If you realized that, you would probably not be rooted to the spot, but would be rushing help to the dying man."

Now we came to the most difficult point for me. I was to stand as though turned to stone, in a state of "tragic inaction." I went all cold inside, and even I realized that I was overacting.

"Yes, there they all are, the old, old, familiar clichés that date back to our ancestors," said Tortsov.

"How can you recognize them?" I asked.

"Eyes starting with horror. The tragic mopping of the brow. Holding the head in both hands. Running all five fingers through the hair. Pressing the hand to the heart. Any one of them is at least three hundred years old.

"Let us clear away all of that rubbish. Clean out all of that play with your forehead, your heart and your hair. Give me, even if it is very slight, some action that has belief in it."

"How can I give you movement when I am supposed to be in a state of dramatic inaction?" I asked.

"What do you think?" he countered. "Can there be activity in dramatic or any other inaction? If there is, of what does it consist?"

That question made me dig into my memory and try to recall what a person would be doing during a period of dramatic inaction. Tortsov reminded me of some passages in *My Life in Art,* and added an incident of which he had personal knowledge.

"It was necessary," he recounted, "to break the news of her husband's death to a woman. After a long and careful preparation I finally pronounced the fateful words. The poor woman was stunned. Yet on her face there was none of that tragic expression which actors like to show on the stage. The complete absence of expression on her face, almost deathly in its extreme immobility, was what was so impressive. It was necessary to stand completely motionless beside her for more than ten minutes in order not to interrupt the process going on within her. At last I made a movement that brought her out of her stupor. Whereupon she fainted dead away.

"A long time afterwards, when it became possible to speak to her about the past, she was asked what went through her mind in those minutes of tragic immobility. It seems that a few moments before receiving the news of his death she was preparing to go out to do some shopping for him. . . . But since he was dead she must do something else. What should it be? In thinking about her occupations, past and present, her mind ran over the memories of her life up to the impasse of the actual moment, with its great question mark. She became unconscious from a sense of complete helplessness.

"I think you will agree that those ten minutes of tragic inaction were full enough of activity. Just think of compressing all of your past life into ten short minutes. Isn't that action?"

"Of course it is," I agreed, "but it is not physical."

"Very well," said Tortsov. "Perhaps it isn't physical. We need not think too deeply about labels or try to be too concise. In every physical act there is a psychological element and a physical one in every psychological act."

The later scenes where I am roused from my stupor and try to revive my brother-in-law proved to be infinitely easier for me to play than that immobility with its psychological activity.

"Now we should go over what we have learned in our last two lessons," said the Director. "Because young people are so impatient, they seek to grab the whole inner truth of a play or a role at once and believe in it.

"Since it is impossible to take control of the whole at once, we must break it up and absorb each piece separately. To arrive at the essential truth of each bit and to be able to believe in it, we must follow the same procedure we used in choosing our units and objectives. When you cannot believe in the larger action you must reduce it to smaller and smaller proportions until you can believe in it. Don't think that this is a mean accomplishment. It is tremendous. You have not been wasting the time you have spent, both in my classes and in Rakhmanov's drills, in centring attention on small physical actions. Perhaps you do not even yet realize that from believing in the truth of one small action an actor can come to feel himself in his part and to have faith in the reality of a whole play.

"I could quote innumerable instances which have occurred in my own experience, where there has been something unexpected injected into the stale, routine acting of a play. A chair falls over, an actress drops her handkerchief and it must be picked up, or the business is suddenly altered. These things necessarily call for small but real actions because they are intrusions emanating from real life. Just as a breath of fresh air will clear the atmosphere in a stuffy room these real actions can put life into stereotyped acting. It can remind an actor of the true pitch which he has lost. It has the power to produce an inner impetus and it can turn a whole scene down a more creative path.

"On the other hand we cannot leave things to chance. It is important for an actor to know how to proceed under ordinary circumstances. When a whole act is too large to handle, break it up. If one detail is not sufficient to convince you of the truth of what you are doing, add others to it, until you have achieved the greater sphere of action which does convince you.

"*A sense of measure* will also help you here.

"It is to these simple but important truths that we have dedicated our work in recent lessons."

6

"This last summer," said the Director, "I went back, for the first time in a number of years, to a place in the country where I used to spend my vacations. The house where I boarded was some distance from the railway station. A short cut to it led through a ravine, past some beehives and a wood. In the old days I came and went so often by this shorter route that I made a beaten track. Later this was all overgrown with tall grass. This summer I went through again. At first it was not so easy to find the path. I often lost my direction and came out onto a main high road, which was full of ruts and holes, because of heavy traffic. Incidentally it would have led me in the opposite direction from the station. So I was obliged to retrace my steps and hunt for the short cut. I was guided by old memories of familiar landmarks, trees, stumps, little rises and falls in the path. These recollections took shape and directed my search. Finally I worked out the right line and was able to go and come to the station along it. As I had to go to town frequently I made use of the short cut almost daily and it soon became a distinct path again.

"During our last few lessons we have been blocking out a line of *physical actions* in the exercise of the burned money. It is somewhat analogous to my path in the country. We recognize it in real life but we have to tread it down all over again on the stage.

"The straight line for you is also overgrown with bad habits which threaten to turn you aside at every step and mislead you onto the rutted and worn highway of stereotyped mechanical acting. To avoid this you must do as I did and establish the right direction by laying down a series of physical actions. These you must tread down until you have permanently fixed the true path of your role. Now go up onto the stage and repeat, several times, the detailed physical actions that we worked out last time.

"Mind you, only physical actions, physical truths, and physical belief in them! Nothing more!"

We played the exercise through.

"Did you notice any new sensations as a result of executing

a whole sequence of physical acts without an interruption?" asked Tortsov. "If you did, the separate moments are flowing, as they should, into larger periods and creating a continuous current of truth.

"Test it by playing the whole exercise from beginning to end, several times, using just the physical actions."

We followed his instructions and really did feel that the detailed bits dovetailed into one continuing whole. This sequence was strengthened by each repetition and the action had the feeling of pushing forward, with increasing momentum.

As we repeated the exercise I kept making one mistake which I feel I ought to describe in detail. Each time I left the scene and went off stage I ceased to play. The consequence was that the logical line of my physical action was interrupted. And it should not have been interrupted. Neither on the stage nor even in the wings should an actor admit such breaks in the continuity of the life of his part. It causes blanks. These in turn become filled with thoughts and feelings which are extraneous to the role.

"If you are unaccustomed to playing for yourself while off stage," said the Director, "at least confine your thoughts to what the person you are portraying would be doing if he were placed in analogous circumstances. This will help to keep you in the part."

After making certain corrections, and after we had gone over the exercise several more times, he asked me: "Do you realize that you have succeeded in establishing, in a solid and permanent manner, the long sequence of individual moments of the true physical action of this exercise?

"This continuous sequence we call, in our theatre jargon, 'the life of a human body.' It is made up, as you have seen, of living physical actions, motivated by an inner sense of truth, and a belief in what the actor is doing. This life of the human body in a role is no small matter. It is one half of the image to be created. although not the more important half."

## 7

After we had gone over the same exercise once more the Director said:

"Now that you have created the *body* of the role we can begin to think about the next, even more important, step, which is the *creation of the human soul* in the part.

"Actually this has already happened inside of you, without your knowing it. The proof is that when you executed all the physical actions in the scene just now you did not do it in a dry, formal way, but with inner conviction."

"How was this change brought about?"

"In a natural way: because the bond between body and soul is indivisible. The life of the one gives life to the other. Every physical act, except simply mechanical ones, has an inner source of feeling. Consequently we have both an inner and outer plane in every role, inter-laced. A common objective makes them akin to one another and strengthens their bonds."

The Director had me go over the scene with the money. As I was counting it I happened to look at Vanya, my wife's hunchback brother, and for the first time I asked myself: why is he forever hanging around me? At this point I felt I could not go on until I had clarified my relations with this brother-in-law of mine.

This is what I, with the Director's help, concocted as a basis for the relationship: the beauty and health of my wife had been bought at the price of the deformity of this, her twin brother. At their birth an emergency operation had to be performed and the boy's life was jeopardized to save the mother and her baby girl. They all survived, but the boy became a half-wit and hunchback. This shadow has always lain on the family and made itself felt. This invention quite changed my attitude toward the unfortunate moron. I was filled with a sincere feeling of tenderness for him and even some remorse for the past.

This gave life at once to the scene of the unhappy creature getting some joy out of the burning of the banknotes. Out of pity for him I did silly things to amuse him. I tapped the packets on the table, made comic gestures and faces as I threw the coloured wrappers off them into the fire. Vanya responded to these improvisations and reacted well to them. His sensitiveness instigated me to go on with more of the same type of inventions. A wholly new scene was created; it was lively, warm and gay. There was an instant response to it from the audience. This was encouraging and drove us on. Then came the moment to go into the next room. To whom? To my wife? Who is she? And there was another question to be solved. I could not go on until I knew all about this person to whom I am supposed to be married. My story about her was extremely sentimental. Nevertheless I really felt that if the circumstances had been what I imagined them to be, then this wife and child would have been infinitely dear to me.

In all this new life imagined for an exercise our old methods of playing it seemed unworthy.

How easy and pleasant it was for me to watch the baby in his bath! Now I did not need to be reminded about the lighted cigarette. I took great care to put it out before I left the living-room.

My return to the table with the money is now both clear and necessary. This is work that I am doing for my wife, my child, and the unfortunate hunchback.

The burning of the money acquired a totally different aspect. All I needed to say to myself was: what should I do if this really happened? I am horror-stricken at the prospect of my future; public opinion will brand me not only as a thief, but also as the murderer of my own brother-in-law. Moreover, I shall be looked upon as an infanticide! No one can restore me in the eyes of the public. Nor do I even know what my wife will think of me after my having killed her brother.

All during these conjectures it was absolutely necessary for me to remain motionless, but my immobility was full of action.

The next scene, the attempt to revive the dead boy, went

off quite by itself. This was natural, in view of my new attitude toward him.

Now the exercise, which had become rather a bore to me, aroused lively sensations. The method of creating both the physical and the spiritual life of a part seemed remarkable. I did feel, however, that the whole basis of the success of this method lay in the magic *ifs* and given circumstances. It was they that produced the inner impulse in me, not the creation of physical details. Why would it not be simpler to work straight from them, instead of putting so much time on physical objectives?

I asked the Director about this, and he agreed.

"Of course," he said, "and that is what I proposed that you do over a month ago when you first played this exercise."

"But then it was difficult for me to arouse my imagination and make it active," I remarked.

"Yes, and now it is wide awake. You find it easy not only to invent fictions but to live them, to feel their reality. Why has that change taken place? Because at first you planted the seeds of your imagination in barren ground. External contortions, physical tenseness and incorrect physical life are bad soil in which to grow truth and feeling. Now you have a correct physical life. Your belief in it is based on the feelings of your own nature. You no longer do your imagining in the air or in space, or in general. It is no longer abstract. We gladly turn to real physical actions and our belief in them because they are within reach of our call.

"We use the conscious technique of creating the physical body of a role and by its aid achieve the creation of the subconscious life of the spirit of a role."

8

In continuing the description of his method the Director illustrated his remarks today by an analogy between acting and travelling.

"Have you ever made a long journey?" he began. "If so, you will recall the many successive changes that take place both in what you feel and what you see. It is just the same on the stage. By moving forward along physical lines we find ourselves constantly in new and different situations, moods, imaginative surroundings, and the externals of production. The actor comes into contact with new people and shares their life.

"All the while his line of physical actions is leading him through the ins and outs of the play. His path is so well built that he cannot be led astray. Yet it is not the path itself that appeals to the artist in him. His interest lies in the inner circumstances and conditions of life to which the play has led him. He loves the beautiful and imaginative surroundings in his part, and the feelings which they arouse in him.

"Actors, like travellers, find many different ways of going to their destination: there are those who really, physically, experience their part, those who reproduce its external form, those who deck themselves with stock tricks and do their acting as though it were a trade, some who make a literary, dry lecture of a part, and those who use the part to show themselves off to advantage before their admirers.

"How can you prevent yourself from going in the wrong direction? At every junction you should have a well trained, attentive, disciplined signal man. *He is your sense of truth which co-operates with your sense of faith in what you are doing, to keep you on the right track.*

"The next question is: what material do we use for building our track?

"At first it would seem that we could not do better than to use real emotions. Yet things of the spirit are not sufficiently substantial. That is why we have recourse to *physical action.*

"However, what is more important than the actions themselves is their truth and our belief in them. The reason is: Wherever you have truth and belief, you have feeling and experience. You can test this by executing even the smallest act in which you really believe and you will find that instantly, intuitively and naturally, an emotion will arise.

"These moments, no matter how short they may be, are much to be appreciated. They are of greatest significance on the stage, both in the quieter parts of a play and in places where you live through high tragedy and drama. You have not far to go to find an example of this: what were you occupied with when you were playing the second half of that exercise? You rushed to the fireplace and pulled out a packet of banknotes: you tried to revive the moron, you ran to save the drowning child. That is the framework of your simple physical actions, inside of which you naturally and logically constructed the physical life of your part.

"Here is another example:

"With what was Lady Macbeth occupied at the culminating point of her tragedy? The simple physical act of washing a spot of blood off her hand."

Here Grisha broke in because he was not willing to believe "that a great writer like Shakespeare would create a masterpiece in order to have his heroine wash her hands or perform some similar natural act."

"What a disillusion indeed," said the Director ironically. "Not to have thought about tragedy! How could he have passed up all of an actor's tenseness, exertion, 'pathos,' and 'inspiration'! How hard to give up all the marvellous bag of tricks and limit oneself to little physical movements, small truths, and a sincere belief in their reality!

"In time you will learn that such a concentration is necessary if you are to possess real feelings. You will come to know that in real life also many of the great moments of emotion are signalized by some ordinary, small, natural movement. Does that astonish you? Let me remind you of the sad moments attendant on the illness and approaching death of someone dear to you. With what is the close friend or wife of the dying man occupied? Preserving quiet in the room, carrying out the doctor's orders, taking the temperature, applying compresses. All these small actions take on a critical importance in a struggle with death.

"We artists must realize the truth that even small physical movements, when injected into 'given circumstances,' acquire great significance through their influence on emotion. The actual wiping off of the blood had helped Lady Macbeth to execute her ambitious designs. It is not by chance that all through her monologue you find in her memory the spot of blood recalled in connection with the murder of Duncan. A small, physical act acquires an enormous inner meaning; the great inner struggle seeks an outlet in such an external act.

"Why is this mutual bond all-important to us in our artistic technique? Why do I lay such exceptional stress on this elementary method of affecting our feelings?

"If you tell an actor that his role is full of psychological action, tragic depths, he will immediately begin to contort himself, exaggerate his passion, 'tear it to tatters,' dig around in his soul, and do violence to his feelings. But if you give him some simple physical problem to solve and wrap it up in interesting, affecting conditions, he will set about carrying it out without alarming himself or even thinking too deeply whether what he is doing will result in psychology, tragedy or drama.

"By approaching emotion in this way you avoid all violence and your result is natural, intuitive, and complete. In the writings of great poets even the simplest acts are surrounded by important attendant conditions and in them lie hidden all manner of baits to excite our feelings.

"There is another simple and practical reason for approaching delicate emotional experiences and strong tragic moments through the truth of physical actions. To reach the great tragic heights an actor must stretch his creative power to the utmost. That is difficult in the extreme. How can he reach the needed state if he lacks a natural summons to his will? This state is brought about only by creative fervor, and that you cannot easily force. If you use unnatural means you are apt to go off in some false direction, and indulge in theatrical instead of in genuine emotion. The easy way is familiar, habitual and mechanical. It is the line of least resistance.

"To avoid that error you must have hold of something substantial, tangible. The significance of physical acts in highly tragic or dramatic moments is emphasized by the fact that the simpler they are, the easier it is to grasp them, the easier to allow them to lead you to your true objective, away from the temptation to mechanical acting.

"Come to the tragic part of a role without any nervous twinges, without breathlessness and violence and above all, not suddenly. Arrive gradually, and logically, by carrying out correctly your sequence of external physical actions, and by believing in them. When you will have perfected this technique of approach to your feelings, your attitude toward the tragic moments will change entirely, and you will cease to be alarmed by them.

"The approach to drama and tragedy, or to comedy and vaudeville, differs only in the given circumstances which surround the *actions* of the person you are portraying. In the circumstances lie the main power and meaning of these actions. Consequently, when you are called upon to experience a tragedy do not think about your emotions at all. Think about what you have to *do*."

When Tortsov had finished speaking there was silence for a few moments until Grisha, ready as always to argue, broke in:

"But I think that artists do not ride around on the earth. In my opinion they fly around above the clouds."

"I like your comparison," said Tortsov with a slight smile. "We shall go into that a little later."

## 9

At today's lesson I was thoroughly convinced of the effectiveness of our method of psycho-technique. Moreover, I was deeply moved by seeing it in operation. One of our classmates, Dasha, played a scene from *Brand,* the one with the abandoned child. The gist of it is that a girl comes home to find that someone has left a child on her doorstep. At first she is upset, but in a moment or two she decides to adopt it. But the sickly little creature expires in her arms.

The reason why Dasha is so drawn to scenes of this sort, with children, is that not long ago she lost a child, born out of wedlock. This was told to me in confidence, as a rumour. But after seeing her play the scene today no doubt remains in my mind about the truth of the story. All during her acting the tears were coursing down her cheeks and her tenderness completely transformed for us the stick of wood she was holding into a living baby. We could feel it inside the cloth that swaddled it. When we reached the moment of the infant's death the Director called a halt for fear of the consequences to Dasha's too deeply stirred emotions.

We all had tears in our eyes.

Why go into an examination of lives, objectives, and physical actions when we could see life itself in her face?

"There you see what inspiration can create," said Tortsov with delight. "It needs no technique; it operates strictly according to the laws of our art because they were laid down by nature herself. But you cannot count on such a phenomenon every day. On some other occasion they might not work and then . . ."

"Oh, yes, indeed they would," said Dasha.

Whereupon, as though she were afraid that her inspiration would wane she began to repeat the scene she had just played. At first Tortsov was inclined to protect her young nervous system by stopping her but it was not long before she stopped herself, as she was quite unable to do anything.

"What are you going to do about it?" asked Tortsov. "You know that the manager who engages you for his company is going to insist that you play not only the first but all the succeeding performances equally well. Otherwise the play will have a successful opening and then fail."

"No. All I have to do is to feel and then I can play well," said Dasha.

"I can understand that you want to get straight to your emotions. Of course that's fine. It would be wonderful if we could achieve a permanent method of repeating successful emotional experiences. But feelings cannot be fixed. They run through your fingers like water. That is why, whether you like it or not, it is necessary to find more substantial means of affecting and establishing your emotions."

But our Ibsen enthusiast brushed aside any suggestion that she use physical means in creative work. She went over all the possible approaches: small units, inner objectives, imaginative inventions. None of them was sufficiently attractive to her. No matter where she turned, or how hard she tried to avoid it, in the end she was driven to accept the physical basis and Tortsov helped to direct her. He did not try to find new physical actions for her. His efforts were to lead her back to her own actions, which she had used intuitively and brilliantly.

This time she played well, and there was both truth and belief in her acting. Yet it could not be compared to her first performance.

The Director then said to her:

"You played beautifully, but not the same scene. You changed your objective. I asked you to play the scene with a real live baby, and you have given me one with an inert stick of wood wrapped in a table cloth. All of your actions were adjusted to that. You handled the stick of wood skilfully, but a living child would necessitate a wealth of detailed movements which you quite omitted this time. The first time, before you swaddled the make-believe baby, you spread out its little arms and legs, you really felt them, you kissed them lovingly, you murmured tender words to it, you smiled at it through your tears. It was truly touching. But just now you left out all these important details. Naturally, because a stick of wood has neither arms nor legs.

"The other time, when you wrapped the cloth around its head you were very careful not to let it press on the baby's cheeks. After he was all bundled up you watched over him, with pride and joy.

"Now try to correct your mistake. Repeat the scene with a *baby,* not a *stick.*"

After a great deal of effort Dasha was finally able to recall consciously what she had felt unconsciously the first time she played the scene. Once she believed in the child her tears came freely. When she had finished playing the Director praised her work as an effective example of what he had just been teaching. But I was still disillusioned and insisted that Dasha had not succeeded in moving us after that first burst of feeling.

"Never mind," said he, "once the ground is prepared and an actor's feelings begin to rise he will stir his audience as soon as he finds an appropriate outlet for them in some imaginative suggestion.

"I do not want to wound Dasha's young nerves but suppose that she had had a lovely baby of her own. She was passionately devoted to him, and suddenly, when only a few months old, he died. Nothing in the world can give her any solace, until suddenly fate takes pity on her and she finds, on her doorstep, a baby even more lovely than her own."

The shot went home. He had barely finished speaking when Dasha began to sob over the stick of wood with twice as much feeling as even the very first time.

I hurried to Tortsov to explain to him that he had accidentally hit upon her own tragic story. He was horrified, and started toward the stage to stop the scene, but he was spellbound by her playing and could not bring himself to interrupt her.

Afterwards I went over to speak to him. "Isn't it true," I said, "that this time Dasha was experiencing her own actual personal tragedy? In that case you cannot ascribe her success to any technique, or creative art. It was just an accidental coincidence."

"Now you tell me whether what she did the first time was art?" countered Tortsov.

"Of course it was," I admitted.

"Why?"

"Because she intuitively recalled her personal tragedy and was moved by it," I explained.

"Then the trouble seems to lie in the fact that I suggested a new *if* to her instead of her finding it herself? I cannot see any real difference," he went on, "between an actor's reviving his own memories by himself and his doing it with the aid of another person. What is important is that the memory should retain these feelings, and, given a certain stimulus, bring them back! Then you cannot help believing in them with your whole body and soul."

"I agree to that," I argued, "yet I still think that Dasha was not moved by any scheme of physical actions but by the suggestion that you made to her."

"I do not for a moment deny that," broke in the Director. "Everything depends on imaginative suggestion. But you must know just when to introduce it. Suppose you go to Dasha and ask her whether she would have been touched by my suggestion if I had made it sooner than I did, when she was playing the scene the second time, wrapping up the stick of wood without any display of feeling at all, before she felt the foundling's little arms and legs, and kissed them, before the transformation had taken place in her own mind and the stick had been replaced by a lovely, living child. I am convinced that at that point the suggestion that that stick with a grimy rag around it was her little boy would only have wounded her sensibilities. To be sure she might have wept over the coincidence between my suggestion and the tragedy in her own life. But that weeping for one who is gone is not the weeping called for in this particular scene where sorrow for what is lost is replaced by joy in what is found.

"Moreover, I believe that Dasha would have been repelled by the wooden stick and tried to get away from it. Her tears would have flowed freely, but quite away from the property baby, and they would have been prompted by her memories of her dead child, which is not what we needed nor what she gave us the first time she played the scene. It was only after she made the mental picture of the child that she could weep over it again as she had at first.

"I was able to guess the right moment and throw in the suggestion that happened to coincide with her most touching memories. The result was deeply moving."

There was, however, one more point I wanted to press, so I asked:

"Wasn't Dasha really in a state of hallucination while she was acting?"

"Certainly not," said the Director emphatically. "What happened was not that she believed in the actual transformation of a wooden stick into a living child, but in the possibility of the occurrence in the play, which, if it happened to her in real life, would be her salvation. She believed in her own maternal actions, love, and all the circumstances surrounding her.

"So you realize that this method of approach to emotions is valuable not only when you create a role but when you wish to relive a part already created. It gives you the means to recall sensations previously experienced. If it were not for them the inspired moments of an actor's playing would flash before us once and then disappear forever."

## 10

Our lesson today was taken up by testing the *sense of truth* of various students. The first to be called on was Grisha. He was asked to play anything at all he liked. So he chose his usual partner, Sonya, and when they had finished the Director said: "What you have just done was correct and admirable from your own point of view, which is that of exceedingly clever technicians, interested only in the external perfection of a performance.

"But my feelings could not go along with you, because

what I look for in art is something natural, something organically creative, that can put human life into an inert role.

"Your make-believe truth helps you to represent images and passions. My kind of truth helps to create the images themselves and to stir real passions. The difference between your art and mine is the same as between the two words *seem* and *be*. I must have real truth. You are satisfied with its *appearance*. I must have true belief. You are willing to be limited to the confidence your public has in you. As they look at you they are sure that you will execute all the established forms with perfection. They rely on your skill as they do on that of an expert acrobat. From your standpoint the spectator is merely an onlooker. For me he involuntarily becomes a witness of, and a party to, my creative work; he is drawn into the very thick of the life that he sees on the stage, and he believes in it."

Instead of making any argument in reply, Grisha caustically quoted the poet Pushkin as having a different point of view about truth in art:

"A host of lowly truths is dearer
       Than fictions which lift us higher than ourselves."

"I agree with you and with Pushkin as well," said Tortsov, "because he is talking about fictions in which we can believe. It is our faith in them that lifts us. This is a strong confirmation of the point of view that on the stage *everything must be real in the imaginary life of the actor*. This I did not feel in your performance."

Whereupon he began to go over the scene in detail and correct it just as he had done with me in the exercise of the burnt money. Then something happened which resulted in a long and most instructive harangue. Grisha suddenly stopped playing. His face was dark with anger, his lips and hands trembled. After wrestling with his emotions for some time, finally he blurted out:

"For months we have been moving chairs around, shutting doors, lighting fires. That's not art; the theatre is not a circus. There physical actions are in order. It is extremely important to be able to catch your trapeze or jump on a horse. Your life depends on your physical skill. But you cannot tell me that the great writers of the world produced their masterpieces so that their heroes could indulge in exercises of physical actions. Art is free! It needs space, and not your little physical truths. We must be free for great flights instead of crawling on the ground like beetles."

When he had finished the Director said:

"Your protest astonishes me. Up to now I have always considered you an actor distinguished for his external technique. Today we find suddenly, that your longings are all in the direction of the clouds. External conventions and lies—that is what clips your wings. What soars is: imagination, feeling, thought. Yet your feelings and imagination seem to be chained right down here in the auditorium.

"Unless you are caught up in a cloud of inspiration and whirled upwards by it you, more than any other here, will feel the need of all the groundwork we have been doing. Yet you seem to fear that very thing and look upon exercises as degrading to an artist.

"A ballerina puffs, blows, and sweats, as she goes through her necessary daily exercises before she can make her graceful flights in the evening's performance. A singer has to spend his mornings bellowing, intoning through his nose, holding notes, developing his diaphragm and searching for new resonance in his head tones if, in the evening, he is to pour out his soul in song. No artists are above keeping their physical apparatus in order by means of necessary technical exercises.

"Why do you set yourself up as an exception? While we are trying to form the closest kind of direct bond between our physical and spiritual natures, why do you try to get rid of the physical side altogether? But nature has refused to give you the very thing you long for: exalted feelings and experiences. Instead she has endowed you with the physical technique to show off your gifts.

"The people who talk most about exalted things are the

very ones, for the most part, who have no attributes to raise them to high levels. They talk about art and creation with false emotions, in an indistinct and involved way. True artists, on the contrary, speak in simple and comprehensible terms. Think about this and also about the fact that, in certain roles, you could become a fine actor and a useful contributor to art."

After Grisha, Sonya was tested. I was surprised to see that she did all the simple exercises extremely well. The Director praised her and then he handed her a paper-cutter and suggested that she stab herself with it. As soon as she smelled tragedy in the air she got up on her stilts and at the climax she brought out such a tremendous amount of noise that we laughed.

The Director said to her:

"In the comedy part you wove a delightful pattern and I believed in you. But in the strong, dramatic places you struck a false note. Evidently your sense of truth is one-sided. It is sensitive to comedy and unformed on the dramatic side. Both you and Grisha should find your real place in the theatre. It is extremely important, in our art, for each actor to find his particular type."

II

Today it was Vanya's turn to be tested. He played the exercise of the burnt money with Maria and me. I felt that he had never done the first half as well as this time. He amazed me by his sense of proportion and convinced me again of his very real talent.

The Director praised him but he went on:

"Why," said he, "do you exaggerate truth to such an undesirable degree in the death scene? You have cramps, nausea, groans, horrible grimaces, and gradual paralysis. You seem, at this point, to be indulging in naturalism for its own sake. You were more interested in external, visual memories of the dissolution of a human body.

"Now in Hauptmann's play of *Hannele*, naturalism has its

place. It is used for the purpose of throwing the fundamental
spiritual theme of the play into high relief. As a means to an
end, we can accept that. Otherwise there is no need of dragging
things out of real life onto the stage which had much better
be discarded.

"From this we can conclude that not every type of truth can
be transferred to the stage. What we use there is *truth transformed into a poetical equivalent by creative imagination.*"

"Exactly how do you define this?" asked Grisha, somewhat
bitterly.

"I shall not undertake to formulate a definition for it," said
the Director. "I'll leave that to scholars. *All I can do is to help
you feel what it is. Even to do that requires great patience, for
I shall devote our whole course to it. Or, to be more exact, it
will appear by itself after you have studied our whole system of
acting and after you yourselves have made the experiment of
initiating, clarifying, transforming simple everyday human
realities into crystals of artistic truth.* This does not happen all
in a minute. You absorb what is essential and discard whatever
is superfluous. You find a beautiful form and expression, appropriate to the theatre. By doing this with the aid of your intuition,
talent, and taste you will achieve a simple, comprehensible
result."

The next student to be tested was Maria. She played the
scene that Dasha did with the baby. She did it both beautifully
and quite differently.

At first she showed an extraordinary amount of sincerity in
her joy at finding the child. It was like having a real live doll
to play with. She danced around with it, wrapped it up, un-
wrapped it, kissed it, caressed it, forgetting entirely that all she
held was a stick of wood. Then suddenly the baby ceased to
respond. At first she looked at him, fixedly, for a long time,
trying to understand the reason for it. The expression on her
face changed. As surprise was gradually replaced by terror, she
became more concentrated, and moved farther and farther away
from the child. When she had gone a certain distance she turned

to stone, a figure of tragic suspense. That was all. Yet how much there was in it of faith, youth, womanliness, true drama! How delicately sensitive was her first encounter with death!

"Every bit of that was artistically true," exclaimed the Director with feeling. "You could believe in it all because it was based on carefully selected elements taken from real life. She took nothing wholesale. She took just what was necessary. No more, no less. Maria knows how to see what is fine and she has a sense of proportion. Both of these are important qualities."

When we asked him how it was that a young, inexperienced actress could give such a perfect performance his reply was:

"It comes mostly from natural talent but especially from an exceptionally keen sense of truth."

At the end of the lesson he summed up:

"I have told you all that I can, at present, about *the sense of truth, falseness, and faith on the stage.* Now we come to the question of how to develop and regulate this important gift of nature.

"There will be many opportunities, because it will accompany us at every step and phase of our work whether it be at home, on the stage, at rehearsal, or in public. This sense must penetrate and check everything that the actor does and that the spectator sees. Every little exercise, whether internal or external, must be done under its supervision and approval.

"Our only concern is that all we do should be in the direction of developing and strengthening this sense. It is a difficult task, because it is so much easier to lie when you are on the stage than to speak and act the truth. You will need a great deal of attention and concentration to aid the proper growth of your sense of truth and to fortify it.

"Avoid falseness, avoid everything that is beyond your powers as yet and especially avoid everything that runs counter to nature, logic, and common sense! That engenders deformity, violence, exaggeration and lies. The more often they get an inning, the more demoralizing it is for your sense of truth. Therefore avoid the habit of falsifying. Do not let the reeds choke the tender flow of truth. Be merciless in rooting out of yourself all tendency to exaggerated, mechanical acting: dispense with throes.

"A constant elimination of these superfluities will establish a special process which is what I shall mean when you hear me cry: Cut 90 per cent!"

# CHAPTER NINE

## Emotion Memory

### I

OUR WORK began today by going over the exercise with the madman. We were delighted because we had not been doing exercises of this sort.

We played it with increased vitality, which was not surprising because each one of us had learned *what* to do and *how* to do it. We were so sure of ourselves we even swaggered a bit. When Vanya frightened us we threw ourselves in the opposite direction, as before. The difference here, however, lay in the fact that we were prepared for the sudden alarm. For that reason, our general rush was much more clearly defined, and its effect was much stronger.

I repeated exactly what I used to do. I found myself under the table, only I was clutching a large book instead of an ash receiver. The others did about the same. Sonya, for instance, ran into Dasha the first time we ever did this scene and accidentally dropped a pillow. This time she did not collide with her but let the pillow fall anyway, in order to have to pick it up.

Imagine our amazement when both Tortsov and Rakhmanov told us that, whereas our playing of this exercise used to be direct, sincere, fresh and true, today it was false, insincere and affected. We were dismayed at such an unexpected criticism. We insisted that we really felt what we were doing.

"Of course you were feeling something," said the Director. "If you were not you would be dead. The point is *what* were you feeling? Let us try to disentangle things and to compare your former with your present acting of this exercise.

"There can be no question but that you preserved the whole

staging, the movements, external actions, the sequence and every little detail of grouping, to an amazingly accurate degree. One could easily be led to think that you had photographed the set. Therefore you have proved that you have remarkably keen memories for the external, factual side of a play.

"Yet, was the way you stood around and grouped yourselves of such great importance? To me, as a spectator, what was going on inside of you was of much greater interest. Those feelings, drawn from our actual experience, and transferred to our part, are what give life to the play. You did not give those feelings. All external production is formal, cold, and pointless if it is not motivated from within. Therein lies the difference between your two performances. In the beginning, when I made the suggestion about the madman, all of you, without exception, became concentrated, each on your own problem of personal safety, and only after that did you begin to act. That was the right and logical process,—the inner experience came first and was then embodied in an external form. Today, on the contrary, you were so pleased with your acting that you never thought about anything except going over and copying all the externals of the exercise. The first time there was a deathly silence—today, it was all jollity and excitement. You were all busy getting things ready: Sonya with her pillow, Vanya with his lampshade, and Kostya with a book instead of an ash tray."

"The property man forgot the ash tray," I said.

"Did you have it prepared *in advance* the first time you played the exercise? Did you know that Vanya was going to yell and frighten you?" asked the Director, with a certain amount of irony. "It's very queer! How did you foresee today that you were going to need that book? It ought to have come into your hand accidentally. It's a pity that that accidental quality could not be repeated today. Another detail: originally, you never relaxed your gaze on the door, behind which the madman was supposed to be. Today you were instantly taken up with our presence. You were interested to see what impression your acting was making on us. Instead of hiding from the crazy man you were showing off to us. The first time you were impelled to act by your inner feelings and your intuition, your human experience. But just now you went through those motions almost mechanically. You repeated a successful rehearsal instead of recreating a new, living scene. Instead of drawing from your memory of life you took your material from the theatrical archives of your mind. What happened inside of you in the beginning naturally resulted in action. Today that action was inflated and exaggerated in order to make an effect.

"The same thing happened to you as to the young man who came to ask V. V. Samoilov whether or not he should go on the stage.

" 'Go out,' said he to the young man. 'Then come back and say over again what you have just told me.'

"The young man came and repeated what he had said the first time, but he was incapable of reliving the same feelings.

"However, neither my comparison to the young man nor your lack of success today should upset you. It is all in the day's work and I shall explain to you why. The *unexpected* is often a most effective lever in creative work. During your first performance of the exercise that quality was obvious. You were genuinely excited by the injection of the idea of a possible lunatic. In this recent repetition the unexpectedness had worn off, because you knew ahead all about it, everything was familiar and clear, even the external form through which you pour your activity. Under the circumstances, it didn't seem worth while, did it, to reconsider the whole scene afresh, to let yourselves be guided by your emotions? A ready-made external form is a terrible temptation to an actor. It is not surprising that novices like you should have felt it and at the same time that you should have proved that you have a good memory for external action. As for *emotion memory*: there was no sign of it today."

When he was asked to explain that term, he said:

"I can best illustrate it as did Ribot, who was the first person to define this type of memories, by telling you a story:

"Two travellers were marooned on some rocks by high tide. After their rescue they narrated their impressions. One remembered every little thing he *did*; how, why, and where he went; where he climbed up and where he climbed down; where he jumped up or jumped down. The other man had no recollection of the place at all. He remembered only the *emotions* he felt. In succession, came *delight, apprehension, fear, hope, doubt,* and finally *panic.*

"The second is just what happened to you the first time you played this exercise. I can clearly recall your dismay, your panic when I introduced the suggestion about the madman.

"I can see you rooted to the spot, as you tried to plan what to do. Your whole attention was riveted on the make-believe objective behind the door, and once you had adjusted yourselves to it you broke out with real excitement and real action.

"If, today, you had been able to do as the second man in Ribot's story did—to revive all the feelings you experienced that first time, and act without effort, involuntarily—then I would have said that you possess *exceptional emotion memories.*

"Unfortunately, such is all too seldom the case. Therefore, I am obliged to be more modest in my demands. I admit that you may begin the exercise and allow its external plan to lead you. But after that you must let it remind you of your former feelings and give yourselves up to them as a guiding force throughout the rest of the scene. If you can do that, I shall say your emotion memories are not exceptional, but that they are good.

"If I must cut down my demands even more, then I should say: play the physical scheme of the exercise, even though it does not recall your former sensations, and even though you do not feel the impulse to look at the given circumstances of the plot with a fresh eye. But then let me see you use your psycho-technique to introduce new imaginative elements that will arouse your dormant feelings.

"If you succeed in this I shall be able to recognize evidences of emotion memory in you. So far, today, you have not offered me any of these possible alternatives."

"Does that mean we have no emotion memory?" I asked.

"No. That is not what you must conclude. We shall make some tests at our next lesson," said Tortsov calmly, as he stood up and prepared to leave the class.

2

Today I was the first to have emotion memory checked.

"Do you remember," asked the Director, "that you once told me about the great impression Moskvin made on you when he came to your town on a tour? Can you recall his performance vividly enough so that the very thought of it now, six years later, brings back the flush of enthusiasm you felt at the time?"

"Perhaps the feelings are not as keen as they once were," I replied, "but I certainly am moved by them very much even now."

"Are they strong enough to make you blush and feel your heart pound?"

"Perhaps, if I let myself go entirely, they would."

"What do you feel, either spiritually or physically, when you recall the tragic death of the intimate friend you told me about?"

"I try to avoid that memory, because it depresses me so much."

"That type of memory, which makes you relive the sensations you once felt when seeing Moskvin act, or when your friend died, is what we call *emotion memory*. Just as your visual memory can reconstruct an inner image of some forgotten thing, place or person, your emotion memory can bring back feelings you have already experienced. They may seem to be beyond recall, when suddenly a suggestion, a thought, a familiar object will bring them back in full force. Sometimes the emotions are as strong as ever, sometimes weaker, sometimes the same strong feelings will come back but in a somewhat different guise.

"Since you are still capable of blushing or growing pale at the recollection of an experience, since you still fear to recall a certain tragic happening, we can conclude that you possess an emotion memory. But it is not sufficiently trained to carry on unaided a successful fight with the theatrical state you allow yourself to get into when you appear on the stage."

Next Tortsov made the distinction between sensation memory, based on experiences, connected with our five senses, and emotion memory. He said that he would occasionally speak of them as running along parallel to one another. This, he said, is a convenient although not a scientific description of their relation to one another.

When he was asked to what extent an actor uses his sensation memories, and what the varying value of each of the five senses is, he said:

"To answer that let us take up each one in turn:

"Of our five senses sight is the most receptive of impressions. Hearing is also extremely sensitive. That is why impressions are readily made through our eyes and ears.

"It is a well known fact that some painters possess the power of inner vision to such a degree that they can paint portraits of people they have seen but who are no longer alive.

"Some musicians have a similar power to reconstruct sounds inwardly. They play over in their minds an entire symphony they have just heard. Actors have this same kind of power of sight and sound. They use it to impress upon themselves, and then later recall, all sorts of visual and audible images,—the face of a person, his expression, the line of his body, his walk, his mannerisms, movements, voice, intonations, dress, racial characteristics.

"Moreover, some people, especially artists, are able not only to remember and reproduce things they have seen and heard in real life, they can also do the same with unseen and unheard things in their own imaginations. Actors of the visual memory type like to see what is wanted of them and then their emotions respond easily. Others much prefer to hear the sound of the voice, or the intonation, of the person they are to portray. With them the first impulse to feeling comes from their auditive memories."

"What about the other senses?" someone asked. "Do we need them, too?"

"Of course we do," said Tortsov. "Think of the opening scene with the three gluttons, in Chekhov's *Ivanov,* or where you have to work yourself up into an ecstasy over a papier maché ragout that is supposed to have been prepared with impressive culinary art by Goldoni's Mistress of the Inn. You have to play that scene so that both your mouth and ours water. To do this you are obliged to have an extremely vivid memory of some delectable food. Otherwise you will overdo the scene and not experience any gustatory pleasure."

"Where would we use the sense of touch?" I asked.

"In a scene such as we find in *Oedipus,* where the king is blinded, and uses his sense of touch to recognize his children.

"Yet the most perfectly developed technique cannot be compared with the art of Nature. I have seen many famous technical actors of many schools and many lands, in my day, and none of them could reach the height to which artistic intuition, under the guidance of nature, is capable of ascending. We must not overlook the fact that many important sides of our complex natures are neither known to us nor subject to our conscious direction. Only nature has access to them. Unless we enlist her aid we must be content with only a partial rule over our complicated creative apparatus.

"Although our senses of smell, taste, and touch are useful, and even sometimes important, in our art, their role is merely auxiliary and for the purpose of influencing our emotion memory. . . ."

### 3

Our lessons with the Director have been suspended temporarily because he has gone away on tour. For the present we are working at dancing, gymnastics, fencing, voice placing, and diction. Meantime something important has happened to me, which threw a great light on the very subject we have been studying—emotion memory.

Not long ago I was walking home with Paul. On a boulevard we ran into a large crowd. I like street scenes, so I pushed into the centre of it, and there my eyes fell on a horrible picture. At my feet lay an old man, poorly dressed, his jaw crushed, both arms cut off. His face was ghastly; his old yellow teeth stuck out through his bloody mustache. A street car towered over its victim. The conductor was fussing with the machinery to show what was wrong with it, and why he was not to blame. A man in a white uniform, with his overcoat thrown over his shoulders, was listlessly dabbing the dead man's nostrils with a bit of cotton on which he poured something out of a bottle. He was from a neighbouring drug store. Not far away some children were playing. One of them came across a bit of bone from the man's hand. Not knowing how to dispose of it he threw it in an ash can. A woman wept, but the rest of the crowd looked on with indifference and curiosity.

This picture made a deep impression on me. What a contrast between this horror on the ground and the light blue, clear, cloudless sky. I went away depressed and it was a long time before I could shake off the mood. In the night I awoke, and the visual memory was even more terrifying than the sight of the accident itself had been. Probably that was because at night everything seems more fearful. But I ascribed it to my emotion memory and its power to deepen impressions.

A few days later I passed by the scene of the accident and involuntarily stopped to recall what had happened so recently. All traces were obliterated. There was one human life less in the world and that was all. However, a small pension would be paid to the family of the deceased and so everyone's sense of justice would be satisfied. Therefore, everything was as it should be. Yet his wife and children were perhaps starving.

As I thought, my memory of the catastrophe seemed to become transformed. At first it had been raw and naturalistic, with all the ghastly physical details, the crushed jaw, the severed arms, the children playing with the stream of blood. Now I was shaken as much by my memory of it all, but in a different way. I was suddenly filled with indignation against human cruelty, injustice, and indifference.

It is just a week since the accident and I passed the scene of it again on my way to school. I stopped for a few moments, to think about it. The snow was white then as now. That's—life. I remembered the dark figure stretched out on the ground—that is—death. The stream of blood, that is the flow of man's transgressions. All around, in brilliant contrast, I see the sky, sun, nature. That's—eternity. The street cars rolling by, filled with passengers, represent the passing generations on their way into the unknown. The whole picture, which was so horrible, so terrifying, has now become majestic, stern . . .

## 4

Today I happened accidentally on a strange phenomenon. In thinking back to that accident on the boulevard I find that the street car tends now to dominate the picture. But it is not the street car of this recent happening—it is one that dates back to a personal experience of my own. This past autumn, late one evening, I was coming back to town from a suburb, on the last trolley. As it was passing through a deserted field it ran off its tracks. The passengers had to combine forces and help to get it back again. How big and heavy it seemed to me then and how weak and insignificant we were in comparison!

Why was this early sensation memory more powerfully and deeply impressed on me than the more recent one? And here is another angle—when I begin to think of the old beggar lying in the street with the apothecary bending over him, I find that my memory turns to quite another happening. It was long ago —I came upon an Italian, leaning over a dead monkey on the sidewalk. He was weeping and trying to push a bit of orange rind into the animal's mouth. It would seem that this scene had affected my feelings more than the death of the beggar. It was buried more deeply into my memory. I think that if I had to stage the street accident I would search for emotional material for my part in my memory of the scene of the Italian with the dead monkey rather than in the tragedy itself.

I wonder why that is?

## 5

Our lessons with the Director were resumed today and I told him about the process of evolution in my feelings about the street accident. First he praised me for my power of observation and then he said:

"That is a capital illustration of what does take place in us. Each one of us has seen many accidents. We retain the memories of them, but only outstanding characteristics that impressed us and not their details. Out of these impressions one large, condensed, deeper and broader sensation memory of related experience is formed. It is a kind of synthesis of memory on a large scale. It is purer, more condensed, compact, substantial and sharper than the actual happenings.

*"Time is a splendid filter for our remembered feelings—besides it is a great artist. It not only purifies, it also transmutes even painfully realistic memories into poetry."*

"Yet the great poets and artists draw from nature."

"Agreed. But they do not photograph her. Their product passes through their own personalities and what she gives them is supplemented by living material taken from their store of emotion memories.

"Shakespeare, for example, often took his heroes and villains, like Iago, from the stories of others and made living creatures of them by adding his own crystallized emotion memories to the picture. Time had so clarified and poetized his impressions that they became splendid material for his creations."

When I told Tortsov about the exchange of persons and things that had taken place in memories, he remarked:

"There is nothing surprising in that—you cannot expect to use your sensation memories the way you do books in a library.

"Can you picture to yourself what our emotion memory is really like? Imagine a number of houses, with many rooms in each house, in each room innumerable cupboards, shelves, boxes, and somewhere, in one of them, a tiny bead. It is easy enough to find the right house, room, cupboard, and shelf. But it is more difficult to find the right box. And where is the sharp eye that will find that tiny bead that rolled out today, glittered for a moment, and then disappeared from sight—only luck will ever find it again.

"That is what it is like in the archives of your memory. It has all those divisions and sub-divisions. Some are more accessible than others. The problem is to recapture the emotion that once flashed by like a meteor. If it remains near the surface and comes back to you, you may thank your stars. But do not count on always recovering the same impression. Tomorrow something quite different may appear in its place. Be thankful for that and do not expect the other. If you learn how to be receptive to these recurring memories, then the new ones as they form will be more capable of stirring your feelings repeatedly. Your soul in turn will be more responsive and will react with new warmth to parts of your role whose appeal had worn thin from constant repetition.

"When the actor's reactions are more powerful, inspiration can appear. On the other hand, don't spend your time chasing after an inspiration that once chanced your way. It is as unrecoverable as yesterday, as the joys of childhood, as first love. Bend your efforts to creating a new and fresh inspiration for today. There is no reason to suppose that it will be less good than yesterday's. It may not be as brilliant. But you have the advantage of possessing it today. It has risen, naturally, from the depths of your soul to light the creative spark in you. Who can say which manifestation of true inspiration is better? They are all splendid, each in its own way, if only because they are *inspired*."

When I pressed Tortsov to say that, since these germs of inspiration are preserved within us, and do not come to us from the outside, we must conclude that inspiration is of secondary rather than primary origin, he refused to commit himself.

"I do not know. Matters of the subconscious are not my field. Moreover I do not think that we should try to destroy the mystery that we are accustomed to wrap around our moments of inspiration. Mystery is beautiful in itself and is a great stimulus to creativeness."

But I was not willing to let it go at that, and asked him if everything we felt while on the stage was not of secondary origin.

"Do we, as a matter of fact, ever feel things there for the first time? I want to know too, whether or not it is a good thing to have original, fresh feelings come to us while we are on the stage—feelings we have never experienced at all in real life?"

"It depends upon the kind," was his answer. "Suppose you are playing the scene in the last act of *Hamlet* where you throw yourself with your sword on your friend Paul here, who enacts the role of the King, and suddenly you are overwhelmed for the first time in your life with a lust for blood. Even though your sword is only a dull, property weapon, so that it cannot draw blood, it might precipitate a terrible fight and cause the curtain to be rung down. Do you think that it would be wise for an actor to give himself up to such spontaneous emotions as that?"

"Does that mean that they are never desirable?" I asked.

"On the contrary, they are extremely desirable," said Tortsov. "But these direct, powerful and vivid emotions do not make their appearance on the stage in the way you think. They do not last over long periods or even for a single act. They flash out in short episodes, individual moments. In that form they are highly welcome. We can only hope that they will appear often, and help to sharpen the sincerity of our emotions, which is one of the most valuable elements in creative work. The unexpected quality of these spontaneous eruptions of feelings is an irresistible and moving force."

Here he added a note of warning:

"The unfortunate part about them is that we cannot control them. They control us. Therefore we have no choice but to leave it to nature and say: 'if they will come, let them come. We will only hope that they will work with the part and not at cross purposes to it.' Of course, an infusion of unexpected, unconscious feelings is very tempting. It is what we dream about, and it is a favourite aspect of creativeness in our art. But you must not conclude from this that you have any right to minimize the significance of *repeated feelings* drawn from emotion memory— on the contrary, you should be completely devoted to them, because they are the only means by which you can, to any degree, influence inspiration.

"Let me remind you of our cardinal principle: Through conscious means we reach the subconscious.

"Another reason why you should cherish those repeated emotions is, that an artist does not build his role out of the first thing at hand. He chooses very carefully from among his memories and culls out of his living experiences the ones that are most enticing. He weaves the soul of the person he is to portray out of emotions that are dearer to him than his everyday sensations. Can you imagine a more fertile field for inspiration? An artist takes the best that is in him and carries it over on the stage. The form will vary, according to the necessities of the play, but the human emotions of the artist will remain alive, and they cannot be replaced by anything else."

"Do you mean to say," broke in Grisha, "that in every kind of role, from Hamlet to Sugar in *The Blue Bird,* we have to use our own, same, old feelings?"

"What else can you do?" said Tortsov. "Do you expect an actor to invent all sorts of new sensations, or even a new soul, for every part he plays? How many souls would he be obliged to house? On the other hand, can he tear out his own soul, and replace it by one he has rented, as being more suitable to a certain part? Where can he get one? You can borrow clothing, a watch, *things* of all sorts, but you cannot take *feelings* away from another person. My feelings are inalienably mine, and yours belong to you in the same way. You can understand a part, sympathize with the person portrayed, and put yourself in his place, so that you will act as he would. That will arouse feelings in the actor that are *analogous* to those required for the part. But those feelings will belong, not to the person created by the author of the play, but to the actor himself.

*"Never lose yourself on the stage. Always act in your own person, as an artist. You can never get away from yourself. The moment you lose yourself on the stage marks the departure from truly living your part and the beginning of exaggerated false acting.* Therefore, no matter how much you act, how many parts you take, you should never allow yourself any exception to the rule of using your own feelings. To break that rule is the equivalent of killing the person you are portraying, because you deprive him of a palpitating, living, human soul, which is the real source of life for a part."

Grisha could not bring himself to believe that we must play ourselves always.

"That is the very thing you must do," affirmed the Director. *"Always and forever, when you are on the stage, you must play yourself. But it will be in an infinite variety of combinations of objectives, and given circumstances which you have prepared for your part, and which have been smelted in the furnace of your emotion memory.* This is the best and only true material for inner creativeness. Use it, and do not rely on drawing from any other source."

"But," argued Grisha, "I cannot possibly contain all the feelings for all the roles in the world."

"The roles for which you haven't the appropriate feelings are those you will never play well," explained Tortsov. "They will be excluded from your repertory. Actors are not in the main divided by types. The differences are made by their inner qualities."

When we asked him how one person could be two widely contrasting personalities he said:

"To begin with the actor *is* not one or the other. He has, in his own person, either a vividly or indistinctly developed inner and outer individuality. He may not have in his nature either the villainy of one character or the nobility of another. But the seed of those qualities will be there, because we have in us the elements of all human characteristics, good and bad. An actor should use his art and his technique to discover, by natural means, those elements which it is necessary for him to develop for his part. In this way the soul of the person be portrays will be a combination of the living elements of his own being.

"Your first concern should be to find the means of drawing on your emotional material. Your second, that of discovering methods of creating an infinite number of combinations of human souls, characters, feelings, passions for your parts."

"Where can we find those means and those methods?"

"First of all, learn to use your emotion memory."

"How?"

"By means of a number of inner and outer stimuli. But this is a complicated question, so we shall take it up next time."

# 6

We had our lesson today on the stage, with the curtain down. It was supposed to be in "Maria's apartment," but we could not recognize it. The dining-room was where the living-room had been. The former dining-room had been converted into a bed-room. The furniture was all poor and cheap. As soon as the students recovered from their surprise they all clamoured to have the original apartment back, because they said they were depressed by this one, and could not work in it.

"I am sorry nothing can be done about it," said the Director. "The other furniture was needed for a current play, so they gave us in exchange whatever they could spare, and they arranged things as best they knew how. If you don't like it the way it is, change anything you wish to make it more comfortable."

This started a general moving, and soon the place was torn to pieces.

"Stop!" cried Tortsov, "and tell me what sensation memories all this chaos brings to the surface in you."

"When there is an earthquake," said Nicholas, who had been a surveyor, "they move furniture around this way."

"I don't know how to define it," said Sonya, "but somehow it makes me think of the time when the floors are being done over."

As we continued to push the furniture around, various arguments arose. Some were searching for one mood, others for another, according to the effect produced on their emotion memories by this or that grouping of the things in the room. In the end the arrangement was tolerable. But we asked for more light. Whereupon we were given a demonstration in lighting and sound effects.

First we had the light of a sunny day, and we felt very cheerful. Off stage there was a symphony of noises, automobile horns, street car bells, factory whistles, and the faraway sound of an engine—all the audible evidence of a day in a city.

Gradually the lights were dimmed. It was pleasant, calm, but slightly sad. We were inclined to be thoughtful, our lids grew heavy. A strong wind came up, then a storm. The windows rattled in their frames, the gale howled, and whistled. Was it rain or snow beating on the panes? It was a depressing sound. The street noises had died away. A clock ticked loudly in the next room. Somebody began to play the piano, fortissimo at first and then more softly and sadly. The noises in the chimney increased the sense of melancholy. With the coming of evening lights were turned on, the piano playing ceased. At some distance a clock struck twelve. Midnight. Silence reigned. A mouse gnawed the floor. We could hear an occasional automobile horn or railroad whistle. Finally all sounds stopped and the calm and darkness was absolute. In a little while grey shadows heralded the dawn. As the first rays of sunlight fell into the room, I felt a great relief.

Vanya was the most enthusiastic of all about the effects.

"It was better than in real life," he assured us.

"There the changes are so gradual," added Paul, "that you are not aware of the changing mood. But when you compress twenty-four hours into a few minutes you feel the whole power over you of the varying tones of light."

"As you have noticed," said the Director, "surroundings have a big influence over your feelings. And this happens on the stage as well as in real life. In the hands of a talented director all these means and effects become creative and artistic media.

"When the external production of a play is inwardly tied up with the spiritual life of the actors it often acquires more significance on the stage than in real life. If it meets the needs of the play and produces the right mood it helps the actor to formulate the inner aspect of his role, it influences his whole psychic state and capacity to feel. Under such conditions the setting is a definite stimulus to our emotions. Therefore if an actress is to play Marguerite, tempted by Mephistopheles while she is at prayer, the director must give her the means of producing the atmosphere of being in church. It will help her to feel her part.

"For the actor playing Egmont, in prison, he must create a mood suggestive of enforced solitary confinement."

"What happens," asked Paul, "when a director creates a splendid external production which, however, does not fit the inner needs of a play?"

"Unfortunately that is a rather frequent occurrence," answered Tortsov, "and the result is always bad, because his mistake leads the actors in the wrong direction and sets up barriers between them and their parts."

"What if the external production is just plain bad?" asked someone.

"The result is even worse. The artists who work with the director, in back of the scenes, will achieve the diametrically opposite effect from the right one. Instead of attracting the attention of the actors toward the stage they will repel them, and throw them into the power of the audience beyond the footlights. Consequently the external production of a play is a sword in the hands of a director, that cuts both ways. It is equally capable of doing good and harm.

"Now I am going to put a problem to you," the Director went on. "Does every good set help an actor and appeal to his emotion memory? For example: imagine a beautiful set, designed by some artist highly gifted in the use of colour, line and perspective. You look at the set from the auditorium and it creates a complete illusion. And yet if you come up close to it you are disillusioned, you are ill at ease with it. Why? Because if a set is made from the painter's point of view, in two and not in three dimensions, it has no value in the theatre. It has width and height but lacks the depth, without which, as far as the stage is concerned, it is lifeless.

"You know from your own experience what a bare, empty stage feels like to an actor; how difficult it is to concentrate attention on it, and how hard it is to play even a short exercise or simple sketch.

"Just try to stand up in such a space and pour out the role of Hamlet, Othello, or Macbeth! How difficult it is to do it without the help of a director, a scheme of movements, without properties that you can lean on, sit on, move towards or group yourselves around! Because each situation that is prepared for you helps you to give a plastic outward form to your inner mood. Therefore, we absolutely need that third dimension, a depth of form in which we can move, live, and act."

7

"Why are you hiding away in a corner?" asked the Director of Maria, when he came onto the stage today.

"I . . . want to get away,—I—can't stand it . . ." she muttered, as she tried to get farther and farther away from the distracted Vanya.

"Why are you sitting together here so cosily?" he asked, of a group of students clustered in the sofa near the table.

"We . . . er . . . were listening to some anecdotes," stammered Nicholas.

"What are you and Grisha doing over there by the lamp?" he asked Sonya.

She was embarrassed and did not know what to say, but finally brought out something about reading a letter together.

He then turned to Paul and me and asked:

"Why are you two pacing up and down?"

"We were just talking things over," I replied.

"In a word," he concluded, "you have all chosen appropriate ways of responding to the moods you were in. You have produced the right setting and used it for your purpose. Or, is it possible that the setting you found suggested the mood and the action?"

He sat down by the fireplace and we faced him. Several pulled up their chairs to be nearer him, to hear better. I settled myself at the table to take notes. Grisha and Sonya sat off by themselves, so that they could whisper to each other.

"Now tell me just why each of you is sitting in that particular spot," he demanded, and we were again obliged to account for our movements. He was satisfied that each one had made use of the setting in accordance with what he had to do, his mood and his feelings.

The next step was to scatter us in various parts of the room, with pieces of furniture to help form groups. Then he asked us to note whatever moods, emotion memories, or repeated sensations had been suggested to us by the arrangement. We also had to say under what circumstances we would use such a setting. After that the Director arranged a series of sets, and in each case we were called upon to say: under what emotional circumstances, conditions, or in what mood, we would find it in keeping with our inner requirement to use the sets according to his indications. In other words: whereas we had, at first, chosen our setting to correspond to our mood and object, now he was doing that for us, and our part was to produce the right objective and induce the appropriate feelings.

The third test was one of responding to an arrangement prepared by some one else. This last problem is one that an actor is frequently called upon to solve; consequently it is necessary for him to be capable of doing it.

Then he began some exercises in which he put us in positions that were in direct conflict with our purposes and moods. All of which exercises led us to appreciate a good, comfortable, full background arranged for the sake of the sensations it aroused. In summing up what we had accomplished, the Director said that an actor looks for a suitable mise-en-scene to correspond to his mood, his objective and that also those same elements create the setting. They are, in addition, a stimulus to the emotion memory.

"The usual impression is that a director uses all of his material means, such as the set, the lighting, sound effects, and other accessories, for the primary purpose of impressing the public. On the contrary. We use these means more for their effect on the actors. We try in every way to facilitate the concentration of their attention on the stage.

"There are still many actors," he continued, "who in defiance of any illusion we can create, by means of light, sounds, or colour, still feel their interest more centred in the auditorium than on the stage. Not even the play itself and its essential meaning can bring back their attention to our side of the footlights. So that this may not happen to you, try to learn to look at and see things on the stage, to respond and give yourselves up to what is going on around you. In a word, make use of everything that will stimulate your feelings.

"Up to this point," the Director went on, after a slight pause, "we have been working from the stimulus to the feeling. Often, however, the reverse process is necessary. We use it when we wish to fix accidental inner experiences.

"As an example I shall tell you about what happened to me at one of the early performances of Gorki's *Lower Depths*. The role of Satin had been comparatively easy for me, with the exception of his soliloquy in the last act. That demanded the impossible of me,—to give a universal significance to the scene, to say the soliloquy with such profound implications of deeper meaning that it became the central point, the denouement of the whole play.

"Each time that I reached this danger spot, I seemed to put brakes on my inner feelings. And that hesitation stopped the free flow of creative joy in my part. After the soliloquy I invariably felt like a singer who has missed his high note.

"To my surprise this difficulty disappeared at either the third or fourth performance. When I tried to find the reason for this, I decided that I must go over in detail everything that happened to me the entire day before my appearance in the evening.

"The first item was that I received a shockingly big bill from my tailor, and was upset. Then I lost the key to my desk. In an ugly mood I sat down to read the review of the play, and found that what was bad had been praised, while the good parts were not appreciated. This depressed me. I spent the whole day mulling over the play—a hundred times I tried to analyse its inner meaning. I recalled every sensation I had at every point of my part, and I was so wrapped up that when evening came, instead of being all wrought up as usual, I was quite unaware of the public and indifferent to any idea of success or failure. I merely pursued my way logically and in the right direction, and found that I had gone past the danger spot of the soliloquy without ever noticing it.

"I consulted an experienced actor who is also an excellent psychologist, and asked him to help me clarify what had occurred, so that I could fix the experience of that evening. His attitude was:

" 'You cannot repeat an accidental sensation you may have on the stage, any more than you can revive a dead flower. It is better to try to create something new than to waste your efforts on dead things. How to go about it? First of all, don't worry about the flower, just water the roots, or plant new seeds.

" 'Most actors work in the opposite direction. If they achieve some accidental success in a part they want to repeat it and they go at their feelings directly. But that is like trying to raise flowers without the co-operation of nature, and you cannot do that unless you are willing to be satisfied with artificial blossoms.'

"So then what?

" 'Don't think about the feeling itself, but set your mind to work on what makes it grow, what the conditions were that brought about the experience.

" 'You do the same,' said this wise actor to me. *'Never begin with results. They will appear in time as the logical outcome of what has gone before.'*

"I did as he advised. I tried to get down to the roots of that soliloquy, to the fundamental idea of the play. I realized that my version had had no real kinship at all with what Gorki had written. My mistakes had built up an impassable barrier between me and the main idea.

"This experience illustrates the method of working from the aroused emotion back to its original stimulus. By using this method an actor can at will repeat any desired sensation, because he can trace the accidental feeling back to what stimulated it, in order to retrace his path back from the stimulus to the feeling itself."

8

The Director began, today, by saying:

"The broader your emotion memory, the richer your material for inner creativeness. That, I think, requires no further elaboration. It is, however, necessary, in addition to the richness of the emotion memory, to distinguish certain other characteristics; namely, its power, its firmness, the quality of the material it retains, to the extent that these affect our practical work in the theatre.

"Our whole creative experiences are vivid and full in direct proportion to the power, keenness and exactness of our memory. If it is weak the feelings it arouses are pale, intangible and transparent. They are of no value on the stage because they will not carry across the footlights."

From his further remarks it appears that there are many degrees of power in emotion memory and both its effects and combinations are varied. On this point he said:

"Imagine that you have received some insult in public, perhaps a slap in the face, that makes your cheek burn whenever you think of it. The inner shock was so great that it blotted out all the details of this harsh incident. But some insignificant thing will instantly revive the memory of the insult, and the emotion will recur with redoubled violence. Your cheek will grow red or you will turn pale and your heart will pound.

"If you possess such sharp and easily aroused emotional material you will find it easy to transfer it to the stage and play a scene analogous to the experience you had in real life which left such a shocking impression on you. To do this you will not need any technique. It will play itself because nature will help you.

"Here is another example: I have a friend who is extraordinarily absent-minded. He dined once with some friends he had not seen for a year. In the course of the dinner he made a reference to the health of his host's adorable little boy.

"His words were greeted with a stony silence, and his hostess fainted dead away. The poor man had completely forgotten that the boy had died since he last saw his friends. He says that he will never forget as long as he lives what he felt on that occasion.

"However, the sensations which my friend felt were different from those experienced by a person who had had his face slapped because in this case they did not obliterate all the details attendant on the incident. My friend retained a very accurate memory not only of his feelings, but of the happening itself and of the attending circumstances in which it occurred. He definitely remembers the frightened expression on the face of a man across the table, the glazed eyes of the woman next to him, and the cry that broke from the other end of the table.

"In the case of a really weak emotion memory the psycho-technical work is both extensive and complicated.

"There is one other of the many-sided aspects of this form of memory that we actors do well to take cognizance of, and I shall speak of it in detail.

"Theoretically you might suppose that the ideal type of emotion memory would be one that could retain and reproduce impressions in all the exact details of their first occurrence, that they would be revived just as they really were experienced. Yet if that were the case what would become of our nervous systems? How would they stand the repetition of horrors with all the original painfully realistic details? Human nature could not stand it.

"Fortunately things actually happen in a different way. Our emotion memories are not exact copies of reality—occasionally some are more vivid, but usually they are less so, than the original. Sometimes impressions once received continue to live in us, grow and become deeper. They even stimulate new processes and either fill out unfinished details or else suggest altogether new ones.

"In a case of this kind a person can be perfectly calm in a dangerous situation and then faint away when he remembers it later. That is an example of the increased power of the memory over the original happening and of the continuing growth of an impression once had.

"There remains now—in addition to the power and intensity of these memories—their quality. Suppose that instead of being the person to whom something happened, you are merely an onlooker. It is one thing to receive an insult in public yourself and to experience a keen sense of embarrassment on your own account, and it is quite another thing to see this happen to someone else, to be upset by it, to be in a position to side freely with the aggressor or his victim.

"There is, of course, no reason why the onlooker should not experience very strong emotions. He may even feel the incident more keenly than the participating parties. But that is not what I am interested in at present. All I want to point out now is that their feelings are different.

"There is another possibility—a person might not participate in an incident either as a principal or an onlooker. He might only hear or read about it. Even that would not prevent his receiving deep and powerful impressions. It would all depend on the strength of the imagination of the person who wrote the description or told about it, and also on that of the person reading or hearing the story.

"Again, the emotions of a reader or hearer differ in quality from those of an onlooker or principal in such an event.

"An actor has to deal with all these types of emotional material. He works it over and adjusts it to the needs of the person whom he portrays.

"Now let us suppose that you were a witness when that man was slapped in public, and that the incident left strong traces in your memory. It would be easier for you to reproduce those feelings if on the stage you played the part of a witness. But imagine that, instead, you were called upon to play the man who was slapped. How would you adapt the emotion you experienced as a witness to the role of the man insulted?

"The principal feels the insult; the witness can share only **sympathetic feelings. But** sympathy then might be transformed **into direct reaction.That is exactly what** happens to us when we **are working on a role.** From the very moment when the actor feels that change take place in him he becomes an active principal in the life of the play—real human feelings are born in him —*often this transformation from human sympathy into the real feelings of the person in the part occurs spontaneously.*

"The actor may feel the situation of the person in the part so keenly, and respond to it so actively, that he actually puts himself in the place of that person. From that point of view he then sees the occurrence through the eyes of the person who was slapped. He wants to act, to participate in the situation, to resent the insult, just as though it were a matter of personal honour with him. In that case the transformation of the emotions of the witness to those of the principal takes place so completely that the strength and quality of the feelings involved are not diminished.

"You can see from this that we use not only our own past emotions as creative material but we use feelings that we have had in sympathizing with the emotions of others. It is easy to state a priori that it is utterly impossible that we should have sufficient emotional material of our own to supply the needs of all the parts we shall be called upon to play in a whole lifetime on the stage. No one person can be the universal soul in Chekhov's *Sea Gull,* which has had all human experiences, including murder and one's own death. Yet we have to live all these things on the stage. So we must study other people, and get as close to them emotionally as we can, until sympathy for them is transformed into feelings of our own.

"Isn't that what happens to us every time we begin the study of a new role?"

## 9

"(1) If you remember the exercise with the madman," said the Director, "you will recall all the imaginative suggestions. Each contained a stimulus for your emotion memory. They gave you an inner impetus through things that had never happened to you in real life. You also felt the effect of the external stimuli.

"(2) Do you remember how we broke up that scene from *Brand* into units and objectives, and how the men and women in the class divided into furious opposition on it? That was another type of inner stimulus.

"(3) If you remember our demonstration of objects of attention, on the stage and in the audience, you will realize now that living objects can be a real stimulus.

"(4) Another important source of stimulation of emotion is true physical action and your *belief* in it.

"(5) As time goes on you will become acquainted with many new inner sources of stimulation. The most powerful of them lies in the text of the play, the implications of thought and feeling that underlie it and affect the inter-relationship of the actors.

- "(6) You are now aware too of all the external stimuli that surround us on the stage, in the form of settings, arrangement of furniture, lighting, sound and other effects, which are calculated to create an illusion of real life and its living *moods*.

"If you total up all these and add to them those that you are still to learn about, you will find that you have many. They represent your psycho-technical store of riches, which you must learn how to use."

When I told the Director that I was most anxious to do that very thing but did not know how to go about it, his advice was:

"Do as a hunter does in stalking game. If a bird does not rise of its own accord you could never find it among all the leaves of the forest. You have to coax it out, whistle to it, use various *lures*.

"Our artistic emotions are, at first, as shy as wild animals and they hide in the depths of our souls. If they do not come to the surface spontaneously you cannot go after them and find them. All you can do is to concentrate your attention on the most effective kind of lure for them. The very things for your purpose are these stimuli to your emotion memory we have just been discussing.

"The bond between the lure and the feeling is natural and normal and one that should be extensively employed. The more you test its effect and analyse its results in emotions aroused, the better you will be able to judge what your sensation memory retains, and you will be in a stronger position to develop it.

"At the same time we must not overlook the question of the quantity of your reserves in this respect. You should remember that you must constantly be adding to your store. For this purpose you draw, of course, principally upon your own impressions, feelings and experiences. You also acquire material from life around you, real and imaginary, from reminiscences, books, art, science, knowledge of all kinds, from journeys, museums and above all from communication with other human beings.

"Do you realize, now that you know what is required of an actor, why a real artist must lead a full, interesting, beautiful, varied, exacting and inspiring life? He should know, not only what is going on in the big cities, but in the provincial towns, far-away villages, factories, and the big cultural centres of the world as well. He should study the life and psychology of the people who surround him, of various other parts of the population, both at home and abroad.

"We need a broad point of view to act the plays of our times and of many peoples. We are asked to interpret the life of human souls from all over the world. An actor creates not only the life of his times but that of the past and future as well. That is why he needs to observe, to conjecture, to experience, to be carried away with emotion. In some cases his problem is even more complex. If his creation is to interpret current life he can observe his surroundings. But if he has to interpret the past, the future, or an imaginary epoch, he has either to reconstruct or to recreate something out of his imagination—a complicated process.

"Our ideal should always be to strive for what is *eternal* in art, that which will never die, which will always remain young and close to human hearts.

"Our goal should be the heights of accomplishment built by the great classics. Study them and learn to use living emotional material for their rendering.

"I have told you all that I can at present about *emotion memory*. You will learn more and more about it as we pursue our program of work."

# CHAPTER TEN

# Communion

I

WHEN THE Director came in he turned to Vassili and asked:
"With whom or with what are you in communion at this moment?"

Vassili was so absorbed in his own thoughts that he did not immediately recognize the purport of the question.

"I?" he replied, almost mechanically. "Why, not with anyone or anything."

"You must be a marvel," was the Director's joking remark, "if you are able to continue in that state for long."

Vassili excused himself by assuring Tortsov that since no one was either looking at or addressing him he could not be in contact with anyone.

It was now Tortsov's turn to be surprised. "Do you mean," said he, "that someone must look at or talk with you to be in communication with you? Close your eyes and ears, be silent, and try to discover with whom you are in mental communication. Try to find one single second when you will not be in some contact with some object."

I tried that myself and noted what went on inside of me.

I visualized the previous evening when I had heard a famous string quartet and I followed my movements step by step. I went into the foyer, greeted some friends, found my seat, and watched the musicians tune up. They began to play and I listened. But I could not put myself into a state of emotional relationship to them.

That, I concluded, must have been a blank space in the flow

of communion between me and my surroundings. But the Director was firm in his disagreement with that conclusion.

"How can you," said he, "look upon a time when you were
absorbing music, as a blank space?"

"Because although I listened," I insisted, "I really did not
hear the music, and although I tried to penetrate its meaning I
did not succeed. So I felt that no contact was established."

"Your association with and acceptance of the music had not
yet begun because the preceding process had not yet been
achieved and it distracted your attention. When that was done
you would either give yourself up to the music or become interested in something else. But there was no break in the continuity of your relationship to something."

"Perhaps that was so," I admitted, and pursued my recollections. Absent-mindedly I made a movement which, it seemed
to me, attracted the attention of the concert-goers near me. After
that I sat very quiet and pretended to be listening to the music
but as a matter of fact I really did not hear it because I was
watching what was going on around me.

My eye wandered over in the direction of Tortsov and I
noticed that he had not been aware of my accidental movement.
I looked around the hall for the elder Shustov, but neither he
nor any of the other actors from our theatre was there. Then I
tried to visualize all of the audience, but by this time my attention became so scattered that I was unable to control or direct it.
The music was conducive to all sorts of imaginings. I thought
about my neighbours, about my relatives, who live far away in
other cities, and about my dead friend.

The Director told me afterwards that all those things came
into my head because I felt the need either of sharing my
thoughts and feelings with the objects of my meditation or of
absorbing them from these objects.

Finally my attention was drawn to the lights on the chandelier overhead and I gave myself up to a lengthy contemplation
of them. That, I was convinced, must have been a blank moment

because, by no stretch of the imagination, could you call looking at those lights a form of intercourse.

When I told Tortsov about it he explained my state of mind in this way:

"You were trying to find out *how* and *of what* that object was made. You absorbed its form, its general aspect, and all sorts of details about it. You accepted these impressions, entered them in your memory, and proceeded to think about them. That means that you drew something from your object, and we actors look upon that as necessary. You are worried about the inanimate quality of your object. Any picture, statue, photograph of a friend, or object in a museum is inanimate, yet it contains some part of the life of the artist who created it. Even a chandelier can, to a certain degree, become an object of lively interest, if only because of our absorption in it."

"In that case," I argued, "we can be in association with any old thing that our eye happens to fall on?"

"I doubt if you would have the time to absorb from or to give out even a particle of yourself to everything that flashes by you. Yet without absorbing from others or giving of yourself to others there can be no intercourse on the stage. To give to or to receive from an object something, even briefly, constitutes a moment of spiritual intercourse.

"I have said more than once that it is both possible to look at and to see, and to look at and not to see. On the stage, you can look at, see and feel everything that is going on there. But it is also possible to look at what surrounds you on this side of the footlights, while your feelings and interest are centred in the auditorium, or in some place beyond the walls of the theatre.

"There are mechanical tricks which actors use to cover up their inner lack but they only emphasize the blankness of their stare. I need not tell you that that is both useless and harmful. The eye is the mirror of the soul. The vacant eye is the mirror of the empty soul. It is important that an actor's eyes, his look, reflect the deep inner content of his soul. So he must build up great inner resources to correspond to the life of a human soul in his part. All the time that he is on the stage he should be sharing these spiritual resources with the other actors in the play.

"Yet an actor is only human. When he comes on the stage it is only natural that he should bring with him his everyday thoughts, personal feelings, reflections and realities. If he does this, the line of his own personal, humdrum life is not interrupted. He will not give himself up wholly to his part unless it carries him away. When it does so, he becomes completely identified with it and is transformed. But the moment he becomes distracted and falls under the sway of his own personal life, he will be transported across the footlights into the audience or beyond the walls of the theatre, wherever the object is that maintains a bond of relationship with him. Meanwhile he plays his part in a purely mechanical way. When those lapses are frequent, and subject to interpolations from the actor's personal life, they ruin the continuity of the role because they have no relation to it.

"Can you imagine a valuable necklace in which, after every three golden links, there is one of tin, and then two golden links tied together with string? What would anyone want with such a necklace? And who can want a constantly breaking line of communication on the stage, which either deforms, or kills acting? Yet if communication between persons is important in real life, it is ten times more so on the stage.

"This truth derives from the nature of the theatre, which is based on the inter-communication of the dramatis personae. You could not possibly conceive of a playwright who would present his heroes either in a state of unconsciousness or asleep, or at any time when their inner life was not functioning.

"Nor could you imagine that he would bring two people onto the stage who not only did not know each other but who refused to become acquainted, to exchange thoughts and feelings, or who would even conceal these from each other by sitting in silence at opposite ends of the set.

"Under those circumstances, there would be no reason for a spectator to come into the theatre at all, since he could not get what he came for; namely, to sense the emotions and discover the thoughts of the people participating in the play.

"How different it is if, when these same actors come onto the stage, one of them wants to share his feelings with another, or to convince him of something he believes, while the other is making every effort to take in those feelings and those thoughts.

"When the spectator is present during such an emotional and intellectual exchange, he is like a witness to a conversation. He has a silent part in their exchange of feelings, and is excited by their experiences. But the spectators in the theatre can understand and indirectly participate in what goes on on the stage only while this intercourse continues among the actors.

"If actors really mean to hold the attention of a large audience they must make every effort to maintain an uninterrupted exchange of feelings, thoughts, and actions among themselves. And the inner material for this exchange should be sufficiently interesting to hold spectators. The exceptional importance of this process makes me urge you to devote special attention to it and to study with care its various outstanding phases."

2

"I shall start with *self-communion*," began Tortsov. "When do we talk to ourselves?

"Whenever we are so stirred up that we cannot contain ourselves; or when wrestling with some idea difficult to assimilate; when we are making an effort to memorize something, and trying to impress it on our consciousness by saying it aloud; or when we relieve our feelings, either gay or sad, by voicing them.

"These occasions are rare in ordinary life, yet frequent on the stage. When I have occasion to commune with my own feelings on the stage, in silence, I enjoy it. It is a state familiar to me off the stage, and I am quite at home in it. But when I am obliged to pronounce long, eloquent soliloquies I have no notion what to do.

"How can I find a basis for doing on the stage what I do not

do off of it? How can I address my very self? A man is a
large creature. Should one speak to his brain, his heart, his imagination, his hands or feet? From what to what should that inner
stream of communication flow?

"To determine that we must choose a subject and an object.
Where are they? Unless I can find those two inwardly connected centres I am powerless to direct my roving attention,
always ready to be drawn toward the public.

"I have read what the Hindus say on this subject. They believe in the existence of a kind of vital energy called Prana,
which gives life to our body. According to their calculation the
radiating centre of this Prana is the solar plexus. Consequently,
in addition to our brain which is generally accepted as the nerve
and psychic centre of our being, we have a similar source near
the heart, in the solar plexus.

"I tried to establish communication between these two
centres, with the result that I really felt not only that they
existed, but that they actually did come into contact with one
another. The cerebral centre appeared to be the seat of consciousness and the nerve centre of the solar plexus—the seat of
emotion.

"The sensation was that my brain held intercourse with my
feelings. I was delighted because I had found the subject and the
object for which I was searching. From the moment I made the
discovery I was able to commune with myself on the stage, either
audibly or in silence, and with perfect self-possession.

"I have no desire to prove whether Prana really exists or not.
My sensations may be purely individual to me, the whole thing
may be the fruit of my imagination. That is all of no consequence provided I can make use of it for my purposes and it
helps me. If my practical and unscientific method can be of use
to you, so much the better. If not, I shall not insist on it."

After a slight pause Tortsov continued:

"The process of mutual intercourse with your partner in a
scene is much easier to achieve. But here again we run into a
difficulty. Suppose one of you is on the stage with me and we

are in direct communication. But I am extremely tall. Just look at me! I have a nose, mouth, arms, legs and a big body. Can you communicate with all of these parts of me at once? If not, choose some one part that you wish to address."

"The eyes," someone suggested, and added, "because they are the mirror of the soul."

"You see, when you want to communicate with a person you first seek out his soul, his inner world. Now try to find my living soul: the real, live me."

"How?" I asked.

The Director was astonished. "Have you never put out your emotional antennae to feel out the soul of another person? Look at me attentively, try to understand and sense my inner mood. Yes, that is the way. Now tell me how you find me."

"Kind, considerate, gentle, lively, interested," I said.

"And now?" he asked.

I looked at him closely and suddenly found not Tortsov but Famusov (the famous character in the classic play *Woe From Too Much Wit*), with all his familiar earmarks, those extraordinarily naïve eyes, fat mouth, puffy hands and the soft gestures of a self-indulgent old man.

"And now with whom are you in communication?" asked Tortsov with Famusov's voice.

"With Famusov, of course," I answered.

"And what has become of Tortsov?" he said, returning instantly to his own personality. "If you had not been addressing your attention to the Famusov nose or hands which I had transformed by a technical method, but to the spirit within, you would have found that it had not changed. I can't expel my soul from my body and hire another to replace it. You must have failed to get into communication with that living spirit. In that case, what were you in contact with?"

That was just what I was wondering, so I set myself to remembering what change my own feelings underwent as my object was transformed from Tortsov to Famusov, how they turned from the respect which the one inspires, to the irony and good-humoured laughter which the other causes. Of course, I must have been in contact with his inner spirit throughout and yet I could not be clear about it.

"You were in contact with a new being," he explained, "which you may call Famusov-Tortsov, or Tortsov-Famusov. In time you will understand these miraculous metamorphoses of a creative artist. Let it suffice now that you understand that *people always try to reach the living spirit of their object* and that they do not deal with noses, or eyes, or buttons the way some actors do on the stage.

"All that is necessary is for two people to come into close contact and a natural, mutual exchange takes place. I try to give out my thoughts to you, and you make an effort to absorb something of my knowledge and experience."

"But that does not mean that the exchange is mutual," argued Grisha. "You, the subject, transmit your sensations to us, but all we, the objects, do is to receive. What is reciprocal in that?"

"Tell me what you are doing this minute," Tortsov replied. "Aren't you answering me? Aren't you voicing your doubts and trying to convince me? That is the confluence of feelings you are looking for."

"It is now, but was it, while you were talking?" Grisha clung to his point.

"I don't see any difference," answered Tortsov. "We were exchanging thoughts and feelings then and we are continuing to do so now. Obviously in communicating with one another the giving out and the taking in occur alternately. But even while I was speaking and you were merely listening I was aware of your doubts. Your impatience, astonishment and excitement, all carried over to me.

"Why was I absorbing those feelings from you? Because you could not contain them. Even when you were silent, there was a meeting of feelings between us. Of course, it did not become explicit until you began to speak. Yet it proves how constant the flow of these interchanging thoughts and feelings is. It is especially necessary on the stage to maintain that flow unbroken, because the lines are almost exclusively in dialogue.

"Unfortunately, that unbroken flow is all too rare. Most actors, if indeed they are aware of it at all, use it only when they are saying their own lines. But let the other actor begin to say his and the first one neither listens nor makes an attempt to absorb what the second is saying. He ceases to act until he hears his next cue. That habit breaks up constant exchange because that is dependent on the give and take of feelings both during the speaking of the lines, and also during the reply to those already spoken, and even during silences, when the eyes carry on.

"Such fragmentary connection is all wrong. When you speak to the person who is playing opposite you, learn to follow through until you are certain your thoughts have penetrated his consciousness. Only after you are convinced of this and have added with your eyes what could not be put into words, should you continue to say the rest of your lines. In turn, you must learn to take in, each time afresh, the words and thoughts of your partner. You must be aware today of his lines even though you have heard them repeated many times in rehearsals and performances. This connection must be made each time you act together, and this requires a great deal of concentrated attention, technique, and artistic discipline."

After a slight pause the Director said that we would now pass to the study of a new phase: *communion with an imaginary, unreal, non-existent object*, such as an apparition.

"Some people try to delude themselves into thinking that they really do see it. They exhaust all of their energy and attention on such an effort. But an experienced actor knows that the point does not lie in the apparition itself, but in his inner relation to it. Therefore he tries to give an honest answer to his own question: what should I do if a ghost appeared before me?

"There are some actors, especially beginners, who use an imaginary object when they are working at home because they lack a living one. Their attention is directed towards convincing themselves of the existence of a non-existent thing, rather than concentrating on what should be their inner objective. When they form this bad habit they unconsciously carry the same method over onto the stage and eventually become unaccustomed to a living object. They set an inanimate make-believe one up between themselves and their partners. This dangerous habit sometimes becomes so ingrained that it may last a lifetime.

"What torture to play opposite an actor who looks at you and yet sees someone else, who constantly adjusts himself to that other person and not to you. Such actors are separated from the very persons with whom they should be in closest relationship. They cannot take in your words, your intonations, or anything else. Their eyes are veiled as they look at you. Do avoid this dangerous and deadening method. It eats into you and is so difficult to eradicate!"

"What are we to do when we have no living object?" I asked.

"Wait until you find one," answered Tortsov. "You will have a class in drill so that you can exercise in groups of two or more. Let me repeat: I insist that you do not undertake any exercises in communication except with living objects and under expert supervision.

"Even more difficult is mutual communion with a collective object; in other words, with the public.

"Of course, it cannot be done directly. The difficulty lies in the fact that we are in relation with our partner and simultaneously with the spectator. With the former our contact is direct and conscious, with the latter it is indirect, and unconscious. The remarkable thing is that with both our relation is mutual."

Paul protested, and said:

"I see how the relation between actors can be mutual, but not the bond between the actors and the public. They would have to contribute something to us. Actually, what do we get from them? Applause and flowers! And even these we do not receive until after the play is over."

"What about laughter, tears, applause during the perform-ance, hisses, excitement! Don't you count them?" said Tortsov.

"Let me tell you of an incident which illustrates what I mean. At a children's matinee of *The Blue Bird,* during the trial of the children by the trees and the animals, I felt someone nudge me. It was a ten-year-old boy. 'Tell them that the Cat is listening. He pretended to hide, but I can *see* him,' whispered an agitated little voice, full of worry and concern for Mytyl and Tyltyl. I could not reassure him, so the little fellow crept down to the footlights and whispered to the actors playing the parts of the two children, warning them of their danger.

"Isn't that real response?

"If you want to learn to appreciate what you get from the public let me suggest that you give a performance to a com-pletely empty hall. Would you care to do that? No! Because to act without a public is like singing in a place without resonance. To play to a large and sympathetic audience is like singing in a room with perfect acoustics. The audience constitute the spiritual acoustics for us. They give back what they receive from us as living, human emotions.

"In conventional and artificial types of acting this problem of relation to a collective object is solved very simply. Take the old French farces. In them the actors talk constantly to the public. They come right out in front and address either short individual remarks or long harangues which explain the course of the play. This is done with impressive self-confidence, assur-ance, and aplomb. Indeed, if you are going to put yourself in direct relation to the public, you had better dominate it.

"There is still another angle: dealing with mob scenes. We are obliged to be in direct, immediate relationship with a mass object. Sometimes we turn to individuals in the crowd; at others, we must embrace the whole in a form of extended mutual ex-change. The fact that the majority of those making up a mob scene are naturally totally different from one another and that they contribute the most varied emotions and thoughts to this mutual intercourse, very much intensifies the process. Also the group quality excites the temperament of each component member and of all of them together. This excites the principals and that makes a great impression on the spectators."

After that Tortsov discussed the undesirable attitude of mechanical actors toward the public.

"They put themselves in direct touch with the public, passing right by the actors playing opposite them. That is the line of least resistance. Actually that is nothing more nor less than exhibitionism. I think you can be trusted to distinguish between that and a sincere effort to exchange living human feelings with other actors. There is a vast difference between this highly creative process and ordinary mechanical, theatrical gestures. They are both opposite and contradictory.

"We can admit all but the theatrical type, and even that you should study if only to combat it.

"One word, in conclusion, about the active principle underlying the process of communication. Some think that our external, visible movements are a manifestation of activity and that the inner, invisible acts of spiritual communion are not. This mistaken idea is the more regrettable because every manifestation of inner activity is important and valuable. Therefore learn to prize that inner communion because it is one of the most important sources of action."

### 3

"If you want to exchange your thoughts and feelings with someone you must offer something you have experienced yourself," the Director began. "Under ordinary circumstances life provides these. This material grows in us spontaneously and derives from surrounding conditions.

"In the theatre it is different, and this presents a new difficulty. We are supposed to use the feelings and thoughts created by the playwright. It is more difficult to absorb this spiritual material than to play at external forms of non-existing passions in the good old theatrical way.

"It is much harder truly to commune with your partner than

to *represent* yourself as being in that relation to him. Actors love to follow the line of least resistance, so they gladly replace real communion by ordinary imitations of it.

"This is worth thinking about, because I want you to understand, see, and feel what we are most likely to send out to the public in the guise of exchange of thoughts and feelings."

Here the Director went up on the stage and played a whole scene in a way remarkable for talent and mastery of theatre technique. He began by reciting some poetry, the words of which he pronounced hurriedly, effectively, but so incomprehensibly that we could not understand a word.

"How am I communicating with you now?" he asked.

We did not dare criticize him, so he answered his own question. "In no way at all," he said. "I mumbled some words, scattered them around like so many peas, without even knowing what I was saying.

"That is the first type of material often offered to the public as a basis of relationship—thin air. No thought is given either to the sense of the words themselves or to their implications. The only desire is to be effective."

Next he announced that he would do the soliloquy from the last act of *Figaro*. This time his acting was a miracle of marvellous movements, intonations, changes, infectious laughter, crystalline diction, rapid speech, brilliant inflections of a voice with an enchanting timbre. We could hardly keep from giving him an ovation. It was all so theatrically effective. Yet we had no conception of the inner content of the soliloquy as we had grasped nothing of what he said.

"Now tell me in what relation I was to you this time," he asked again. And again we were unable to answer.

"I showed you myself, in a part," Tortsov answered for us, "and I used the Figaro soliloquy for that purpose, its words, gestures, and everything that went with it. I did not show you the role itself, but myself in the role and my own attributes: my form, face, gestures, poses, mannerisms, movements, walk, voice, diction, speech, intonations, temperament, technique—everything except feelings.

"For those who have an externally expressive apparatus what I did just now would not be difficult. Let your voice resound, your tongue emit words and phrases distinctly, your poses be plastic, and the whole effect will be pleasing. I acted like a diva in a café chantant, constantly watching you to see whether I was making good. I felt that I was so much merchandise and that you were the buyers.

"This is a second example of how not to act, despite the fact that this form of exhibitionism is widely used and immensely popular."

He went on to a third example.

"You have just seen me presenting myself. Now I shall show you a part, as presented by the author, but this does not mean that I shall live the part. The point of this performance will lie not in my feelings but in the pattern, the words, external facial expressions, gestures, and business. I shall not create the role. I shall merely present it in an external manner."

He played a scene in which an important general accidentally found himself alone at home with nothing to do. Out of boredom he lined up all the chairs in the place so that they looked like soldiers on parade. Then he made neat piles of everything on all the tables. Next he thought of something rather spicy; after that he looked aghast over a pile of business correspondence. He signed several letters without reading them, yawned, stretched himself, and then began his silly activities all over again.

All the while Tortsov was giving the text of the soliloquy with extraordinary clarity; about the nobility of highly placed persons and the dense ignorance of everyone else. He did it in a cold, impersonal way, indicating the outer form of the scene without any attempt to put life or depth into it. In some places he rendered the text with technical crispness, in others he underscored his pose, gesture, play, or emphasized some special detail of his characterization. Meantime he was watching his public out of the corner of his eye to see whether what he was doing carried across. When it was necessary to make pauses he drew them out. Just the bored way actors do when they play a well-made part for the 500th time. He might as well have been a gramophone or a movie operator showing the same film ad infinitum.

"Now," he continued, "there remains the illustration of the right way and means to be used in establishing contact between the stage and the public.

"You have already seen me demonstrate this many times. You know that I always try to be in direct relation to my partner, to transmit to him my own feelings, analogous to those of the character I am playing. The rest, the complete fusion of the actor with his part, happens automatically.

"Now I shall test you. I shall make a note of incorrect communication between you and your partners by ringing a bell. By incorrect I mean that you are not in direct contact with your object, that you are showing off the part or yourself, or that you are recording your lines impersonally. All such mistakes will get the bell.

"Remember that there are only three types which will get my silent approval:

1) Direct communication with an object on the stage, and indirect communication with the public.
2) Self-communion.
3) Communication with an absent or imaginary object."

Then the test began.

Paul and I played well as we thought and were surprised to have the bell rung on us frequently.

All the others were tested in the same way. Grisha and Sonya were last, and we thought the Director would be ringing incessantly; yet actually he did it much less than we expected that he would.

When we asked him why, he explained:

"It just means that many who boast are mistaken and others,

whom they criticize, prove capable of establishing the right contact with one another. In either case it is a matter of percentage. But the conclusion to be drawn is that there is no completely right or completely wrong relationship. The work of an actor is mixed; there are good and bad moments in it.

"If you were to make an analysis you would divide your results by percentages, allowing the actor so much for contact with his partner, so much for contact with the public, so much for demonstrating the pattern of his part, so much for showing himself off. The relation of these percentages to one another in the final total determines the degree of accuracy with which the actor was able to achieve the process of communion. Some will rate higher in their relations with their partners, others in their ability to commune with an imaginary object, or themselves. These approach the ideal.

"On the negative side some types of relation between subject and object are less bad than others. It is, for example, less bad to exhibit the psychological pattern of your role impersonally than to exhibit yourself or give a mechanical performance.

"There are an infinite number of combinations. Consequently it is best for you to make a practice of: 1) finding your real object on the stage and getting into active communication with it, and 2) recognizing false objects, false relationships and combatting them. Above all give special attention to the quality of the spiritual material on which you base your communication with others."

4

"Today we shall check your external equipment for intercommunication," announced the Director. "I must know whether you really appreciate the means at your disposal. Please go up on the stage, sit down in pairs, and start some kind of an argument."

I reasoned that Grisha would be the easiest person with whom to pick a quarrel, so I sat down by him, and it was not long before my purpose was accomplished.

Tortsov noticed that in making my points to Grisha I used my wrists and fingers freely, so he ordered them to be bandaged.

"Why do that?" I asked.

"So that you will understand how often we fail to appreciate our tools. I want you to be convinced that whereas the eyes are the mirror of the soul, the tips of the fingers are the eyes of the body," he explained.

Having no use of my hands I increased my intonation. But Tortsov requested me to speak without raising my voice or adding extra inflections. I had to use my eyes, facial expression, eyebrows, neck, head and torso. I tried to replace the means I had been deprived of. Then I was bound down to my chair and only my mouth, ears, face, and eyes were still free.

Soon even these were bound up and all that I could do was roar. Which did not help.

At this point the external world ceased to exist for me. Nothing was left to me except my inner vision, my inner ear, my imagination.

I was kept in this state for some time. Then I heard a voice that seemed to come from far off.

It was Tortsov, saying:

"Do you want some one organ of communication back? If so, which one?"

I tried to indicate that I would think about it.

How could I choose the most necessary organ? Sight expresses feelings. Speech expresses thought. Feelings must influence the vocal organs because the intonation of the voice expresses inner emotion, and hearing, too, is a great stimulus to them. Yet hearing is a necessary adjunct of speech. Besides, they both direct the use of the face and the hands.

Finally I exclaimed angrily, "An actor cannot be crippled! He has to have all of his organs!"

The Director praised me and said:

"At last you are talking like an artist who appreciates the real value of each one of those organs of communication. May we see disappear forever the actor's blank eye, his immobile face and brow, his dull voice, speech without inflection, his contorted body with its stiff backbone and neck, his wooden arms, hands, fingers, legs in which there is no motion, his slouching gait and painful mannerisms!

"Let us hope our actors will devote as much care to their creative equipment as a violinist does to his beloved Stradivarius or Amati."

## 5

"Up to this point we have been dealing with the external, visible, physical process of communion," the Director began. "But there is another, important aspect which is inner, invisible and spiritual.

"My difficulty here is that I have to talk to you about something I feel but do not know. It is something I have experienced and yet I cannot theorize about it. I have no ready-made phrases for something I can explain only by a hint, and by trying to make you feel, for yourselves, the sensations that are described in a text.

> " 'He took me by the wrist and held me hard;
> Then goes he to the length of all his arm,
> And with his other hand thus o'er his brow,
> He falls to such perusal of my face
> As he would draw it. Long stay'd he so;
> At last, a little shaking of mine arm
> And thrice his head thus waving up and down,
> He raised a sigh so piteous and profound
> That it did seem to shatter all his bulk
> And end his being: that done, he lets me go:
> And with his head over his shoulder turn'd,
> He seem'd to find his way without his eyes;
> For out o' doors he went without their help,
> And to the last bended their light on me.'

"Can you sense, in those lines, the wordless communion between Hamlet and Ophelia? Haven't you experienced it in similar circumstances, when something streamed out of you, some current from your eyes, from the ends of your fingers or out through your pores?

"What name can we give to these invisible currents, which we use to communicate with one another? Some day this phenomenon will be the subject of scientific research. Meantime let us call them rays. Now let us see what we can find out about them through study and making notes of our own sensations.

"When we are quiescent this process of irradiation is barely perceptible. But when we are in a highly emotional state these rays, both given and received, become much more definite and tangible. Perhaps some of you were aware of these inner currents during the high spots of your initial test performance, as for example when Maria called for help, or when Kostya cried out 'Blood, Iago, blood!', or during any one of the various exercises you have been doing.

"It was only yesterday that I was witness to a scene between a young girl and her fiancé. They had quarreled, were not speaking and they were seated as far apart as possible. She pretended she did not even see him. But she did it in a way to attract his attention. He sat motionless, and watched her with a pleading gaze. He tried to catch her eye so that he might guess her feelings. He tried to feel out her soul with invisible antennae. But the angry girl withstood all attempts at communication. Finally he caught one glance as she turned for an instant in his direction.

"This, far from consoling him, depressed him more than ever. After a while he moved to another place, so that he could look straight at her. He longed to take her hand, to touch her and transmit the current of his feelings to her.

"There were no words, no exclamations, no facial expressions, gestures or actions. That is direct, immediate communion in its purest form.

"Scientists may have some explanation of the nature of this unseen process. All I can do is to describe what I myself feel and how I use these sensations in my art."

Unfortunately our lesson was interrupted at this point.

6

We were divided into pairs and I sat with Grisha. Instantly we started to send rays to each other in a mechanical way.

The Director stopped us.

"You are already using violent means when that is what you should avoid in such a delicate, susceptible process. Your muscular contractions would preclude any possibility of accomplishing your purpose.

"Sit back," said he in a tone of command. "More! Still more! Much, much more! Sit in a comfortable, easy position! That is not relaxed enough! Nor that! Arrange yourselves restfully. Now look at each other. Do you call that looking? Your eyes are popping out of your heads. Ease up! More! No tenseness.

"What are you doing?" Tortsov asked Grisha.

"I am trying to carry on our dispute about art."

"Do you expect to express such thoughts through your eyes? Use words and let your eyes supplement your voice. Perhaps then you will feel the rays that you are directing toward each other."

We continued our argument. At one point Tortsov said to me:

"During that pause, I was conscious of your sending out rays. And you, Grisha, were preparing to receive them. Remember, it occurred during that long drawn out silence."

I explained that I had been unable to convince my partner of my point of view and I was just preparing a new argument.

"Tell me, Vanya," said Tortsov, "could you feel that look of Maria's? Those were real rays."

"They were shot at me!" was his wry response.

The Director turned back to me.

"Besides listening I want you now to try to absorb something vital from your partner. In addition to the conscious, explicit discussion and intellectual exchange of thoughts, can you feel a parallel interchange of currents, something you draw in through your eyes and put out again through them?

"It is like an underground river, which flows continuously

under the surface of both words and silences and forms an invisible bond between subject and object.

"Now I wish you to make a further experiment. You will put yourself in communication with me," said he, taking Grisha's place.

"Fix yourself comfortably, don't be nervous, don't hurry, and don't force yourself. Before you try to transmit anything to another person you must prepare your material.

"A little while ago this type of work seemed complicated to you. Now you do it easily. The same will be true of this present problem. Let me have your feelings without any words, just through your eyes," he ordered.

"But I cannot put all the shadings of my feelings into the expression of my eyes," I explained.

"We can't do anything about that," he said, "so never mind all the shadings."

"What will remain?" I asked with dismay.

"Feelings of sympathy, respect. You can transmit them without words. But you cannot make the other person realize that you like him because he is an intelligent, active, hardworking and high-minded young man."

"What am I trying to communicate to you?" I asked Tortsov, as I gazed at him.

"I neither know nor care to know," was his reply.

"Why not?"

"Because you are staring at me. If you want me to sense the general meaning of your feelings, you must be experiencing what you are trying to transmit to me."

"Now can you understand? I cannot present my feelings more clearly," I said.

"You look down on me for some reason. I cannot know the exact cause for this without words. But that is beside the point. Did you feel any current issuing from you freely?"

"Perhaps I did in my eyes," I replied, and I tried to repeat the same sensation.

"No. This time you were just thinking about how you could

push that current out. You tensed your muscles. Your chin
and neck were taut and your eyes began to start from their
sockets. What I want from you you can accomplish much more
simply, easily and naturally. If you want to envelop another
person in your desires you don't need to use your muscles. Your
physical sensation from this current should be barely perceptible, but the force you are putting behind it would burst a
blood vessel."

My patience crumbled and I exclaimed:

"Then I do not understand you at all!"

"You take a rest now and I shall try to describe the type
of sensation I want you to feel. One of my pupils likened it
to the fragrance of a flower. Another suggested the fire in a
diamond. I have felt it when standing at the crater of a volcano.
I felt the hot air from the tremendous internal fires of the
earth. Does either of these suggestions appeal to you?"

"No," I said stubbornly, "not at all."

"Then I shall try to get at you by an inverse method," said
Tortsov patiently. "Listen to me.

"When I am at a concert and the music does not affect me
I think up various forms of entertainment for myself. I pick
out a person in the audience and try to hypnotize him. If my
victim happens to be a beautiful woman I try to transmit my
enthusiasm. If the face is ugly I send over feelings of aversion.
In such instances I am aware of a definite, physical sensation.
That may be familiar to you. In any case that is the thing we
are looking for at present."

"And you feel it yourself when you are hypnotizing someone else?" asked Paul.

"Yes, of course, and if you have ever tried to use hypnosis
you must know exactly what I mean," said Tortsov.

"That is both simple and familiar to me," said I with relief.

"Did I ever say it was anything extraordinary?" was Tortsov's surprised rejoinder.

"I was looking for something very—special."

"That is what always happens," remarked the Director.

"Just use a word like creativeness and immediately you all climb up on your stilts.

"Now let us repeat our experiment."

"What am I radiating?" I asked.

"Disdain again."

"And now?"

"You want to caress me."

"And now?"

"That again is a friendly feeling, but it has a touch of irony in it."

I was delighted at his having guessed my intentions.

"Did you understand that feeling of an out-going current?"

"I think I did," I replied, with slight indecision.

"In our slang, we call that *irradiation*.

"The absorbing of those rays is the inverse process. Suppose we try it."

We exchanged roles: he began to communicate his feelings to me and I to guess them.

"Try to define in words your sensation," he suggested after we had finished the experiment.

"I should express it by a simile. It is like a piece of iron being drawn by a magnet."

The Director approved. Then he asked me if I had been conscious of the inner bond between us during our silent communion.

"It seemed to me that I was," I replied.

"If you can establish a long, coherent chain of such feelings it will eventually become so powerful that you will have achieved what we call grasp. Then your giving out and absorption will be much stronger, keener and more palpable."

When he was asked to describe more fully what he meant by grasp Tortsov continued:

"It is what a bull-dog has in his jaw. We actors must have that same power to seize with our eyes, ears and all our senses. If an actor is to listen, let him do it intently. If he is called upon to smell, let him smell hard. If he is to look at something.

let him really use his eyes. But of course this must all be done without unnecessary muscular tension."

"When I played that scene from *Othello,* did I show any grasp?" I asked.

"There were one or two moments," admitted Tortsov. "But that is too little. The whole role of Othello calls for complete grasp. For a simple play you need an ordinary grasp, but for a Shakespeare play you have to have an absolute grasp.

"In everyday life we don't need complete grasp, but on the stage, above all in playing tragedy, it is a necessity. Just make the comparison. The greater part of life is devoted to unimportant activities. You get up, you go to bed, you follow a routine which is largely mechanical. That is not stuff for the theatre. But there are purple patches of terror, supreme joy, high tides of passion and outstanding experiences. We are challenged to fight for freedom, for an idea, for our existence and our rights. That is material we can use on the stage if, for its expression, we have a powerful inner and outer grasp. Grasp does not in any way signify unusual physical exertion, it means greater inner activity.

"An actor must learn to become absorbed in some interesting, creative problem on the stage. If he can devote all of his attention and creative faculties to that he will achieve true grasp.

"Let me tell you a story about an animal trainer. He was in the habit of going to Africa to pick out monkeys to train. A large number would be gathered together at some point and from these he would choose those he considered the most promising for his purpose. How did he make his choice? He took each monkey separately and tried to interest it in some object, a bright handkerchief, which he would wave before him, or some toy that might amuse him with its colour or sound. After the animal's attention was centred on this object the trainer would begin to distract him by presenting some other thing, a cigarette, perhaps, or a nut. If he succeeded in getting the monkey to switch from one thing to another he would reject him. If, on the other hand, he found that the animal could not be distracted from the first object of his interest and would make an effort to go after it when removed, the trainer would buy him. His choice was established by the monkey's evident capacity to grasp and hold something.

"That is how we often judge our students' power of attention and ability to remain in contact with one another—by the strength and continuity of their grasp."

## 7

The Director began our lesson by saying:

"Since these currents are so important in the interrelationship of actors, can they be controlled by technical means? Can we produce them at will?

"Here again we are in the situation of having to work from the outside, when our desires do not come spontaneously from the inside. Fortunately an organic bond exists between the body and the soul. Its power is so great that it can all but recall the dead to life. Think of a man apparently drowned. His pulse has stopped and he is unconscious. By the use of mechanical movements his lungs are forced to take in and give out air! That starts the circulation of his blood, and then his organs resume their customary functions, so life is revived in this man practically dead.

"In using artificial means we work on the same principle. External aids stimulate an inner process.

"Now let me show you how to apply these aids."

Tortsov sat down opposite me and asked me to choose an object, with its appropriate, imaginative basis, and to transmit it to him. He allowed the use of words, gestures, and facial expressions.

This took a long time until finally I understood what he wanted and was successful in communicating with him. But he kept me for some time watching and becoming accustomed to the accompanying physical sensations. When I had mastered the exercise he restricted, one after another, my means of expression, words, gestures and so on, until I was obliged to carry on my communion with him solely by giving out and absorbing rays.

After that he had me repeat the process in a purely mechanical, physical way without allowing any feelings to participate. It took time for me to separate the one from the other and when I succeeded he asked how I felt.

"Like a pump bringing up nothing but air," I said. "I felt the outgoing currents, principally through my eyes, and perhaps partly from the side of my body towards you."

"Then continue to pour out that current, in a purely physical and mechanical way, as long as you possibly can," he ordered.

It was not long before I gave up what I called a perfectly "senseless" proceeding.

"Then why didn't you put some sense into it?" he asked. "Weren't your feelings clamouring to come to your aid and your emotion memory suggesting some experience you could use as material for the current you were sending out?"

"Of course, if I were obliged to continue this mechanical exercise, it would be difficult not to use something to motivate my action. I should need some basis for it."

"Why don't you transmit what you feel at this very moment, dismay, helplessness, or find some other sensation?" suggested Tortsov.

I tried to transmit my vexation and exasperation to him.

My eyes seemed to say: "Let me alone, will you? Why persist? Why torture me!"

"How do you feel now?" asked Tortsov.

"This time I feel as though the pump had something besides air to bring up."

"So your 'senseless' physical giving out of rays acquired a meaning and purpose after all!"

Then he went on to other exercises based on receiving rays. It was the inverse procedure and I shall describe only one new point: before I could absorb anything from him I had to feel out, through my eyes, what he wanted me to draw from him.

This required attentive search, feeling my way into his mood and making some kind of connection with it.

"It is not simple to do by technical means what is natural and intuitive in ordinary life," said Tortsov. "However, I can give you this consolation, that when you are on the stage and playing your part this process will be accomplished far more easily than in a classroom exercise.

"The reason is: for our present purpose you had to scrape together some accidental material to use, while on the stage all your given circumstances have been prepared in advance, your objectives have been fixed, your emotions ripened and ready for the signal to come to the surface. All you need is a slight stimulus and the feelings prepared for your role will gush out in continuous, spontaneous flow.

"When you make a siphon to empty water out of a container, you suck the air out once and the water flows out by itself. The same thing happens to you: give the signal, open the way and your rays and currents will pour out."

When he was asked about developing this ability through exercises he said:

"There are the two types of exercises that we have just been doing:

"The first teaches you to stimulate a feeling which you transmit to another person. As you do this you note the accompanying physical sensations. Similarly you learn to recognize the sensation of absorbing feelings from others.

"The second consists of an effort to feel the mere physical sensations of giving out and absorbing feelings, without the accompanying emotional experience. For this, great concentration of attention is imperative. Otherwise you might easily confuse these sensations with ordinary muscular contractions. If these occur choose some inner feeling which you wish to radiate. But above all avoid violence and physical contortion. Radiation and absorption of emotions must take place easily, freely, naturally, and without any loss of energy.

"But do not do these exercises alone, or with an imaginary

person. Always use a living object, actually with you, and wishing to exchange feelings with you. Communion must be mutual. Also do not attempt these exercises except under the supervision of my assistant. You need his experienced eye to keep you from going wrong and from the danger of confusing muscular tenseness with the right process."

"How difficult it seems," I exclaimed.

"Difficult to do something that is normal and natural?" said Tortsov. "You are mistaken. Anything normal can be done easily. It is much more difficult to do something which is contrary to nature. Study its laws and do not try for anything that is not natural.

"All the first stages of our work seemed difficult to you, the relaxation of muscles, the concentration of attention, and the rest, yet now they have become second nature.

"You should be happy because you have enriched your technical equipment by this important stimulus to communion."

# CHAPTER ELEVEN

## Adaptation

I

THE FIRST suggestion that the Director made, after seeing the big placard "ADAPTATION" that his assistant had put up, was to Vanya. He gave this problem:

"You want to go somewhere. The train leaves at two o'clock. It is already one o'clock. How are you going to manage to slip away before classes are over? Your difficulty will lie in the necessity of deceiving not only me but all of your comrades as well. How will you go about it?"

I suggested that he pretend to be sad, thoughtful, depressed or ill. Then everyone would ask: "What's the matter with you?" That would give an opportunity to cook up some story in a way that would oblige us to believe he really was ill and to let him go home.

"That's it!" exclaimed Vanya joyously, and he proceeded to go through a course of antics. But after he had cut a few capers, he tripped and screamed with pain. He stood rooted to the floor with one leg up and his face twisted with suffering.

At first we thought he was fooling us, and that this was part of his plot. But he was apparently in such real pain that I believed in it, and was about to go over to help him when I felt a little doubt and thought that for the tiniest part of a second I saw a twinkle in his eye. So I stayed with the Director, while all the others went to his rescue. He refused to let anyone touch his leg. He tried to step on it but he yelled so with pain that Tortsov and I looked at each other as much as to say, is this real or is it fooling? Vanya was helped off the stage with great difficulty. They held him up by the armpits and he used his good leg.

Suddenly Vanya began to do a fast dance, and burst into laughter.

"That was great! That I really did feel!" he chortled.

He was rewarded with an ovation and I was once more aware of his very real gifts.

"Do you know why you applauded him?" asked the Director. "It was because he found the right *adaptation* to the circumstances that were set for him, and successfully carried through his plan.

"We shall use this word, *adaptation,* from now on to mean both the *inner and outer human means that people use in adjusting themselves to one another in a variety of relationships and also as an aid in effecting an object.*"

He further explained what he meant by adjusting or conforming oneself to a problem.

"It is what Vanya has just done. To get out of his classes early he used a contrivance, a trick, to help him solve the situation he was in."

"Then adaptation means deceit?" asked Grisha.

"In a certain way, yes; in another, it is a vivid expression of inner feelings or thoughts: third, it can call the attention to you of the person with whom you wish to be in contact: fourth, it can prepare your partner by putting him in a mood to respond to you: fifth, it can transmit certain invisible messages, which can only be felt and not put into words. And I could mention any number of other possible functions, for their variety and scope is infinite.

"Take this illustration:

"Suppose that you, Kostya, hold some high position and I have to ask a favour of you. I must enlist your aid. But you do not know me at all. How can I make myself stand out from the others who are trying to get help from you?

"I must rivet your attention on me and control it. How can I strengthen and make the most of the slight contact between us? How can I influence you to take a favourable attitude toward me? How can I reach your mind, your feelings, your attention, your imagination? How can I touch the very soul of such an influential person?

"If only I can make him conjure up a picture in his mind's eye that in any way approximates the dreadful reality of my circumstances, I know his interest will be aroused. He will look into me more attentively, his heart will be touched. But to reach this point I must penetrate into the being of the other person, I must sense his life, I must adapt myself to it.

"What we are primarily aiming at, in using such means, is to express our states of mind and heart in higher relief. There are, however, contrasting circumstances in which we make use of them to hide or mask our sensations. Take a proud sensitive person who is trying to appear amiable to hide his wounded feelings. Or, a prosecuting attorney who covers himself most cleverly with various subterfuges in order to veil his real object in cross-examining a criminal.

"We have recourse to methods of adaptation in all forms of communion, even with ourselves, because we must necessarily make allowances for the state of mind we are in at any given moment."

"But after all," argued Grisha, "words exist to express all these things."

"Do you suppose that words can exhaust all the nicest shadings of the emotions you experience? No! When we are communing with one another words do not suffice. If we want to put life into them, we must produce feelings. They fill out the blanks left by words, they finish what has been left unsaid."

"Then the more means you use, the more intense and complete your communion with the other person will be?" someone suggested.

"It is not a question of quantity but of quality," explained the Director.

I asked what qualities were best suited to the stage.

"There are many types," was his answer. "Each actor has

his own special attributes. They are original with him, they spring from varied sources and they vary in value. Men, women, old people, children, pompous, modest, choleric, kind, irritable, and calm people all have their own types. Each change of circumstance, setting, place of action, time—brings a corresponding adjustment. You adjust yourself differently in the dead of night, alone, from the way you do in daylight and in public. When you arrive in a foreign country you find ways of adapting yourself in a way suitable to the surrounding circumstances.

"Every feeling you express, as you express it, requires an intangible form of adjustment all its own. All types of communication as, for example, communication in a group, with an imaginary, present or absent object, require adjustments peculiar to each. We use all of our five senses and all the elements of our inner and outer make-up to communicate. We send out rays and receive them, we use our eyes, facial expression, voice and intonation, our hands, fingers, our whole bodies, and in every case we make whatever corresponding adjustments are necessary.

"You will see actors who are gifted with magnificent powers of expression in all phases of human emotions and the means they use are both good and right. Yet they may be able to transmit all this only to a few people, during the intimacy of rehearsals. When the play goes on and their means should grow in vividness, they pale and fail to get across the footlights in a sufficiently effective, theatrical form.

"There are other actors who possess the power to make vivid adjustments, but not many. Because they lack variety their effect loses strength and keenness.

"Finally there are actors whom nature has maltreated by endowing them with monotonous, and insipid, although correct powers of adjustment. They can never reach the front rank of their profession.

"If people in ordinary walks of life need and make use of a large variety of adaptations, actors need a correspondingly greater number because we must be constantly in contact with one another and therefore incessantly adjusting ourselves. In all the examples I have given the quality of the adjustment plays a great part: vividness, colourfulness, boldness, delicacy, shading, exquisiteness, taste.

"What Vanya did for us was vivid to the point of boldness. But there are other methods of adaptation. Now let me see Sonya, Grisha, and Vassili go up on the stage and play me the exercise of the burnt money."

Sonya stood up rather languidly with a depressed look on her face, apparently waiting for the two men to follow her example. But they sat tight. An embarrassing silence ensued.

"What is the matter?" asked Tortsov.

No one answered and he waited patiently. Finally Sonya could not stand the silence any longer, so she made up her mind to speak. To soften her remarks she used some feminine mannerisms because she had found that men were usually affected by them. She dropped her eyes and kept rubbing the number plate on the orchestra seat in front of her to disguise her feelings. For a long time she could not bring out any words. To hide her blushes she put a handkerchief to her face and turned away.

The pause seemed endless: to fill it up and to lessen the embarrassment caused by the situation, also to lend a humorous touch to it, she forced out a little mirthless laugh.

"We are so bored by it. Really we are," she said. "I don't know how to tell you—but please, give us another exercise—and we will act."

"Bravo! I agree! And now you don't have to do that exercise because you have already given me what I wanted," exclaimed the Director.

"What did she show you?" we asked.

"While Vanya showed us a bold adaptation, Sonya's was more exquisite, fine-grained, and contained both internal and external elements. She very patiently used all the gamut of her powers of persuasion to get me to take pity on her. She made effective use of her resentment and tears. Whenever she could, she put in a touch of flirtation to gain her objective. She kept readjusting herself in order to make me feel and accept all the shadings of the changing emotions she was experiencing. If one did not succeed, she tried another and a third, hoping to find the most convincing way to penetrate to the heart of her problem.

"You must learn to adapt yourselves to circumstances, to time, and to each individual person. If you are called upon to deal with a stupid person you must adjust yourself to his mentality, and find the simplest means with which to reach his mind and understanding. But if your man is shrewd, you should proceed more cautiously and use subtler means so that he won't see through your wiles.

"To prove to you how important these adaptations are in our creative work, let me add that many actors of limited emotional capacity produce greater effects through their vivid powers of adjustment than those who feel more deeply and powerfully yet cannot transmit their emotions in any but pale forms."

2

"Vanya," ordered the Director, "go up on the stage with me and play a variation of what you did last time."

Our lively young friend bounced off and Tortsov slowly followed, whispering to us as he went: "Watch me draw him out!" Out loud he added: "So you want to get away from school early. That is your main, your fundamental objective. Let me see you accomplish it."

He sat down near a table, took a letter out of his pocket and became wholly absorbed in reading it. Vanya stood close by, his whole attention concentrated on finding the most ingenious possible way to outwit him.

He tried the most varied kinds of stunts but Tortsov, as if on purpose, paid no attention to him. Vanya was indefatigable in his efforts. For a long while he sat absolutely motionless with an agonized expression on his face. If Tortsov had even so much as looked at him then he must have taken pity on him. Suddenly Vanya got up and rushed off into the wings. In a little while he came back, walking with the uncertain step of an invalid and wiping his brow as if a cold sweat were pouring from it. He sat down heavily near Tortsov, who continued to ignore him. But he was acting truthfully and we responded with approval to all he did.

After that Vanya nearly passed out with fatigue: he even slid out of his chair on to the floor and we laughed at his exaggerations.

But the Director was unmoved.

Vanya thought up more things to make us laugh harder. Even so Tortsov was silent and paid no attention to him. The more Vanya exaggerated, the louder we laughed. Our merriment encouraged him to think of more and more amusing things to do, until finally we roared.

That was just what Tortsov was waiting for.

"Do you realize what has just happened?" he asked as soon as he could quiet us. "Vanya's central objective was to get out of school ahead of time. All of his actions, words, efforts to appear ill and to gain my sympathetic attention were means which he was using to accomplish his main purpose. In the beginning what he did conformed properly to that purpose. But alas! As soon as he heard the laughter from the audience he changed his whole direction and began to adapt his actions, not to me who was paying no attention to him, but to you, who showed your delight in his stunts.

"His objective now became, how to amuse the spectators. What basis could he find for this? Where would he look for his plot? How could he believe in and live in it? His only resort must be to the theatrical—that is why he went wrong.

"At this point his means became false by being used for their own sakes instead of in their proper role of auxiliaries. That sort of wrong acting is frequently seen on the stage. I know any number of actors who are capable of making brilliant adjustments and yet who use these means to entertain their public rather than to convey their feelings. They turn their powers of adaptation, just as Vanya did, into individual vaudeville numbers. The success of these separate entities turns their heads. They are willing to sacrifice their role, as a whole, to the excitement of obtaining a burst of applause, shouts of laughter. Very often these particular moments have nothing to do with the play. Naturally, under such circumstances, these adaptations lose all meaning.

"So you see they can even be a dangerous temptation to an actor. There are whole roles that are permeated with opportunities for misusing adaptations. Take Ostrovski's play *Enough Stupidity in Every Wise Man* and the role of old man Mamayev. Because he has no occupation he spends all his time giving advice to anyone he can get hold of. It is not easy to stick to a single objective throughout a five act play: to preach and preach to others and to convey to them constantly the same thoughts and feelings. Under the circumstances it is extremely easy to lapse into monotony. To avoid that, many actors, in this part, concentrate their efforts on all sorts of changing adaptations of the main idea of preaching to others. This endless variety of adjustments is, of course, valuable, but it can be harmful if the emphasis is put on the variations rather than on the objective.

"If you study the inner workings of an actor's mind you will find that what happens is that instead of saying to himself, 'I shall aim at such and such an objective by means of a severe tone,' what he really says is: 'I want to be severe.' But as you know, you must not be severe, or anything else, just for its own sake.

"If you do your true feelings and actions will disappear and be replaced by artificial, theatrical ones. It is all too typical of actors that in the presence of the persons whom the play gives them to communicate with, they seek out some other object for their attentions, on the other side of the footlights, and proceed to adjust themselves to that object. Their external communication may seem to be with the persons on the stage, but their real adjustments are being made to the spectators.

"Suppose you live on the top floor of a house and across the wide street lives the object of your affections. How can you tell her of your love? You can blow kisses, press your hand to your heart. You can appear to be in a state of ecstasy, sadness, or longing. You can use gestures to enquire whether or not you may call on her and so on. All these adjustments to your problem must be expressed in strong colours, otherwise they will never get across the intervening space.

"Now comes an exceptionally favourable opportunity: there is not a soul on the street; she stands, alone, at her window; in all the other windows the blinds are down. There is nothing to keep you from calling over. Your voice must be pitched to bridge the distance.

"The next time you meet her she is walking along the street on the arm of her mother. How can you make use of this close encounter to whisper a word, perhaps to beg her to come to some rendez-vous? To be in keeping with the circumstances of the meeting you will need some expressive but barely perceptible gesture of the hand, or perhaps only the eyes. If you must use words let them be scarcely audible.

"You are just about to act when you suddenly see your rival across the street. You are seized with a desire to show him your success. You forget the mamma and shout loving words at the top of your lungs.

"Most actors constantly do with impunity what we would look upon as inexplicably absurd in an ordinary human being. They stand side by side with their partners on the stage and yet they adjust their whole facial expressions, voices, gestures and actions to the distance, not between them and the other actors, but between them and whoever is sitting in the last row of the orchestra."

"But I really should consider the poor devil who can't afford to sit in the front rows, where he can hear everything," broke in Grisha.

"Your first duty," answered Tortsov, "is to adapt yourself to your partner. As for the poor people in the last rows, we have a special way of reaching them. We have our voices placed properly and we use well prepared methods of pronouncing vowels and consonants. With the right kind of diction you can speak as softly as if you were in a small room and those poor people will hear you better than if you yell, especially if you have aroused their interest in what you are saying, and have made them penetrate the inner meaning of your lines. If you rant, your intimate words, that should be conveyed in a gentle tone, will lose their significance and the spectators will not be inclined to look beyond them."

"Nevertheless the spectator has to see what is going on," persisted Grisha.

"For that very purpose we make use of sustained, clear-cut, coherent, logical action. That is what makes the spectator understand what is happening. But if the actors are going to contradict their own inner feelings by gesticulations and poses that may be attractive but are not truly motivated, then the public will tire of following them because they have no vital relation either to the spectators or to the characters in the play, and they become easily bored by repetition. I say all this by way of explaining that the stage, with all its attendant publicity, tends to lead actors away from natural, human adaptations to situations, and tempts them to conventional, theatrical ways. Those are the very forms that we must fight against with every means at our disposal until we have chased them out of the theatre."

3

Tortsov prefaced his remarks today by the statement:

"*Adaptations are made consciously* and *unconsciously.*

"Here is an illustration of intuitive adjustment as an expression of supreme sorrow. In *My Life in Art* there is a description of how a mother received the news of the death of her son. In the very first moments she expressed nothing but began hurriedly to dress. Then she rushed to the street door and cried, 'Help!'

"An adjustment of that sort cannot be reproduced either intellectually or with the aid of any technique. It is created naturally, spontaneously, unconsciously, at the very moment when emotions are at their height. Yet that type, so direct, vivid and convincing, represents the effective method we need. It is only by such means that we create and convey to an audience of thousands all the finer, barely perceptible shades of feeling. But to such experiences the only approach is through intuition and the subconscious.

"How such feelings stand out on the stage! What an ineradicable impression they make on the memories of the spectators!

"In what does their power lie?

"In their overwhelming *unexpectedness.*

"If you follow an actor through a role, step by step, you may expect him, at a certain important point, to give his lines in a loud, clear-cut, serious tone of voice. Suppose that instead of that, he quite unexpectedly uses a light, gay and very soft tone as an original way of handling his part. The surprise element is so intriguing and effective that you are persuaded that this new way is the only possible way of playing that bit. You say to yourself: 'How is it I never thought of that nor imagined that those lines were so significant?' You are amazed and delighted by this unexpected adaptation by the actor.

"Our subconscious has its own logic. Since we find subconscious adaptations so necessary in our art I shall go into some detail in discussing them.

"The most powerful, vivid, and convincing adaptations are the products of that wonder-working artist—nature. They are almost wholly of subconscious origin. We find that the greatest artists use them. However, even these exceptional people cannot produce them at any given time. They come only in moments of inspiration. At other times their adaptations are only partially subconscious. Take into consideration the fact that as long as we are on the stage we are in unending contact with one another, therefore our adjustments to each other must be constant. Then think of how many actions and moves this means, and guess what proportion of subconscious moments they may include!"

After a pause the Director went on:

"It is not only when we are concerned with a constant interchange of thoughts and feelings and adjustments that the subconscious comes into the picture. It comes to our aid at other times as well. Let us test this out on ourselves. I suggest that for five minutes you do not talk about or do anything."

After this period of silence Tortsov questioned each student as to what took place inside of him, what he was thinking about and feeling during that time.

Someone said that for some reason he suddenly remembered his medicine.

"What has that to do with our lesson?" Tortsov enquired.

"Nothing whatsoever."

"Perhaps you felt a pain and that reminded you of the medicine?" he pursued.

"No, I was not aware of any pain."

"How did such an idea pop into your head?"

There was no answer.

One of the girls had been thinking about a pair of scissors.

"What relation did they have to what we are doing?" asked Tortsov.

"None that I can think of."

"Perhaps you noticed some defect in your dress, decided to remedy it, and that put you in mind of the scissors?"

"No, my clothes are all in order. But I left my scissors in a box with some ribbons and I locked the box up in my trunk. It suddenly flashed through my mind, I hope I don't forget where I put them."

"Then you just thought about the scissors and afterwards reasoned out why that happened?"

"Yes, I did think about the scissors first."

"But you still do not know where the idea came from in the first place?"

Pursuing his investigations Tortsov found that Vassili, during the period of silence, had been thinking about a pineapple and it occurred to him that its scaly surface and pointed leaves made it very similar to certain types of palm trees.

"What put a pineapple into the foreground of your mind? Had you eaten some recently?"

"No."

"Where did you all get such thoughts, about medicines, scissors, and pineapple?"

When we admitted that we did not know the Director said:

"All of these things come out of your subconscious. They are like shooting stars."

After a moment's reflection he turned to Vassili and said:

"I do not yet understand why, when you were telling us about that pineapple, you kept twisting yourself into such strange physical positions. They did not add anything to your story about the pineapple and the palm. They were expressing something else. What was it? What lay behind the intensely reflective expression in your eyes and the sombre look on your face? What was the meaning of the pattern you drew in the air with your fingers? Why did you look at us all in turn so significantly and shrug your shoulders? What relation had all this to the pineapple?"

"Do you mean to say I was doing all those things?" asked Vassili.

"I certainly do, and I want to know what you meant."

"It must have been astonishment," said Vassili.

"Astonishment at what? At the miracles of nature?"

"Perhaps."

"Then those were the adjustments to the idea suggested by your mind?"

But Vassili was silent.

"Can it be that your mind, which is really an intelligent one, could suggest such absurdities?" said Tortsov. "Or was it your feelings? In that case you gave an external physical form to the suggestion made by your subconscious? In either case, both when you had the idea of the pineapple, and when you

adjusted yourself to that idea, you passed through that unknown region of the subconscious.

"From some stimulus or other an idea comes into your head.
At that instant it crosses the subconscious. Next you consider
that idea, and later when both the idea and your thoughts about
it are put into tangible physical form you pass again, for an
infinitesimal length of time, through the subconscious. Each
time you do that your adjustments, in whole or in part, absorb
something essential from it.

"In every process of inter-communication, necessarily involving adjustments, both the subconscious and intuition play a
large, if not the principal part. In the theatre their significance
is extraordinarily enhanced.

"I do not know what science says on this subject. I can
only share with you what I have felt and observed in myself.
After prolonged investigation I can now assert that in ordinary life I do not find any conscious adjustment without some
element, however slight, of the subconscious in it. On the stage,
on the other hand, where one would suppose that subconscious
intuitive adjustments preponderate, I am constantly finding completely conscious adaptations. These are the actors' rubber
stamps. You find them in all roles that have been worn thread-
bare. Every gesture is self-conscious to a high degree."

"Then may we conclude that you are not willing to coun-
tenance any conscious adjustments on the stage?" I asked.

"Not those I have just mentioned and which have become
nothing more than stencils. And yet I must admit that I am
aware of the conscious character of certain adjustments when
they have been suggested by outside sources, by the director,
other actors, or friends, proffering sought or unsought advice.
Such adaptations should be used with utmost care and wisdom.

"Never accept them in the form in which they are presented
to you. Do not allow yourself simply to copy them. You must
adapt them to your own needs, make them your own, truly part
of you. To accomplish this is to undertake a large piece of work
involving a whole new set of given circumstances and stimuli.

"You should go about it in the same way as an actor does who sees in real life some typical characteristic that he wishes to embody in a role. If he merely copies it he will fall into the error of superficial and routine acting."

"What other types of adaptations exist?" I asked.

"*Mechanical* or *motor* adjustments," answered Tortsov.

"You mean—stencils?"

"No. I am not speaking of them. They should be exterminated. *Motor* adjustments are subconscious, semi-conscious, and conscious in origin. They are normal, natural, human adaptations that are carried to a point of becoming purely mechanical in character.

"Let me illustrate. Let us assume that in playing a certain character part you make use of real, human adjustments in your relations to others on the stage. Yet a large part of those adjustments grow out of the character you are portraying and do not stem directly from you. Those supplementary adaptations have appeared spontaneously, involuntarily, unconsciously. But the director has pointed them out to you. After which you are aware of them, they become conscious, and habitual. They grow into the very flesh and blood of the character you are playing, every time you live through the part. Finally these supplementary adjustments become motor activities."

"Then they are stereotypes?" someone asked.

"No. Let me repeat. A rubber stamp piece of acting is conventional, false and lifeless. It has its origin in theatrical routine. It conveys neither feelings, thoughts nor any images characteristic of human beings. Motor adjustments, on the contrary, were intuitive, originally, but they have become mechanical, without sacrificing their quality of naturalness. Because they remain organic and human, they are the antithesis of the rubber stamp."

## 4

"The next step is the question of what *technical means* we can employ to stimulate adaptations," announced the Director as he came into class today. Then he proceeded to lay out a program of work for the lesson.

"I shall begin with *intuitive adaptations*.

"There is no *direct approach* to our subconscious, therefore we make use of various stimuli that induce a process of living the part, which in turn inevitably creates interrelationship and conscious or unconscious adjustments. That is the indirect approach.

"What else, you ask, can we accomplish in that region into which our consciousness cannot penetrate? We refrain from interfering with nature and avoid contravening her laws. Whenever we can put ourselves into a wholly natural and relaxed state, there wells up within us a flow of creation that blinds our audience by its brilliance.

"In dealing with *semi-conscious adjustments* the conditions are different. Here we have some use for our psycho-technique. I say *some* for even here our possibilities are restricted.

"I have one practical suggestion to make and I think I can explain it better by an illustration. Do you remember when Sonya coaxed me out of making her do the exercise, how she repeated the same words over and over again, using a great variety of adaptations? I want you to do the same thing, as a sort of exercise, but do not use the same adjustments. They have lost their effectiveness. I want you to find fresh ones, conscious or unconscious, to take their place."

On the whole we repeated the old stuff.

When Tortsov reproached us for being so monotonous, we complained that we did not know what material to use as a basis for creating fresh adaptations.

Instead of answering us he turned to me and said:

"You write shorthand. Take down what I am going to dictate:

"Calm, excitement, good humour, irony, mockery, quarrelsomeness, reproach, caprice, scorn, despair, menace, joy, benignity, doubt, astonishment, anticipation, doom. . . ."

He named all these states of mind, mood, emotions and many more. Then he said to Sonya:

"Put your finger on any one word in that list and, whatever it is, use it as the basis for a new *adaptation*."

She did as she was told, and the word was: *benignity*.

"Now use some fresh colours in the place of the old ones," suggested the Director.

She was successful in striking the right note and finding appropriate motivation. But Leo outshone her. His booming voice was positively unctuous and his whole fat face and figure exuded benignity.

We all laughed.

"Is that sufficient proof for you of the desirability of introducing fresh elements into an old problem?" asked Tortsov.

Sonya then put her finger on another word on the list. This time the choice rested on *quarrelsomeness*. With truly feminine capacity for nagging she went to work. This time she was outdone by Grisha. No one can compete with him when it comes to argumentative persistence.

"There is fresh proof of the efficacy of my method," said Tortsov with satisfaction. Then he proceeded to go through similar exercises with all the other students.

"Put what other human characteristics or moods you choose on that list and you will find them all useful in supplying you with fresh colours and shadings for almost every interchange of thought and feelings. Sharp contrasts and the element of unexpectedness are also helpful.

"This method is extremely effective in dramatic and tragic situations. To heighten the impression, at a particularly tragic point, you can suddenly laugh as though to say: 'The way destiny pursues me is nothing short of ridiculous!' or, 'In such despair I cannot weep, I can only laugh!'

"Just think what is required of your facial, vocal and physical apparatus if it is to respond to the finest shadings of such subconscious feelings. What flexibility of expression, what sensitiveness, what discipline! Your powers of expression as an artist will be tested to the limit by the adjustments you must make in your relation to other actors on the stage. For this reason you must give appropriate preparation to your body, face, and voice. I mention this now only in passing, and because I hope it will make you more aware of the necessity of your exercises in physical culture, dancing, fencing, and voice placing. In time we shall go more fully into the cultivation of external attributes of expression."

Just as the lesson was over, and Tortsov was getting up to leave, the curtain was suddenly drawn, and we saw Maria's living-room, all decorated. When we went up onto the stage to see it, we found placards on the walls, reading:

1) Inner tempo-rhythm.
2) Inner characterization.
3) Control and finish.
4) Inner ethics and discipline.
5) Dramatic charm.
6) Logic and coherence.

"There are a number of signs around here," said Tortsov, "but, for the present, my remarks about them must be brief. There are many necessary elements in the creative process which we have not yet sorted out. My problem is: how can I talk about them without departing from my habitual method, which is first to make you feel what you are learning by vivid practical example and later come to theories? How can I discuss with you now *invisible inner tempo-rhythm* or *invisible inner characterization*? What example can I give you to illustrate my explanations in practice?

"It seems to me that it would be simpler to wait until we take up *external tempo-rhythm and characterization,* because you can demonstrate them with *physical actions* and at the same time *experience them inwardly.*

"Or again: how can I speak concretely about *control* when you have neither a play nor a part demanding sustained control in its presentation? By the same token, how can I talk about *finish* when we have nothing on which we can put a finish?

"Nor is there any point now, in taking up *ethics in art* or *discipline on the stage* during creative work, when most of you have never even stood behind the footlights except at the test performance.

"Finally, what can I say to you about *charm* when you have never felt its power over, and effect on, an audience of thousands?

"All that is left on the list is *logic, coherence.* On that subject, it seems to me, I have already spoken often and at length. Our whole program has been permeated by it and will continue to be."

"When have you discussed it?" I asked with surprise.

"What do you mean, *when?*" exclaimed Tortsov, astonished in his turn. "I have talked about it on every possible occasion. I have insisted on it when we were studying *magic ifs, given circumstances,* when you were carrying out projects in *physical action,* and especially in establishing *objects for the concentration of attention,* in choosing *objectives* derived from *units.* At every step I have demanded the most stringent kind of *logic* in your work.

"What there is still left to be said on this subject will be fitted in from time to time as our work progresses. So I shall not make any special statements now. I fear to, in fact. I am afraid of falling into philosophy and of straying from the path of practical demonstration.

"That is why I have merely mentioned these various elements, in order to make the list complete. In time we shall come to them, and work on them in a practical way, and eventually we shall be able to deduce theories from that work.

"This brings us temporarily to the end of our study of the internal elements necessary to the creative process in an actor. I shall add only that the elements I have listed today are just as important and necessary in bringing about the right inner spiritual state as those we worked on earlier in greater detail."

# CHAPTER TWELVE

# Inner Motive Forces

I

"NOW THAT we have examined all the 'elements,' and methods of psycho-technique, we can say that our inner instrument is ready. All we need is a virtuoso to play on it. Who is that master?"

"We are," answered several of the students.

"Who are 'we'? Where is that invisible thing called 'we' to be found?"

"It is our imagination, attention, feelings." We ran over the list.

"Feelings! That's the most important," exclaimed Vanya.

"I agree with you. Feel your part and instantly all your inner chords will harmonize, your whole bodily apparatus of expression will begin to function. Therefore we have found the first, and most important master—*feeling*," said the Director. Then he added:

"Unfortunately it is not tractable nor willing to take orders. Since you cannot begin your work, unless your feelings happen to function of their own accord it is necessary for you to have recourse to some other master. Who is it?"

"Imagination!" decided Vanya.

"Very well. *Imagine* something and let me see your creative apparatus set in motion."

"What shall I imagine?"

"How should I know?"

"I must have some objective, some supposition——"

"Where will you get them?"

"His mind will suggest them," put in Grisha.

"Then the mind is the second master we are seeking. It initiates and directs creativeness."

"Is imagination incapable of being a master?" I enquired.

"You can see for yourself that it requires guidance."

"What about attention?" asked Vanya.

"Let us study it. What are its functions?"

"It facilitates the work of the feelings, mind, imagination and will," contributed various students.

"Attention is like a reflector," I added. "It throws its rays on some chosen object and arouses in it the interest of our thoughts, feelings and desires."

"Who points out the object?" asked the Director.

"The mind."

"Imagination."

"Given circumstances."

"Objectives."

"In that case, all of these elements choose the object and initiate the work, whereas attention must limit its action to an auxiliary role."

"If attention is not one of the masters, what is it?" I pursued.

Instead of giving us a direct answer Tortsov proposed that we go up on the stage and play the exercise we were so tired of, about the madman. At first the students were silent, looked around at each other and tried to make up their minds to get up. Finally, one after another we arose and went slowly toward the stage. But Tortsov checked us.

"I am glad that you mastered yourselves, but although you gave evidence of will power in your actions that is not sufficient for my purpose. I must arouse something more lively in you, more enthusiastic, a kind of artistic *wish*—I want to see you eager to go on the stage, full of excitement and animation."

"You will never get that from us with that old exercise," burst out Grisha.

"Nevertheless, I shall try," said Tortsov with decision.

"Are you aware that while you were expecting the escaped lunatic to break in by the front door he has actually sneaked up the back stairs and is pounding at the back door? It is a flimsy affair. Once it gives way . . . What will you do in these new circumstances, decide!"

The students were thoughtful, their attention all concentrated, while they considered their problem and its solution, the erection of a second barricade.

Then we rushed to the stage and things began to hum. It was all very like the early days in our course when we first played this same exercise.

Tortsov summed up as follows:

"When I suggested that you play this exercise you tried to make yourselves do it, against your desires, but you could not force yourselves to become excited over it.

"Then I introduced a fresh supposition. On the basis of that you created for yourselves a new objective. This new wish, or wishes, was 'artistic' in character and put enthusiasm into the work. Now tell me, who was the master to play on the instrument of creation?"

"You were," was the decision of the students.

"To be more exact, it was my *mind*," corrected Tortsov. "But your mind can do the same thing and be a motive power, in your psychic life, for your creative process.

"Therefore we have proved that the second master is the *mind*, or intellect," concluded Tortsov. "Is there a third?

"Could it be the *sense of truth* and our *belief* in it? If so, it would suffice to believe in something and all of our creative faculties would spring into action."

"Believe in what?" was asked.

"How should I know? That is your affair."

"First we must create the life of a human spirit and then we can believe in that," remarked Paul.

"Therefore our *sense of truth* is not the master we are seeking. Can we find it in *communion* or *adaptation*?" asked the Director.

"If we are to have communication with one another we must have thoughts and feelings to exchange"

"Quite right."

"It's units and objectives!" was Vanya's contribution.

"That is not an element. It represents merely a technical method of arousing inner, living desires and aspirations," explained Tortsov. "If those longings could put your creative apparatus to work and direct it spiritually then . . ."

"Of course they can," we chorused.

"In that case we have found our third master—*will. Consequently we have three impelling movers in our psychic life, three masters who play on the instrument of our souls.*"

As usual Grisha had a protest to make. He claimed that up to the present no stress had been laid on the part that the *mind* and the *will* play in creative work, whereas we had heard a great deal about *feeling*.

"You mean that I should have gone over the same details with respect to each one of these three motive forces?" asked the Director.

"No, of course not. Why do you say the *same* details?" retorted Grisha.

"How could it be otherwise? Since these three forces form a triumvirate, inextricably bound up together, what you say of the one necessarily concerns the other two. Would you have been willing to listen to such repetition? Suppose I were discussing creative *objectives* with you, how to divide, choose and name them. Don't *feelings* participate in this work?"

"Of course they do," agreed the student.

"Is *will* absent?" asked Tortsov.

"No, it has a direct relation to the problem," we said.

"Then I would have had to say practically the same thing twice over. And now what about the *mind*?"

"It takes part both in the division of the objectives and in naming them," we replied.

"Then I should have repeated the same thing a third time!

"You ought to be grateful to me for having preserved your patience and saved your time. However, there is a grain of justification for Grisha's reproach.

"I do admit that I incline toward the *emotional side of creativeness* and I do this purposely because we are too prone to leave out feeling.

"We have altogether too many calculating actors and scenic productions of intellectual origin. We see too rarely true, living, emotional creativeness."

2

"The power of these motive forces is enhanced by their interaction. They support and incite one another with the result that they always act at the same time and in close relationship. When we call our mind into action by the same token we stir our will and feelings. It is only when these forces are co-operating harmoniously that we can create freely.

"When a real artist is speaking the soliloquy 'to be or not to be,' is he merely putting before us the thoughts of the author and executing the business indicated by his director? No, he puts into the lines much of his own conception of life.

"Such an artist is not speaking in the person of an imaginary Hamlet. He speaks in his own right as one placed in the circumstances created by the play. The thoughts, feelings, conceptions, reasoning of the author are transformed into his own. And it is not his sole purpose to render the lines so that they shall be *understood*. For him it is necessary that the spectators *feel* his inner relationship to what he is saying. They must follow his own creative *will* and desires. Here the motive forces of his psychic life are united in action and interdependent. This combined power is of utmost importance to us actors and we should be gravely mistaken not to use it for our practical ends. *Hence, we need to evolve an appropriate psycho-technique. Its basis is to take advantage of the reciprocal interaction of the members of this triumvirate in order not only to arouse them by natural means but also to use them to stir other creative elements.*

"Sometimes they go into action spontaneously, subconsciously. On such favourable occasions we should give ourselves up to the flow of their activity. But what are we to do when they do not respond?

"In such cases we can turn to one member of the triumvirate, perhaps the mind, because it responds more readily to commands. The actor takes the thoughts in the lines of his part and arrives at a conception of their meaning. In turn, this conception will lead to an opinion about them, which will correspondingly affect his feelings and will.

"We have already had many practical demonstrations of this truth. Think back to the beginnings of the exercise with the madman. The mind provided the plot and the circumstances in which to place it. These created the conception of the action and together they affected your feelings and will. As a result you played the sketch splendidly. This instance is an admirable example of the part of the *mind* in initiating the creative process. But it is possible to approach a play or a role on the side of feelings if the emotions give an immediate response. When they do so respond, everything falls into place in natural order: a *conception* is forthcoming, a *reasoned form* arises and in combination they stir your *will*.

"When, however, the feeling does not rise to the bait, what direct stimulus can we use? The direct stimulus for the mind we can find in the thoughts taken from the text of the play. For the feelings we must seek out the tempo-rhythm that underlies the inner emotions and the external actions of a part.

"It is impossible for me to discuss this important question now because you must first have a certain amount of preparation to enable you to grasp deeply enough what is significant and necessary. Moreover, we cannot immediately pass to the study of this problem because it would necessitate making a big jump ahead and would interfere with the orderly development of our program of work. That is why I shall leave this point and take up the method of arousing the *will* to creative action.

"In contrast to the mind, which is directly affected by thought, and to feelings, which respond immediately to tempo-rhythm, there is no direct stimulus by which we can influence the will."

"What about an objective?" I suggested. "Doesn't that influence your creative desire and therefore your will?"

"That depends. If it is not particularly alluring it won't. Artificial means would have to be used to sharpen it up, make it lively and interesting. On the other hand, a fascinating objective does have a direct and immediate effect. But—not on the will. Its attraction is to the emotions. First you are carried away by your feelings, desires are subsequent. Therefore its influence on your will is indirect."

"But you have been telling us that will and feeling were inseparable, so if an objective acts on the one, it naturally affects the other at the same time," said Grisha, eager to point out a discrepancy.

"You are quite right. Will and feeling are like Janus, two-faced. Sometimes emotion is in the ascendant, at others, will or desire preponderates. Consequently some objectives influence the will more than the feeling and others enhance the emotions at the expense of the desire. In one way or another, directly or indirectly, the objective is a magnificent stimulus and one which we are eager to use."

After a few moments of silence Tortsov continued:

"Actors whose feelings over-balance their intellects, will naturally, in playing Romeo or Othello, emphasize the emotional side. Actors in whom will is the most powerful attribute, will play Macbeth or Brand and underscore ambition or fanaticism. The third type will unconsciously stress, more than is necessary, the intellectual shadings of a part like Hamlet or Nathan der Weise.

"It is, however, necessary not to allow any one of the three elements to crush out either of the others and thereby upset the balance and necessary harmony. Our art recognizes all three types and in their creative work all three forces play leading parts. The only type that we reject as too cold and reasoning is that which is born of arid calculation."

There was silence for a while and then Tortsov concluded the lesson with the following statement:

"Now you are wealthy. You have at your disposal a great number of elements to use in creating the life of a human soul in a part.

"That is a great achievement and I congratulate you!"

# CHAPTER THIRTEEN

# The Unbroken Line

I

"YOUR INNER instrument is at concert pitch!" announced the Director at the beginning of the lesson.

"Imagine that we have decided to produce a play in which each of you is promised a splendid part. What would you do when you went home, after the first reading?"

"Act!" blurted out Vanya.

Leo said he would try to think himself into his part and Maria said she would go off somewhere into a corner and try to feel hers.

I decided I would start with the suppositions offered by the play and put myself into them. Paul said he would divide the play up into small units.

"In other words," explained the Director, "you would all use your inner forces to feel out the soul of the part.

"You will have to read the play over many times. Only on the rarest occasions can an actor seize the essentials of a new part instantly and be so carried away by it that he can create its whole spirit in one burst of feeling. More often his mind first grasps the text in part, then his emotions are slightly touched and they stir vague desires.

"In the beginning his understanding of the inner significance of a play is necessarily too general. Usually he will not get to the bottom of it until he has thoroughly studied it by following the steps the author took when he wrote it.

"When the first reading of the text leaves no impression, either intellectual or emotional—what is the actor to do?

"He must accept the conclusions of others and make a

stronger effort to penetrate the meaning of the text. With persistence he will evolve some vague conception of the part which he must then develop. Finally, his inner motive forces will be drawn into action.

"Until his goal is clear the direction of his activities will remain unformed. He will feel only individual moments in his role.

"It is not surprising that in this period the flow of his thoughts, desires and emotions appears and disappears. If we were to chart its course the pattern would be disjointed and broken. It is only when he comes to a deeper understanding of his part and a realization of its fundamental objective that a line gradually emerges as a continuous whole. Then we have the right to speak of the beginning of creative work."

"Why just then?"

Instead of an answer the Director began to make certain unrelated movements with his arms, head, and body. Then he asked:

"Can you say that I was dancing?"

We answered in the negative. Whereupon, still seated, he went through a series of motions that flowed harmoniously from one into another in unbroken sequence.

"Could a dance be made out of that?" he asked.

We agreed unanimously that it could. Then he sang several notes, with long pauses between.

"Is that a song?"

"No," we replied.

"Is this?" Whereupon he poured out a lovely, resonant melody.

"Yes!"

Next he drew some accidental and unrelated lines on a piece of paper and asked if that were a design. When we denied that it was he drew a few, long, graceful, curving patterns which we readily admitted could be called a design.

"Do you see that in every art we must have an *unbroken*

*line?* That is why, when the line emerges as a whole, I say that creative work has begun."

"But can there really be a line that is never broken either in real life or, much less, on the stage?" objected Grisha.

"Possibly that line can exist," explained the Director, "but not in a normal person. In healthy people there must be some interruptions. At least, so it seems. Yet during those breaks, a person continues to exist. He does not die. Therefore some sort of a line continues.

"Let us agree that *the normal, continuing line is one in which there are some necessary interruptions.*"

Toward the end of the lesson the Director explained that we need not one but many lines to represent the direction of our various inner activities.

"On the stage, if the inner line is broken an actor no longer understands what is being said or done and he ceases to have any desires or emotions. The actor and the part, humanly speaking, live by these unbroken lines. That is what gives life and movement to what is being enacted. Let those lines be interrupted and life stops. Let it be revived, and life goes on. But this spasmodic dying away and reviving is not normal. A role must have continuous being and its unbroken line."

2

"At our last lesson we found that in our art, as in any other, we must have a whole, unbroken line. Would you like me to show you how it is made?"

"Of course!" we exclaimed.

"Then tell me," said he, turning to Vanya, "what you did today, from the moment you got up until you came here?"

Our lively comrade made strenuous efforts to concentrate on the question, but he found it difficult to turn his attention backwards. To help him the Director gave him the following advice:

"In recalling the past, do not try to go forward toward the present. Go backwards from the present to the point in the past which you wish to reach. It is easier to go backwards, especially when you are dealing with the recent past."

As Vanya did not immediately grasp the idea, the Director prompted him:

"Now you are here talking with us. What did you do before that?"

"I changed my clothes."

"Changing your clothes is a short, independent process. It contains all sorts of elements. It constitutes what we may call a *short line*. There are many of them in any role. For example:

"What were you doing before you changed?"

"I was fencing and doing gymnastics."

"And before that?"

"I smoked a cigarette."

"And still earlier?"

"I was at my singing lesson."

He pushed Vanya farther and farther into the past until he reached the moment when he first woke up.

"We now have collected a series of short lines, episodes in your life since early morning, bringing us down to the present moment. All of them have been retained in your memory. In order to fix them I suggest that you go over the sequence several times in the same order."

After this was done the Director was satisfied that Vanya not only felt those few hours of the immediate past but that he had fixed them in his memory.

"Now do the same thing in the reverse order, starting with the moment when you first opened your eyes this morning."

Vanya did that, too, several times.

"Now tell me whether this exercise has left an intellectual or emotional imprint on you which you could consider a rather extended *line of your life* today? Is it an integrated whole made up of *individual acts* and feelings, thoughts and sensations?"

He went on: "I am convinced that you understand how to recreate the line of the past. Now, Kostya, let me see you do the same thing in the future, taking the latter half of today."

"How do I know what is going to happen to me in the immediate future?" I asked.

"Don't you know that after this lesson you have other occupations, that you will go home, and have dinner? Have you nothing in prospect for this evening, no calls to make, no play, movie, or lecture? You do not know that your intentions will be carried out but you can suppose that they will be. Then you must have some idea about the rest of the day. Don't you feel that solid line as it stretches out into the future, fraught with cares, responsibilities, joys and griefs?

"In looking ahead there is a certain movement, and where there is movement a line begins.

"If you join this line with the one that has gone before you will create *one whole unbroken line that flows from the past, through the present, into the future, from the moment you wake in the morning until you close your eyes at night.* That is how little individual lines flow together and form one large current that represents the *life of a whole day.*

"Now suppose you are in a provincial stock company and that you have been given the role of Othello to prepare in a week's time. Can you feel that all your life for those days will be poured into one main direction, to solve your problem honourably? There would be one dominating idea that would absorb everything leading up to the moment of that terrifying performance."

"Of course," I admitted.

"Can you feel the larger line that goes through that whole week of preparation for the part of Othello?" the Director pushed me still farther.

"And if there exist lines that run through days and weeks, can't we assume that they also exist in terms of months, years, or even a lifetime?

"All these large lines represent the welding together of smaller ones. That is what happens in every play and with every part. In reality life builds the line but on the stage it is the artistic imagination of the author that creates it in the likeness of truth. However, he gives it to us only in bits, and with breaks in it."

"Why is that?" I asked.

"We have already talked about the fact that the playwright gives us only a few minutes out of the whole life of his characters. He omits much of what happens off the stage. He often says nothing at all about what has happened to his characters while they have been in the wings, and what makes them act as they do when they return to the stage. We have to fill out what he leaves unsaid. Otherwise we would have only scraps and bits to offer out of the life of the persons we portray. You cannot live that way so we must create for our parts comparatively unbroken lines."

# 3

Tortsov began today by asking us to settle ourselves as comfortably as possible in "Maria's drawing-room" and talk about anything we wished. Some sat at the round table and others along the wall, where there were some attachments for electric lights.

Rakhmanov, the Assistant Director, was so busy getting us all arranged that it was obvious we were to have another of his "demonstrations".

As we talked we noticed that various lights came on and off and it was evident that this happened in relation to *who* was talking and *about whom* we spoke. If Rakhmanov spoke a light went on near him. If we mentioned something lying on the table, that object was instantly illuminated. At first I could not understand the meaning of the lights that appeared and disappeared outside of our living room. Finally I concluded that they had to do with periods of time. For example, the light in the corridor went on when we referred to the past, one in the dining-room when we mentioned the present, the one in the big hall when we spoke of the future. I also noticed that as soon as one light went off another came on. Tortsov explained that *that represented the unbroken chain of changing objects on which we concentrate our attention either coherently or in a haphazard manner in real life.*

"This is similar to what occurs during a performance. It is important that the sequence of the objects you focus on should form a *solid line. That line must remain on our side of the footlights, and not stray once into the auditorium.*

"The life of a person or of a part," explained the Director, "consists of an unending change of objects, circles of attention, either on the plane of reality or of the imagination, in the realm of memories of the past or dreams about the future. The unbroken quality of this line is of utmost importance to an artist, and you should learn to establish it in yourselves. By means of electric lights I am going to illustrate how it can flow without a break from one end of a role to the other.

"Go down into the orchestra," he said to us, asking Rakhmanov to go to the lighting switches and help him.

"This is the plot of the play I shall give. We are to have an auction at which two Rembrandts will be sold. While waiting for the bidders to arrive I shall sit at this round table with an expert on paintings and come to an understanding about the figure at which we shall start the sale. To do this we must examine both pictures." (A light on either side of the stage went on and off and the light in Tortsov's hand was extinguished.)

"Now we make mental comparisons with other Rembrandts in museums, abroad." (A light in the vestibule, representing the imagined paintings abroad, came on and off, alternating with the two lights on the stage which stood for the pictures to be auctioned.)

"Do you see those small lights near the door? Those are the unimportant buyers. They have attracted my attention and I greet them. However, I do this without great enthusiasm.

"If no more substantial buyers than these appear I shall not be able to run up the price of the pictures! That is what is going on in my mind." (All the other lights went out except a spot surrounding Tortsov, to indicate the small circle of attention. It moved with him as he paced nervously up and down.)

"See! The whole stage and the rooms beyond are now flooded with large lights. Those are the representatives of foreign museums, whom I go to greet with special deference."

He proceeded to demonstrate not only his meeting with the museum directors but the auction itself. His attention was sharpest when the bidding was fiercest and the excitement at the end was reproduced by a veritable bacchanalia of lights! The big lights went on together and separately, making a lovely pattern, something like an apotheosis of fireworks.

"Could you feel that the living line on the stage was unbroken?" he asked us.

Grisha claimed that Tortsov had not succeeded in proving what he wanted to.

"You will excuse me for saying so but you proved the opposite of your contention. This illumination did not show us an unbroken line—but an unending chain of different points."

"An actor's attention is constantly passing from one object to another. It is that constant change of foci that constitutes the unbroken line," explained Tortsov. "If an actor should cling to one object during a whole act or a whole play he would be spiritually unbalanced and the victim of an *idée fixe*."

All the other students were in agreement with the Director's point of view and felt that the demonstration was vivid and successful.

"So much the better!" he said with satisfaction. "This was to show you what should always happen on the stage. Now I shall demonstrate what should not take place and yet what usually does.

"Look. The lights appear on the stage only at intervals while they burn almost incessantly down in the auditorium.

"Tell me: does it seem normal to you that an actor's mind and feelings should wander away, for long spaces of time, into the audience and beyond the premises of the theatre? When they come back to the stage it is only for a brief moment, then they fade away again.

"In that sort of acting the actor and his part only occasionally belong to each other. To avoid that use all your inner force to build an unbroken line."

# CHAPTER FOURTEEN

# The Inner Creative State

## I

"WHEN YOU have assembled the lines along which your inner forces move, where do they go? How does a pianist express his emotions? He goes to his piano. Where does a painter go? To his canvas, his brushes and colours. So, an actor turns to his spiritual and physical creative instrument. His mind, will, and feelings combine to mobilize all of his inner 'elements.'

"They draw life from the fiction which is the play and make it seem more real, its objectives better founded. All this helps him to feel the role, its innate truthfulness, to believe in the actual possibility of what is happening on the stage. In other words this triumvirate of inner forces takes on the tone, colour, shadings and moods of the elements they command. They absorb their spiritual content. They also give out energy, power, will, emotion and thought. They graft these living particles of the role onto the 'elements'. From these grafts there gradually grow what we call the 'elements of the artist in the role'."

"Where are they headed?" was asked.

"To some point far away, to which the plot of the play lures them. They move forward toward creative objectives, pushed by inner longings, ambition, and by movements inherent in the character of their parts. They are drawn by the objects on which they have concentrated their attention, into contact with the other characters. They are fascinated by the artistic truthfulness of the play. And note that all these things are on the stage.

"The farther along they move together, the more unified the line of their advance. Out of this fusing of elements arises an important inner state which we call——" here Tortsov paused

246

to point to the placard hanging on the wall and read: "*The Inner Creative Mood*."

"Whatever is that?" exclaimed Vanya, already alarmed.

"It is simple," I volunteered. "Our inner motive forces combine with the elements to carry out the purposes of the actor. Is that right?" here I appealed to Tortsov.

"Yes, with two modifications. The first is that the common fundamental objective is still far off and that they combine forces to search for it. The second is a matter of terms. Up to now we have used the word 'elements' to cover artistic talent, qualities, natural gifts and several methods of psycho-technique. Now we can call them 'Elements of the Inner Creative Mood'."

"That's beyond me!" Vanya decided and made a gesture of despair.

"Why? It is an almost entirely normal state."

"*Almost?*"

"It is better than the normal state, in some ways, and in others—less good."

"Why *less* good?"

"On account of the conditions of an actor's work, which has to be done in public, his creative mood smacks of the theatre, and of self-exhibition, which the normal type does not."

"In what way is it *better?*"

"It includes the feeling of *solitude in public* which we do not know in ordinary life. That is a marvelous sensation. A theatre full of people is a splendid sounding board for us. For every moment of real feeling on the stage there is a response, thousands of invisible currents of sympathy and interest, streaming back to us. A crowd of spectators oppresses and terrifies an actor, but it also rouses his truly creative energy. In conveying great emotional warmth it gives him faith in himself and his work.

"Unfortunately a natural creative mood is seldom spontaneous. In exceptional cases it does come and then an actor will give a magnificent performance. In the too-frequent case, when an actor cannot get into the right inner state, he says: I am not in the mood. That means his creative apparatus is either not functioning properly, is not functioning at all, or has been replaced by mechanical habits. Is it the abyss of the proscenium arch that has disordered his functions? Or has he gone before the public with a half-finished part, with lines and actions even he cannot believe in?

"It is also possible the actor has not freshened up a well-prepared but old role. Yet he should do this every time he re-creates it. Otherwise he is likely to go out onto the stage and present only a shell.

"There is another possibility: the actor may have been drawn away from his work by lazy habits, inattention, poor health, or personal worries.

"In any one of those cases the combination, selection and quality of elements will be wrong, and for various reasons. There is no necessity to go into these cases individually. You know that when an actor comes out on the stage before an audience he may lose his self-possession from fright, embarrassment, shyness, agitation, a sense of overwhelming responsibility or unsurmountable difficulties. At that moment he is incapable of speaking, listening, looking, thinking, wishing, feeling, walking, or even moving, in an ordinary human way. He feels a nervous need to gratify the public, to show himself off and to hide his own state.

"Under those circumstances his component elements disintegrate and separate. That, of course, is not normal. On the stage, as in real life, the elements should be indivisible. The difficulty is that work in the theatre contributes to make a creative mood unstable. The actor is left to act without direction. He is in contact with the audience, instead of with his partner in the play. He adapts himself to their pleasure and not to the task of sharing his thoughts and feelings with his fellow actors.

"Unfortunately inner defects are not visible. The spectators do not see, they only sense them. Only experts in our profession understand them. But it is why ordinary theatre-goers do not respond and do not come back.

"The danger is heightened by the fact that if one element in the composition is lacking or wrong the whole suffers. You can test my words: you can create a state in which all the component parts are working together in perfect harmony, like a well-trained orchestra. Put in one false element and the tone of the whole is ruined.

"Suppose you have chosen a plot you cannot believe. It is inevitable that if you force yourself the result will be self-deception, which must disorganize your whole mood. The same is true of any other of the elements.

"Take concentrating on an object. If you look at it and do not see it you will be drawn away by the magnet of other things, away from the stage, even away from the theatre.

"Try choosing some artificial instead of a real objective, or using your role to display your temperament. The moment you introduce a false note *truth becomes a theatrical convention. Belief becomes faith in mechanical acting. Objectives change from human to artificial; imagination* evaporates and is replaced by *theatrical claptrap.*

"Add these undesirable things together and you will create an atmosphere in which you can neither live nor do anything except contort yourself, or imitate something.

"Beginners in the theatre, lacking in experience and technique, are the most likely to go wrong. They easily acquire any number of artificial habits. If they achieve a normal, human state it is accidental."

"Why can we so easily become artificial when we have acted only once in public?" I asked.

"I shall answer you in your own words," Tortsov replied. "Do you remember our very first lesson when I asked you to sit on the stage and instead of simply sitting you started to exaggerate? At the time you exclaimed: 'How strange! I have been on the stage only once, and the rest of the time I have been leading a normal life and yet I find it easier to be affected than to be natural.' The reason lies in the necessity of doing our artistic work in public where theatrical artificiality is constantly warring with truth. How can we protect ourselves against the one and strengthen the other? That we shall discuss in our next lesson."

2

"Let us take up the problem of how to avoid falling into habits of inner artificiality and to achieve a true inner creative state. To this double problem there is one answer: each of them precludes the existence of the other. By creating the one you destroy the other.

"Most actors before each performance put on costumes and make-up so that their external appearance will approximate that of the character they are to play. But they forget the most important part, which is the inner preparation. Why do they devote such particular attention to their external appearance? Why do not they put make-up and a costume on their souls?

"The inner preparation for a part is as follows: instead of rushing into his dressing-room at the last moment, an actor should (especially if he has a big part) arrive there two hours ahead of his entrance and begin to get himself in form. You know that a sculptor kneads his clay before he begins to use it, and a singer warms up his voice before his concert. We need to do something similar to tune our inner strings, to test the keys, the pedals, and the stops.

"You know this type of exercise through your drill work. The first necessary step is the relaxation of muscular tension. Then comes: Choose an object—that picture? What does it represent? How big is it? Colours? Take a distant object! Now a small circle, no further than your own feet! Choose some physical objective! Motivate it, add first one and then other imaginative fictions! Make your action so truthful that you can believe in it! Think up various suppositions and suggest possible circumstances into which you put yourself. Continue this until you have brought all of your 'elements' into play and then choose one of them. It makes no difference which. Take whichever appeals to you at the time. If you succeed in making that one function concretely (no generalities!) it will draw all the others along in its train.

"We must exercise great care, each time we have a creative piece of work to do, to prepare the various elements out of which we compose a true inner creative mood.

"We are so constituted that we need all our organs and members, heart, stomach, kidneys, arms and legs. We are uncomfortable when any one of them is removed and replaced by something artificial, a glass eye, a false nose or ear or tooth, a wooden leg or arm. Why not believe the same of our inner make-up? Artificiality in any form is just as disturbing to your inner nature. So go through your exercises every time you are to do anything creative."

"But," began Grisha in his usual argumentative tone, "if we did that we should have to go through two whole performances every evening. One for our own benefit, and a second for the public."

"No, that is not necessary," said Tortsov reassuringly. "To prepare yourself, go over the fundamental parts of your role. You do not need to develop them fully.

"What you must do is to ask: am I sure of my attitude toward this or that particular place? Do I really feel this or that action? Should I change or add to such and such imaginative detail? All these preparatory exercises test your expressive apparatus.

"If your role has matured to the point where you can do all this, the time needed to carry it out will be short. Unfortunately not every role reaches this stage of perfection.

"Under less favourable circumstances this preparation is difficult, but it is necessary even when it involves the expenditure of time and attention. Moreover an actor must constantly practise to achieve a true creative mood at all times, whether he is performing, rehearsing or working at home. His mood will be unstable at first, until his part is well rounded out, and again later, when it gets worn, it loses its keenness.

"This wavering back and forth makes it necessary to have a

pilot to direct us. As you become more experienced you will find the work of this pilot largely automatic.

"Suppose an actor is in perfect possession of his faculties on the stage. His mood is so complete that he can dissect its component parts without getting out of his role. They are all functioning properly, facilitating one another's operations. Then there is a slight discrepancy. Immediately the actor investigates to see which part is out of order. He finds the mistake and corrects it. Yet all the time he can easily continue to play his part even while he is observing himself.

"Salvini said: 'An actor lives, weeps, and laughs on the stage, and all the while he is watching his own tears and smiles. It is this double function, this balance between life and acting that makes his art.'"

# 3

"Now that you know the meaning of the inner creative state let us look into the soul of an actor at the time when that state is being formed.

"Suppose he is on the point of undertaking a most difficult and complex Shakespearean role—Hamlet. To what can it be compared? To an immense mountain filled with every kind of wealth. You can estimate its value only by uncovering its deposits of ore, or mining deep for precious metals, or marble. Then there is its natural external beauty. Such an undertaking is beyond the powers of any one person. The prospector must call in specialists, a large, organized force of helpers, he must have financial resources, and time.

"He builds roads, sinks shafts, burrows tunnels, and, after careful investigation, concludes that the mountain contains incalculable riches. But the search for the delicate and minute creations of nature must be made in unexpected places. An enormous amount of work will be done before the treasure is obtained. This enhances the appreciation of its value and the further men penetrate the greater their amazement at its extent. The higher they rise on the mountain side, the wider the horizon becomes. Still higher the mountain top is wreathed in clouds and we never know what happens up there in space beyond human ken.

"Suddenly someone cries: 'Gold! Gold!' Time goes by and the picks stop. The workmen move on, disappointed, to another place. The vein has disappeared, all their efforts were fruitless; their energy wilts. The prospectors and surveyors are lost and do not know where to turn. After a while another cry is heard and they all start off enthusiastically until the venture again proves disappointing. This happens again and again until finally they really find the rich vein."

After a short pause the Director continued:

"A struggle like this goes on for years when an actor is working on Hamlet, because the spiritual riches in this part are hidden. He must dig deep to find the motive forces of that most subtle of human souls.

"A great work of literature by and about a genius calls for infinitely detailed and intricate research.

"To grasp the spiritual delicacy of a complex soul it is not enough to use one's mind or any one 'element' by itself. It requires an artist's whole power and talent, as well as the harmonious co-operation of his inner forces, with those of the author.

"When you have studied the spiritual nature of your part you can decide, and then feel, its underlying purpose. For such work an actor's inner motive forces must be strong, sensitive, and penetrating. The elements of his inner creative state must be deep, delicate, and sustained. Unfortunately, we frequently see actors skimming thoughtlessly over the surface of parts and not digging into great roles."

After another brief interval Tortsov said:

"I have described the *larger creative state*. But it also exists on a smaller scale.

"Vanya, please go up onto the stage and look for a small slip of pale blue paper . . . which no one lost there."

"How can I do it that way?"

"Very simply. To carry out your purpose you will have to understand and feel just how it would be done in real life. You must organize all of your inner forces, and, to create your objective, you must propose certain given circumstances. Then answer the question of how you would search for the paper if you really needed to."

"If you really had lost a slip of paper, I really would find it," said Vanya, whereupon he executed the whole action very well. The Director approved.

"You see how easy it is. All you needed was the stimulus of the simplest sort of suggestion and it released the whole harmonious process of establishing your inner creative state on the stage. The small problem, or objective, leads directly and immediately to action, but even though the scale is small the elements involved are the same as in a larger and more complicated undertaking, such as playing Hamlet. The functions of the various elements will vary in importance and length of time in operation, but they all collaborate in some degree with one another.

"Generally speaking, the quality of power and endurance of an actor's inner creative state varies in direct ratio to the size and significance of his objective. The same can be said of the equipment used to achieve his purpose.

"Also the degree of power and endurance can be classified as small, medium, or large. So we get an infinite number of aspects, qualities, and degrees of creative moods in which one 'element' or another preponderates.

"Under certain conditions this variety is increased. If you have a clear-cut definite objective you quickly acquire a solid and correct inner state. If, on the other hand, it is indefinite, vague, your inner mood is likely to be fragile. In either case the quality of the objective is the determining factor.

"Sometimes, for no reason at all, perhaps even at home, you feel the power of a creative mood and you look about for a way of putting it to use. In that case it will provide its own objective.

"In *My Life in Art* a story is told about an old, retired actress now dead, who used to play all sorts of scenes to herself, alone at home, because she had to satisfy that very feeling and give an outlet to her creative impulses.

"Sometimes an objective exists subconsciously and is even carried out subconsciously without either the knowledge or the will of the actor. Often it is only afterwards that he realizes fully what it is that has happened."

# CHAPTER FIFTEEN

# The Super-Objective

I

TORTSOV began the lesson today with the following remarks:

"Dostoyevski was impelled to write *The Brothers Karamazov* by his lifelong *search for God*. Tolstoy spent all of his life struggling for *self-perfection*. Anton Chekhov wrestled with the *triviality* of bourgeois life and it became the *leit motiv* of the majority of his literary productions.

"Can you feel how these larger, vital purposes of great writers have the power to draw all of an actor's creative faculties and to absorb all the details and smaller units of a play or part?

"In a play the whole stream of individual, minor objectives, all the imaginative thoughts, feelings, and actions of an actor, should converge to carry out the *super-objective* of the plot. The common bond must be so strong that even the most insignificant detail, if it is not related to the *super-objective,* will stand out as superfluous or wrong.

"Also this impetus toward the super-objective must be continuous throughout the whole play. When its origin is *theatrical* or *perfunctory* it will give only an approximately correct direction to the play. If it is human and directed toward the accomplishment of the basic purpose of the play it will be like a main artery, providing nourishment and life to both it and the actors.

"Naturally, too, the greater the literary work, the greater the pull of its super-objective."

"But if a play lacks the touch of genius?"

"Then the pull will be distinctly weaker."

"And in a bad play?"

"Then the actor has to point up the super-objective himself, make it deeper and sharper. In doing that the name he gives to it will be extremely significant.

"You already know how important it is to choose the right name for an objective. You remember that we found the verb form preferable because it gave more impetus to action. The same is true to an even greater extent in defining the super-objective.

"Suppose we are producing Griboyedov's *Woe From Too Much Wit* and we decide that the main purpose of the play can be described by the words 'I wish to strive for Sophy.' There is a great deal in the plot that would confirm that definition. The drawback would be that in handling the play from that angle the theme of social denunciation would appear to have only an episodic, accidental value. But you can describe the super-objective in the terms of 'I wish to struggle, not for Sophy, but for my country!' Then Chatski's ardent love of his country and his people will move into the foreground.

"At the same time the indictment of society theme will become more prominent, giving the whole play a deeper inner significance. You can deepen its meaning still further if you use: 'I wish to struggle for freedom' as the main theme. In that set-up the hero's accusations become more severe and the whole play loses the personal, individual tone it had when the theme was connected with Sophy; it is no longer even national in scope, but broadly human, and universal in its implications.

"In my own experience I have had some even more vivid proofs of the importance of choosing the right name for the super-theme. One instance was when I was playing *Le Malade Imaginaire* of Molière. Our first approach was elementary and we chose the theme 'I wish to be sick.' But the more effort I put into it and the more successful I was, the more evident it became that we were turning a jolly, satisfying comedy into a pathological tragedy. We soon saw the error of our ways and changed to: 'I wish to be thought sick.' Then the whole comic side came to the fore and the ground was prepared to show up the way in which the charlatans of the medical world exploited the stupid Argan, which was what Molière meant to do.

"In Goldoni's *La Locandiera* we made the mistake of using 'I wish to be a misogynist,' and we found that the play refused to yield either humour or action. It was only when I discovered that the hero really loved women and wished only to be accounted a misogynist that I changed to 'I wish to do my courting on the sly' and immediately the play came to life.

"In this last instance the problem concerned my part rather than the whole play. However, it was only after prolonged work, when we realized that the Mistress of the Inn was really the Mistress of our Lives, or, in other words, *Woman,* that the whole inner essence of the play became evident.

"Often we do not come to a conclusion about this main theme until we have put on a play. Sometimes the public helps us to understand its true definition.

"The main theme must be firmly fixed in an actor's mind throughout the performance. It gave birth to the writing of the play. It should also be the fountain-head of the actor's artistic creation."

2

The Director began today by telling us that the main inner current of a play produces a state of inner grasp and power in which actors can develop all the intricacies and then come to a clear conclusion as to its underlying, fundamental purpose.

"That inner line of effort that guides the actors from the beginning to the end of the play we call the *continuity* or the *through-going action*. This through line galvanizes all the small units and objectives of the play and directs them toward the super-objective. From then on they all serve the common purpose.

"To emphasize the enormous practical significance of the *through-going action* and the *super-objective* in our creative process the most convincing proof I can offer is an instance that came to my personal knowledge. A certain actress, who enjoyed great popular success, became interested in our system of acting and decided to give up the stage for a while to perfect herself in this new method. She worked with various teachers and for several years. Then she returned to the stage.

"To her amazement she was no longer successful. The public found that she had lost her most valuable attribute, which was a direct outburst of inspiration. This had been replaced by dryness, naturalistic detail, perfunctory ways of acting and other similar defects. You can easily imagine the situation in which this actress now found herself. Each time she appeared she felt as though she were going through some test. It interfered with her playing and increased her sense of distraction and dismay, amounting almost to despair. She tested herself in various out-of-town theatres, thinking that perhaps the public in the capital was hostile to or prejudiced against the 'system'. But the result was everywhere the same. The poor actress began to curse the new method and tried to shake it off. She made an effort to go back to her earlier style of acting, but she was unable to do this. She had lost her artificial adeptness and she could no longer stand the absurdities of her old ways in comparison with the new method which she really preferred. So she fell between two stools. It is said that she had made up her mind to leave the stage entirely.

"About this time I happened to have an opportunity to see her play. Afterwards, at her request, I went to her dressing-room. Long after the play had ended and everyone had left the theatre she would not let me go, but implored me, in a desperately emotional way, to tell her what the cause was of the change that had taken place in her. We went over every detail of her part, how it had been prepared, all of the technical equipment that she had acquired through her study of the 'system'. Everything was correct. She understood every part of it, by itself. But she had not grasped the creative basis of the system as a whole. When I asked her about the through line of action and the super-objective, she admitted that she had heard about them in a general way but that she had no practical knowledge of them.

" 'If you play without the through line of action,' I said to her, 'you are merely going through certain disjointed exercises of parts of the system. They are useful in classroom work but they do not do for a whole performance of a part. You have passed over the important fact that all these exercises have the principal purpose of establishing fundamental lines of direction. That is why the splendid bits of your role have produced no effect. Break up a beautiful statue and the small scraps of marble cannot be overwhelming in their effect.'

"The next day, at rehearsal, I showed her how to prepare her units and objectives in relation to the main theme and direction of her part.

"She went about her work passionately and asked for several days to get a firm hold on it. I checked her work each day and finally went to the theatre to see her act the part over again in the new spirit. Her success was overpowering. I cannot describe to you what happened that evening in the theatre. This gifted actress was rewarded for all of her sufferings and doubts over a period of years. She threw herself into my arms, kissed me and wept for joy, she thanked me for giving her back her talent. She laughed and danced and took innumerable curtain calls, from a public that was not willing to let her go.

"That shows you the miraculous, life-giving quality of the through line of action and the super-objective."

Tortsov reflected for a few minutes. Then he said:

"Perhaps it would be more graphic if I made a drawing for you."

This is what he drew:

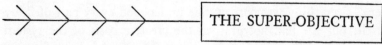

THE THROUGH LINE OF ACTION.

"All the minor lines are headed toward the same goal and fuse into one main current," he explained.

"Let us take the case, however, of an actor who has not established his ultimate purpose, whose part is made up of smaller lines leading in varying directions. Then we have:

"If all the minor objectives in a part are aimed in different directions it is, of course, impossible to form a solid, unbroken line. Consequently the action is fragmentary, uncoordinated, unrelated to any whole. No matter how excellent each part may be in itself, it has no place in the play on that basis.

"Let me give you another case. We have agreed, have we not, that the main line of action and the main theme are organically part of the play and they cannot be disregarded without detriment to the play itself. But suppose we were to introduce an extraneous theme or put what you might call a tendency into the play. The other elements will remain the same but they will be turned aside, by this new addition. It can be expressed this way:

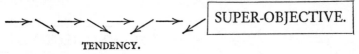

SUPER-OBJECTIVE.

TENDENCY.

"A play with that kind of a deformed, broken backbone cannot live."

Grisha protested violently against that point of view.

"But do you not rob every director," he burst out, "and every actor of all initiative and individual creative capacity, as well as every possibility of renewing old masterpieces by bringing them nearer to the spirit of modern times?"

Tortsov's reply was calm and explanatory:

"You, and many who think as you do, often confuse and misunderstand the meaning of three words: eternal, modern, and momentary. You must be able to make fine distinctions in human spiritual values if you are to get at the true meaning of those words.

"What is modern may become eternal if it deals with questions of freedom, justice, love, happiness, great joy, great suffering. I make no objection to that kind of modernity in the work of a playwright.

"In absolute contrast, however, is momentariness which can never become eternal. It lives only for today and tomorrow it will be forgotten. That is why an external work of art can have nothing in common with what is momentary, no matter how clever the régisseur or how gifted the actors who may try to inject it.

"Violence is always a bad means to use in creative work so that freshening up an old theme by using a transient emphasis can mean only death for both play and part. Yet it is true that we find very rare exceptions. We know that a fruit of one sort can occasionally be grafted on to the stock of another sort and a new fruit produced.

"Sometimes a contemporary idea can be naturally grafted on to an old classic and rejuvenate it. In that case the addition becomes absorbed in the main theme:

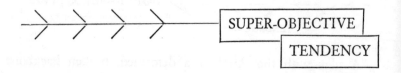

"The conclusion to be drawn from this is: *Above all preserve your super-objective and through line of action. Be wary of all extraneous tendencies and purposes foreign to the main theme.*

"I shall be satisfied if I have succeeded in bringing home to you the primary and exceptional importance of these two things, because I shall feel I have accomplished my main purpose as a teacher and have explained one of the fundamental parts of our system."

After a prolonged pause Tortsov went on:

"Every *action* meets with a *reaction* which in turn intensifies the first. In every play, beside the main action we find its opposite *counteraction*. This is fortunate because its inevitable result is more action. We need that clash of purposes, and all the problems to solve that grow out of them. They cause activity which is the basis of our art.

"Let me take *Brand* as an illustration:

"Suppose that we are agreed that Brand's motto 'All or Nothing' represents the main objective of the play (whether this is correct or not is beside the point at present). A fanatical, fundamental principle of this sort is terrifying. It admits of no compromises, no concessions, no weakening, in executing his ideal purpose in life.

"Now let me try to bind this main theme together with various smaller units in the play, perhaps the same scene we worked over in class, with Agnes and the baby clothes. If I try, mentally, to reconcile this scene with the main theme 'All or Nothing' I can make a great effort of the imagination and somehow bring them together.

"It is much more natural if I take the point of view that Agnes, the mother, represents the line of reaction or the line of counteraction. She is in rebellion against the principal theme.

"If I analyse Brand's part in the scene it is easy to find its relationship to the main theme because he wants his wife to give away the baby clothes to complete her sacrifice to duty. As a fanatic he demands all from her to achieve his ideal of life. Her counteraction only intensifies his direct action. Here we have the clash of two principles.

"Brand's *duty* wrestles with mother *love*; an *idea* struggles with a *feeling*; the fanatic *preacher* with the sorrowing *mother*; the *male* principle with the *female*.

"Therefore, in this scene, the through line of action is in Brand's hands and the counteraction in those of Agnes."

"Now please," said Tortsov, "give me all your attention as I have something important to say!

"Everything that we have undertaken in this first course has been directed toward enabling you to obtain control of the three most important features in our creative process:

1) Inner grasp
2) The through line of action
3) The super-objective."

There was silence for a while and then Tortsov brought the lesson to a close by saying:

"We have covered all these points in general terms. Now you know what we mean by our 'system'."

\*       \*       \*       \*       \*       \*       \*

Our first year's course is almost over. I had expected inspiration but the "system" dashed my hopes.

These thoughts were running in my head as I stood in the vestibule of the theatre, putting on my coat and slowly winding my muffler around my neck.

Suddenly someone nudged me. I turned to find Tortsov.

He had noticed my crestfallen mood and had come to discover its cause. I gave him an evasive answer but he kept after me stubbornly with question after question.

"How do you feel now when you are on the stage?" he asked in an effort to understand my disappointment in the "system".

"That is just the trouble. I don't feel anything out of the ordinary. I am comfortable, I know what to do, I have a purpose in being there, I have faith in my actions and believe in my right to be on the stage."

"What more do you ask for? Do you feel it is wrong?"

Then I confessed my longing to be inspired.

"Don't come to me for that. My 'system' will never manufacture inspiration. It can only prepare a favourable ground for it.

"If I were you, I would give up chasing this phantom, inspiration. Leave it to that miraculous fairy, nature, and devote yourself to what lies within the realm of human conscious control.

"Put a role on the right road and it will move ahead. It will grow broader and deeper and will in the end lead to inspiration."

# CHAPTER SIXTEEN

# On the Threshold of the Subconscious

## I

THE DIRECTOR began with the encouraging remark that we had the longest part of our inner preparatory work behind us.

"All this preparation trains your 'inner creative state', it helps you to find your 'super-objective' and 'through line of action', it creates a conscious psycho-technique, and in the end it leads you —" this he said with a touch of solemnity "—to the 'region of the subconscious'. The study of this important region is a fundamental part of our system.

"Our conscious mind arranges, and puts a certain amount of order into, the phenomena of the external world that surround us. There is no sharply drawn line between conscious and subconscious experience. Our consciousness often indicates the direction in which our subconscious continues to work. Therefore, the fundamental objective of our psycho-technique is to put us in a creative state in which our subconscious will function naturally.

"It is fair to say that this technique bears the same relation to subconscious creative nature as grammar does to poetry. It is unfortunate when grammatical considerations overwhelm the poetic. That happens too often in the theatre, yet we cannot do without grammar. It should be used to help arrange subconscious, creative material because it is only when it has been organized that it can take on an artistic form.

"In the first period of conscious work on a role, an actor feels his way into the life of his part, without altogether understanding what is going on in it, in him, and around him. When he reaches the region of the subconscious the eyes of his soul are opened and he is aware of everything, even minute details, and it all acquires an entirely new significance. He is conscious of new feelings, conceptions, visions, attitudes, both in his role and in himself. Beyond the threshold one's inner life, of its own accord, takes on a simple, full form, because organic nature directs all the important centres of our creative apparatus. Consciousness knows nothing of all this: even our feelings cannot find their way around in this region—and yet without them true creativeness is impossible.

"I do not give you any technical methods to gain control of the subconscious. I can only teach you the indirect method to approach it and give yourselves up to its power.

"We see, hear, understand, and think differently *before* and *after* we cross the 'threshold of the subconscious'. *Beforehand* we have 'true-seeming feelings', *afterwards*—'sincerity of emotions'. On *this* side of it we have the simplicity of a limited fantasy; *beyond*—the simplicity of the larger imagination. Our freedom on *this* side of the threshold is limited by reason and conventions; *beyond* it, our freedom is bold, wilful, active, and always moving forwards. *Over there* the creative process differs each time it is repeated.

"It makes me think of the shore along the ocean. Big waves and small throw themselves up on the sand. Some play around our ankles, others reach our knees, or even sweep us off our feet, while the largest carry us out to sea, and eventually toss us up on the beach again.

"Sometimes the tide of the subconscious barely touches an actor, and then goes out. At other times it envelops his whole being, carrying him into its depths until, at length, it casts him up again on the shore of consciousness.

"All that I am telling you now is in the realm of the emotions, not of reason. You can feel what I say more easily than understand it. Therefore it will be more to the point if, instead of lengthy explanations, I tell you about an actual episode out of my own life which helped me to sense the state I have been describing.

"At a party one evening, in the house of friends, we were

doing various stunts and they decided, for a joke, to operate on me. Tables were carried in, one for operating, the other supposedly containing surgical instruments. Sheets were draped around, bandages, basins, various vessels were brought.

"The 'surgeons' put on white coats and I was dressed in a hospital gown. They laid me on the operating table and bandaged my eyes. What disturbed me was the extremely solicitous manner of the doctors. They treated me as if I were in a desperate condition and did everything with utmost seriousness. Suddenly the thought flashed through my mind: 'What if they really should cut me open?!'

"The uncertainty and the waiting worried me. My sense of hearing became acute and I tried not to miss a single sound. All around I could hear them whispering, pouring water, rattling instruments. Now and then a large basin made a booming noise like the toll of a funeral bell.

" 'Let us begin!' someone whispered.

"Someone took a firm hold on my right wrist. I felt a dull pain and then three sharp stabs. . . . I couldn't help trembling. Something that was harsh and smarted was rubbed on my wrist, then it was bandaged, people rustled around, handing things to the surgeon.

"Finally, after a long pause, they began to speak out loud, they laughed, congratulated me. My eyes were unbandaged and on my left arm lay . . . a new-born baby made out of my right hand, all swaddled in gauze. On the back of my hand they had painted a silly, infantile face.

"The question is: were the feelings that I experienced true and was my belief in them real or were they what we call 'true-seeming'?

"Of course, it wasn't *real truth* and *a real sense of faith*," Tortsov said as he recalled his sensations. "Although we might almost say that, for purposes of the theatre, I really did live those sensations. And yet there was no solid stretch of believing in what I was undergoing. There was a constant wavering back and forth between belief and doubt, real sensations and the illusion of having them. All the while I felt that *if* I really did have an operation I should go through just such moments as I had during this mock operation. The illusion certainly was sufficiently lifelike.

"I felt at times that my emotions were just what they would have been in reality. They recalled sensations familiar to me in real life. I even had presentiments of losing consciousness, if only for a few seconds. They disappeared almost as soon as they came. Yet the illusion left traces. And to this day I am convinced that what happened to me on that evening could happen in real life.

"That was my first experience in the condition which we call the 'region of the subconscious'," said the Director as he finished his story.

"It is a mistake to think that an actor experiences a second state of reality when he is doing creative work on the stage. If that were the case our physical and spiritual organism would be unable to stand the amount of work put on it.

"As you already know, on the stage we live on emotional memories of realities. At times these memories reach a point of illusion that makes them seem like life itself. Although such a thing as complete forgetting of self and unwavering belief in what is happening on the stage is possible, it occurs rarely. We know of separate moments, long or short in duration, when an actor is lost in 'the region of the subconscious'. But during the rest of the time truth alternates with verisimilitude, faith with probability.

"The story I have just told you is an example of the coincidence of emotion memories with the sensations called for by the part. The analogy which results from this coincidence draws the actor closer to the person he is portraying. At such times a creative artist feels his own life in the life of his part, and the life of his part identical with his personal life. This identification results in a miraculous metamorphosis."

After a few moments of reflection Tortsov continued:

"Other things besides such coincidences between real life and a role lead us into the 'region of the subconscious'. Often a sim-ple *external occurrence*, having nothing at all to do with the play, or the part, or the peculiar circumstances of the actor, sud-denly injects a bit of real life into the theatre and instantly sweeps us into a state of subconscious creativeness."

"What kind of an occurrence?" he was asked.

"Anything. Even the dropping of a handkerchief, or the over-turning of a chair. A live incident in the conditioned atmosphere of the stage is like a breath of fresh air in a stuffy room. The actor must pick up the handkerchief, or the chair, spontaneously, because that wasn't rehearsed in the play. He doesn't do it as an actor but in an ordinary, human way and creates a bit of truth that he must believe in. This truth will stand out in sharp con-trast to his conditioned, conventional surroundings. It is in his power to include such accidental moments of reality in his part or to leave them out. He can treat them as an actor and, for that one occasion, fit them into the pattern of his part. Or, he can, for a moment, step out of his part, dispose of the accidental intrusion, and then go back to the convention of the theatre and take up his interrupted action.

"If he can really believe in the spontaneous occurrence and use it in his part, it will help him. It will put him on the road toward the 'threshold of the subconscious'.

"Such occurrences often act as a kind of tuning fork, they strike a living note and oblige us to turn from falseness and arti-ficiality back to truth. Just one such moment can give direction to all the rest of the role.

"Therefore, learn to appreciate any such occurrences. Don't let them slip by. Learn to use them wisely when they happen of their own accord. They are an excellent means of drawing you closer to the subconscious."

2

The Director's opening remark today was:

"Up to now we have been dealing with accidental occurrences which can serve as an approach to the subconscious. But we cannot base any rules on them. What can an actor do if he is not sure of success?

"He has no course open except to turn for assistance to a *conscious psycho-technique*. It can prepare ways and favorable conditions for the approach to the 'region of the subconscious'. You will understand this better if I give you a practical illustration.

"Kostya and Vanya! Please play for us the opening scene of the exercise with the 'burnt money'. You will remember that you begin all creative work by first relaxing your muscles. So please seat yourselves comfortably and rest, just as if you were at home."

We went onto the stage and carried out his instructions.

"That's not enough. Relax more!" called Tortsov from the auditorium. "Make yourselves even more at home. You must feel more at your ease than when you are at home, because we are not dealing with reality, but with 'solitude in public'. So do loosen up your muscles more. Cut 95 percent of that tenseness!

"Perhaps you think that I exaggerate the amount of your excess strain? No, indeed. The effort that an actor makes, when he stands before a large audience, is immeasurable. The worst of it is that all this effort and force is brought about almost unnoticed by, unwished for, and unthought of by the actor.

"Therefore, be quite bold in throwing off as much tenseness as you possibly can. You needn't think for a moment that you will have less than you need. No matter how much you reduce tension, it will never be enough."

"Where do you draw the line?" someone asked.

"Your own physical and spiritual state will tell you what is right. You will sense what is true and normal better when you reach the state that we call 'I am'."

I already felt that Tortsov could not ask for a more relaxed state than the one I was in. Nevertheless he continued to call for still less tension.

As a result I overdid and reached a state of prostration and numbness. That is another aspect of muscular rigidity and I had to struggle against it. To do that I changed poses and tried to get rid of pressure through action. I changed from a quick, nervous rhythm to one which was slow, almost lazy.

The Director not only noticed but approved of what I was doing.

"When an actor is making too much effort it is sometimes a good idea for him to introduce a lighter, more frivolous, approach to his work. That is another way of dealing with tenseness."

But I still was unable to achieve the real sense of ease I feel when I am sprawling on my sofa at home.

At this point Tortsov, in addition to calling for still more relaxation, reminded us that we should not be doing this for its own sake. He recalled the three steps: tenseness, relaxation, justification.

He was quite right because I had forgotten about them, and as soon as I corrected my mistake I felt an entire change come over me. My whole weight was drawn toward the earth. I sank deep into the arm-chair in which I was half lying. Now, it seemed to me, the greater part of my tenseness had disappeared. Even so I did not feel as free as I do in ordinary life. What was the matter? When I stopped to analyse my condition I found that my *attention* was strained and kept me from relaxing. To this the Director said:

"Strained attention shackles you every bit as much as muscular spasms. When your inner nature is in its grip your subconscious process cannot develop normally. You must achieve inner freedom as well as physical relaxation."

"Ninety-five percent off on that too, I suppose," put in Vanya.

"Quite right. The excess of tension is just as great, only you must deal with it more subtly. In comparison with muscles the figments of the soul are as cobwebs to cables. Singly they are easily broken, but you can spin them into stout cords. However, when they are first spun treat them with delicacy."

"How can we handle inner spasms?" one student asked.

"In the same way you deal with muscular contractions. You

first search out the point of tension. Next you try to relieve it and finally you build a basis for freedom from it in an appropriate supposition.

"Make use of the fact that in this case your *attention* is not allowed to wander all over the theatre but is concentrated inside of you. Give it some interesting *object,* something that will help your exercise. Direct it to some attractive objective or action."

I began to go over the objectives in our exercise, all of its given circumstances; mentally I went through all the rooms. Then the unexpected happened. I found myself in an unfamiliar room, one I had not been in before. There was an aged couple, my wife's parents. This unprepared for circumstance affected and stirred me, because it complicated my responsibilities. Two more people to work for, five mouths to feed, not counting myself! This added significance to my work, to tomorrow's checking of accounts, to my own going over of papers now. I sat in the armchair and nervously twisted a bit of string around my fingers.

"That was fine," exclaimed Tortsov approvingly. "That was real freedom from tension. Now I can believe every thing you are doing and thinking about even though I do not know exactly what is in your mind."

He was right. When I checked over my body I found that my muscles were free from contraction. Evidently I had reached the third stage naturally by sitting there and finding a real basis for my work.

"There you have real truth, faith in your actions, the state we call 'I am'. You are on the threshold," he said softly to me. "Only don't be in a hurry. Use your inner vision to see through to the end of each thing you do. If necessary, introduce some new supposition. Stop! Why did you waver then?"

It was easy for me to get back onto the track. I had only to say to myself:

"Suppose they find a large shortage in the accounts?! That would mean a re-checking of all the books and papers. What a ghastly job. And to have to do it all alone, at this hour of the night——!"

Mechanically I pulled out my watch. It was four o'clock. In the afternoon or in the morning? For a moment I assumed it was the latter. I was excited and instinctively threw myself toward my desk and began to work furiously.

Out of the corner of my ear I heard Tortsov make some approving comment and explain to the students that this was the right approach to the subconscious. But I no longer paid any attention to encouragement. I did not need it because I was really living on the stage and could do anything I chose.

Evidently the Director, having achieved his pedagogic purpose was ready to interrupt me but I was eager to cling to my mood and I went right on.

"Oh, I see," said he to the others. "This is a big wave." Nor was I satisfied. I wanted to complicate my situation further and enhance my emotions. So I added a new circumstance: a substantial defalcation in my accounts. In admitting that possibility I said to myself: What would I do? At the very thought my heart was in my mouth.

"The water is up to his waist now," commented Tortsov.

"What can I do?" I said excitedly, "I must get back to the office!" I rushed toward the vestibule. Then I remembered that the office was closed, so I came back and paced up and down trying to gather my thoughts. I finally sat down in a dark corner of the room to think things out.

I could see, in my mind's eye, some severe persons going over the books and counting the funds. They questioned me but I did not know how to answer. An obstinate kind of despair kept me from making a clean breast.

Then they wrote out a resolution, fatal to my career. They stood around in groups, whispering. I stood to one side, an outcast. Then an examination, trial, dismissal, confiscation of property, loss of home.

"He is out in the ocean of the subconscious now," said the Director. Then he leaned over the footlights and said softly to me: "Don't hurry, go through to the very end."

He turned to the other students again and pointed out that,

although I was motionless, you could feel the storm of emotions inside of me.

I heard all these remarks, but they did not interfere with my life on the stage, or draw me away from it. At this point my head was swimming with excitement because my part and my own life were so intermingled that they seemed to merge. I had no idea where one began or the other left off. My hand ceased wrapping the string around my fingers and I became inert.

"That is the very depth of the ocean," explained Tortsov.

I do not know what happened from then on. I know only that I found it easy and pleasant to execute all sorts of variations. I decided once more that I must go to the office, then to my attorney; or I made up my mind I must find certain papers to clear my name, and I hunted through all sorts of drawers.

When I finished playing, the Director said to me, with great seriousness:

"Now you have the right to say that you have found the ocean of the subconscious by your own experience. We can make analogous experiments by using any one of the 'elements of the creative mood' as a starting point, imagination and suppositions, desires and objectives (if they are well defined), emotions (if naturally aroused). You can begin with various propositions and conceptions. If you sense the truth in a play subconsciously, your faith in it will naturally follow, and the state of 'I am'. The important thing to remember in all these combinations is that whatever element you choose to start with you must carry to the limit of its possibilities. You already know that in taking up any one of these links in the creative chain you pull them all along."

I was in a state of ecstasy, not because the Director had praised me but because I had again felt creative inspiration. When I confessed this to Tortsov he explained: "You are not drawing the right conclusion from today's lesson. Something much more important took place than you think. The coming of inspiration was only an accident. You cannot count on it. But you can rely on what actually did occur. The point is, inspiration did not come to you of its own accord. You called for it, by preparing the way for it. This result is of far greater importance.

"The satisfying conclusion that we can draw from today's lesson is that you now have the power to create favourable conditions for the birth of inspiration. Therefore put your thought on what arouses your inner motive forces, what makes for your inner creative mood. Think of your super-objective and the through line of action that leads to it. In short, have in your mind everything that can be consciously controlled and that will lead you to the subconscious. That is the best possible preparation for inspiration. But never try for a direct approach to inspiration for its own sake. It will result in physical contortion and the opposite of everything you desire."

Unfortunately the Director had to postpone further discussion of the subject until the next lesson.


3

Today Tortsov continued to sum up the results of our last lesson. He began:

"Kostya gave you a practical demonstration of the way conscious psycho-technique arouses the subconscious creativeness of nature. At first you might think that we had not accomplished anything new. Work was begun, as it should be, with the freeing of muscles. Kostya's attention was concentrated on his body. But he transferred it skilfully to the supposed circumstances of the exercise. Fresh inner complications justified his sitting there, motionless, on the stage. In him, that basis for his immobility completely freed his muscles. Then he created all sorts of new conditions for his make-believe life. They enhanced the atmosphere of the whole exercise and sharpened the situation with possible tragic implications. This was a source of real emotion.

"Now you ask: What is new in all this? The 'difference' is infinitesimal, and lies in my having obliged him *to carry out each creative act to its fullest limit*. That's all."

"How can that be all?" Vanya blurted.

"Very simply. Carry all of the elements of the inner creative state, your inner motive forces, and your through line of action to the limit of human (not theatrical) activity, and you will inevitably feel the reality of your inner life. Moreover you will not be able to resist believing in it.

"Have you noticed that each time this truth and your belief in it is born, involuntarily, the subconscious steps in and nature begins to function? So when your conscious psycho-technique is carried to its fullest extent the ground is prepared for nature's subconscious process.

"If you only knew how important this new addition is!

"It is all very pleasant to think that every bit of creativeness is full of impatience, exaltation, and complexities. As a matter of actual fact we find that even the smallest action or sensation, the slightest technical means, can acquire a deep significance on the stage only if it is pushed to its limit of possibility, to the boundary of human *truth, faith* and the sense of 'I am'. When this point is reached, your whole spiritual and physical make-up will function normally, just as it does in real life and without regard to the special condition of your having to do your creative work in public.

"In bringing beginners like you to the 'threshold of the subconscious' I take a diametrically opposite view from many teachers. I believe that you should have this experience and use it when you are working on your inner 'elements' and 'inner creative state,' in all your drills and exercises.

"I want you to feel right from the start, if only for short periods, that blissful sensation which actors have when their creative faculties are functioning truly, and subconsciously. Moreover, this is something you must learn through your own emotions and not in any theoretical way. You will learn to love this state and constantly strive to achieve it."

"I can readily see the importance of what you have just told us," I said. "But you have not gone far enough. Please give us now the technical means by which we can push any one element to its very limit."

"Gladly. On the one hand you must first discover what the obstacles are, and learn to deal with them. On the other hand, you must search out whatever will facilitate the process. I shall discuss the difficulties first.

"The most important one, as you know, is the abnormal circumstance of an actor's creative work—it must be done in public. The methods of wrestling with this problem are familiar to you. You must achieve a proper 'creative state'. Do that first of all and when you feel that your inner faculties are ready, give your inner nature the slight stimulus it needs to begin functioning."

"That is just what I don't understand. How do you do it?" Vanya exclaimed.

"By introducing some unexpected, spontaneous incident, a touch of reality. It makes no difference whether it is physical or spiritual in origin. The one condition is that it must be germane to the super-objective and the through line of action. The unexpectedness of the incident will excite you and your nature will rush forward."

"But where do I find that slight touch of truth?" insisted Vanya.

"Everywhere: in what you dream, or think, or suppose or feel, in your emotions, your desires, your little actions, internal or external, in your mood, the intonations of your voice, in some imperceptible detail of the production, pattern of movements."

"And then what will happen?"

"Your head will swim from the excitement of the sudden and complete fusion of your life with your part. It may not last long but while it does last you will be incapable of distinguishing between yourself and the person you are portraying."

"And then?"

"Then, as I have already told you, truth and faith will lead you into the region of the subconscious and hand you over to the power of nature."

After a short pause the Director continued:

"There are other obstacles in your way. One of them is *vagueness. The creative theme of the play may be vague, or the plan of the production may not be clear-cut. A part may be worked out wrong, or its objectives may be indefinite. The actor may be uncertain about the means of expression he has chosen.* If you only knew how doubt and indecision can weigh you down! The only way of dealing with that situation is by clearing up all that is lacking in precision.

"Here is another menace: some actors do not fully realize the limitations placed on them by nature. They undertake problems beyond their powers to solve. The comedian wants to play tragedy, the old man to be a *jeune premier,* the simple type longs for heroic parts and the soubrette for the dramatic. This can only result in forcing, impotence, stereotyped, mechanical action. These are also shackles and your only means of getting out of them is to study your art and yourself in relation to it.

"Another frequent difficulty arises from too conscientious work, too great an effort. The actor puffs; he forces himself to give an external expression to something he does not actually feel. All one can do here is to advise the actor not to try so hard.

"All these are obstacles that you must learn to recognize. The constructive side, the discussion of what helps you to reach the 'threshold of the subconscious' is a complicated question for which we have not sufficient time today."

4

"Now we come to the positive side," said the Director at the beginning of our lesson today. "To the conditions and means which help an actor in his creative work and lead him to the promised land of the subconscious. It is difficult to speak of this realm. It is not always subject to reasoning. What can we do? We can change to a discussion of the super-objective and through line of action."

"Why to them? Why do you choose these two? What is the connection?" came from various perplexed students.

"Principally because they are predominantly conscious in

their make-up and subject to reason. Other grounds for this choice will appear in our lesson today."

He called on Paul and me to play the opening lines of the first scene between Iago and Othello.

We prepared ourselves and played it with concentration and right inner feelings.

"What are you intent on just now?" Tortsov asked.

"My first object is to attract Kostya's attention," answered Paul.

"I was concentrated on understanding what Paul was saying, and trying to visualize his remarks inwardly," I explained.

"Consequently, one of you was drawing the attention of the other in order to attract his notice, and the other was trying to penetrate and visualize the remarks being made to him in order to penetrate and visualize those remarks."

"No, indeed!" we protested vigorously.

"But that is all that could happen in the absence of a super-objective and the through line of action for the whole play. There can be nothing but individual, unrelated actions, undertaken each for his own sake.

"Now repeat what you have just done and add the next scene in which Othello jokes with Iago."

When we had finished Tortsov again asked us what our objective had been.

"Dolce far niente," was my answer.

"What had become of your previous objective, of understanding your colleague?"

"It was absorbed in the next and more important step."

"Now repeat everything up to this point and add still another bit, the first intimations of jealousy."

We did as directed and awkwardly defined our objective as "poking fun at the absurdity of Iago's vow."

"And now where are your former objectives?" probed the Director.

I was going to say that they too had been swallowed up in a

succeeding and more important aim, but I thought better of my answer and remained silent.

"What's the matter? What is troubling you?"

"The fact that at this point in the play the theme of happiness is broken off and the new theme of jealousy begins."

"It does not break off," corrected Tortsov. "It changes with the changing circumstances of the play. First the line passes through a short period of bliss for the newly married Othello, he jokes with Iago, then come amazement, dismay, doubt. He repels the onrushing tragedy, calms his jealousy, and returns to his happy state.

"We are familiar with such changes of moods in reality. Life runs along smoothly, then suddenly doubt, disillusion, grief are injected and still later they blow over and everything is bright once more.

"You have nothing to fear from such changes; on the contrary, learn to make the most of them, to intensify them. In the present instance that is easy to do. You have only to recall the early stages of Othello's romance with Desdemona, the recent blissful past, and then contrast all this with the horror and torture Iago is preparing for the Moor."

"I don't see. What should we recall out of their past?" asked Vanya.

"Think of those wonderful first meetings in the house of Brabantio, the tales of Othello, the secret meetings, the abduction of the bride and the marriage, the separation on the wedding night, the meeting again in Cyprus under a southern sun, the unforgettable honeymoon, and then, in the future—all the result of Iago's hellish intrigue, the fifth act.

"Now go on——!"

We went through the whole scene up to Iago's famous vow, by the sky and by the stars, to consecrate his mind, will, and feelings, his all, to the service of the abused Othello.

"If you work your way through the whole play in this way, your smaller objectives will naturally be absorbed in larger and fewer aims, which will stand like guide posts along the through line of action. This larger objective gathers up all the smaller ones subconsciously and eventually forms the through line of action for the whole tragedy."

The discussion turned next on the right name for the first large objective. No one, not even the Director himself, could decide the question. That was, of course, not surprising, as a real, live, engaging objective cannot be found immediately and by a purely intellectual process. However, for lack of a better one, we did decide on an awkward name for it—"I wish to idealize Desdemona, to give up my whole life to her service."

As I reflected about this larger objective, I found that it helped me to intensify the whole scene as well as other parts of my role. I felt this whenever I began to shape any action toward the ultimate goal—the idealization of Desdemona. All the other inner objectives lost their significance. For example, take the first one: to try to understand what Iago is saying. What was the point of that? No one knows. Why try when it is perfectly clear that Othello is in love, is thinking of no one but her, and will speak of no one else. Therefore all enquiries and thoughts of her are necessary and pleasing to him.

Then take our second objective—dolce far niente. That is no longer necessary or right. In talking about her the Moor is engaged in something important and vital to him, and again for the reason that he wishes to idealize her.

After Iago's first vow I imagine that Othello laughed. It was pleasant for him to think that no stain could touch his crystal-pure divinity. This conviction put him into a *joyful state of mind* and intensified his worship for her. Why? For the same reason as before. I understood better than ever how gradually jealousy took hold of him, how imperceptibly his faith in his ideal weakened and the realization grew and strengthened that wickedness, depravity, snake-like cunning, could be contained in such an angelic form.

"Now where are your former objectives?" queried the Director.

"They have all been swallowed up in our concern over a lost ideal."

"What conclusion can you draw from this work today?" he asked, and then he went on to answer his own question.

"I made the actors playing that scene between Othello and Iago feel for themselves, in actual practice, the process by which the larger objectives absorb the smaller ones. Now Kostya and Paul also know that the more distant goal draws you away from the nearer one. Left to themselves, these smaller objectives naturally pass under the guidance of nature and the subconscious.

"Such a process is easy to understand. When an actor gives himself up to the pursuit of a larger objective, he does it completely. At such times nature is free to function in accordance with her own needs and desires. In other words Kostya and Paul now know through their own experience that an actor's creative work, while on the stage, is really, either in whole or in part, an expression of his creative subconscious."

The Director reflected for a while and then added:

"You will see these larger objectives undergo a transformation, similar to that of the smaller ones, when the super-objective supersedes them all. They fall into place as steps leading to a final, all-embracing goal,—steps that will, to a large extent, be taken subconsciously.

"The through line of action is made up, as you know, of a series of large objectives. If you realize how many, many smaller objectives, transformed into subconscious actions, they contain, then consider the extent of the subconscious activities that flow into the through line of action as it goes across the whole play, giving it a stimulating power to influence our subconscious indirectly."

5

"The creative force of the *through line of action* is in direct proportion to the power of attraction of the super-objective. This not only gives the super-objective a place of primary importance in our work; it also obliges us to devote particular attention to its quality.

"There are many 'experienced directors' who can define a super-objective offhand, because they 'know the game' and are 'old hands' at it. But they are of no use to us.

"There are other directors and playwrights who dig out a purely intellectual main theme. It will be intelligent and right but it will lack charm for the actor. It can serve as a guide but not as a creative force.

"In order to determine the kind of stimulating super-objective we do need to arouse our inner natures, I shall put a number of questions and answer them.

"Can we use a super-objective that is not right from the author's point of view, and yet is fascinating to us actors?

"No. It is not only useless but dangerous. It can only draw the actors away from their parts and the play.

"Can we use a main theme which is merely *intellectual*? No, not a dry product of pure reason. And yet a conscious super-objective, that derives from interesting, creative thinking, is essential.

"What about an *emotional* objective? It is absolutely necessary to us, necessary as air and sunlight.

"And an objective based on *will* that involves our whole physical and spiritual being? It is necessary.

"What can be said of a super-objective that appeals to your creative imagination, which absorbs your whole attention, satisfies your sense of truth, and faith, and all the elements of your inner mood? Any such theme that puts your inner motive forces to work is food and drink for you as an artist.

"Consequently, what we need is a *super-objective which is in harmony with the intentions of the playwright and at the same time arouses a response in the soul of the actors. That means that we must search for it not only in the play but in the actors themselves.*

"Moreover the same theme, in the same part, set for all the actors who play it, will bring a different expression from each of them. Take some perfectly simple, realistic objective, such as: I wish to grow rich! Think of the variety of subtle motives, methods and conceptions you can put into the idea of wealth and its attainment. There is so much, too, that is individual in such a problem and cannot be subject to conscious analysis. Then take a more complicated super-objective, such as lies at the root of a symbolic play by Ibsen or an impressionistic play by Maeterlinck, and you will find that the subconscious element in it is incomparably more profound, complex and individual.

"All these individual reactions are of great significance. They give life and colour to a play. Without them the main theme would be dry and inanimate. What gives that intangible charm to a theme so that it infects all the actors playing one and the same part? Largely it is something we cannot dissect, rising from the subconscious with which it must be in close association."

Vanya was again distressed and asked, "Then how do we get at it?"

"In the same way you deal with the various 'elements'. You push it to the extreme limit of truthfulness and sincere belief in it, to the point where the subconscious comes in of its own accord.

"Here again you must make that small but extraordinarily important little 'addition', just as you did when we discussed the extreme development of the functions of the 'elements', and again when we had up the question of the through line of action."

"It can't be very easy to find such an irresistible super-objective," someone said.

"It is impossible to do it without inner preparation. The usual practice, however, is quite different. The director sits in his study and goes over a play. At almost the first rehearsal he announces the main theme to the actors. They try to follow his direction. Some, by accident, may get hold of the inner essence of the play. Others will approach it in an external, formal way. They may use his theme at first, to give the right direction to their work but later they ignore it. They either follow the pattern of the production, the 'business', or they go after the plot and a mechanical rendering of the action and the lines.

"Naturally, a super-objective that leads to such results has lost all its significance. An actor must find the main theme for himself. If, for any reason, one is given to him by someone else he must filter it through his own being until his own emotions are affected by it.

"To find the main theme, is it sufficient to employ our usual methods of psycho-technique for bringing about a proper inner creative state, and then add the extra touch which leads to the region of the subconscious?

"In spite of the great value I lay on that preparatory work, I must confess that I do not think even the inner state it creates is capable of undertaking the search for the super-objective. You cannot feel around for it outside of the play itself. So you must, even in some small degree, feel the atmosphere of your make-believe existence in the play and then pour those feelings into your already prepared inner state. Just as yeast breeds fermentation, this sense of life in a play will bring your creative faculties to boiling point."

"How do we introduce yeast into our creative state?" said I, puzzled. "How can we make ourselves feel the life of the play before we have even studied it?"

Grisha confirmed me. He said, "Of course, you must study the play and its main theme first."

"Without any preparation, *à froid*?" the Director broke in. "I have already explained to you what that results in, and I have protested against that type of approach to a play or a part.

"My main objection, however, is to putting an actor in an impossible position. He must not be forcibly fed on other people's ideas, conceptions, emotion memories or feelings. Each person has to live through his own experiences. It is important that they be individual to him and analogous to those of the person he is to portray. An actor cannot be fattened like a capon. His own appetite must be tempted. When that is aroused he will demand the material he needs for simple actions; he will then absorb what is given him and make it his own. The director's job is to get the actor to ask and look for the details that will put life into his part. He will not need these details for an intellectual analysis of his part. He will want them for the carrying out of actual objectives.

"Besides, any information and material which he does not need immediately to pursue his aims only clutters up his mind and interferes with his work. He should be careful to avoid this, especially during the early period of creativeness."

"Then what can we do?"

"Yes," Grisha said, echoing Vanya. "You tell us we may not study the play and yet we must know it!"

"Again I must remind you that the work we are discussing is based on the creation of lines formed from small, accessible, physical objectives, small truths, belief in them, which are taken from the play itself and which give to it a living atmosphere.

"Before you have made a detailed study of the play or your part, execute some one small action (I do not care how slight it is), which you do with sincerity and truthfulness.

"Let us say that one of the persons in the play has to come into a room. Can you walk into a room?" asked Tortsov.

"I can," answered Vanya promptly.

"All right then, walk in. But let me assure you that you cannot do it until you know who you are, where you came from, what room you are entering, who lives in the house, and a mass of other given circumstances that must influence your action. To fill all that in so that you can enter the room as you should, will oblige you to learn something about the life of the play.

"Moreover, the actor has to work out these suppositions for himself and give them his own interpretation. If the director tries to force them on him the result is violence. In my way of doing, this cannot happen because the actor asks the director for what he needs as he needs it. This is an important condition for free, individual creativeness.

"An artist must have full use of his own spiritual, human

material because that is the only stuff from which he can fashion
a living soul for his part. Even if his contribution is slight, it is
the better because it is his own.

"Suppose, as the plot unfolds, when you come into that room
you meet a creditor and that you are far behind on the payment
of your debt to him. What would you do?"

"I don't know," exclaimed Vanya.

"You have to know, otherwise you cannot play the part. You
will just say your lines mechanically and act with pretense
instead of truth. You must put yourself into some position
analogous to that of your character. If necessary, you will add
new suppositions. Try to remember when you yourself were ever
in a similar position and what you did. If you never were in one,
create a situation in your imagination. Sometimes you can live
more intensely, more keenly, in your imagination than in real
life. If you make all your preparations for your work in a
human, real way, not mechanically; if you are logical and coherent in your purposes and actions, and if you consider all the
attending conditions of the life of your part, I do not doubt for
a moment that you will know just how to act. Compare what
you have decided on with the plot of the play and you will feel
a certain kinship with it, to a great or small degree. You will
come to feel that, given the circumstances, the opinions, the
social position of the character you are playing, you would be
bound to act as he did.

"That closeness to your part we call perception of yourself in
the part and of the part in you.

"Suppose you go through the whole play, all of its scenes,
bits, objectives, and that you find the right actions and accustom
yourself to executing them from start to finish. You will then
have established an external form of action which we call the
'physical life of a part'. To whom do these actions belong, to
you or to the part?"

"To me, of course," said Vanya.

"The physical aspect is yours and the actions too. But the
objectives, their inner foundation and sequence, all the given

circumstances are mutual. Where do you leave off and where does your part begin?"

"That's impossible to say," answered Vanya, perplexed.

"All you must remember is that the actions you have worked out are not simply external. They are based on inner feelings; they are reinforced by your belief in them. Inside of you, parallel to the line of physical actions, you have an unbroken line of emotions verging on the subconscious. You cannot follow the line of external action sincerely and directly and not have the corresponding emotions."

Vanya made a gesture of despair.

"I see your head is swimming already. That is a good sign because it shows that so much of your role has already become mixed into your own self that you cannot possibly tell where to draw the line between you and your part. Because of that state you will feel yourself closer than ever to your part.

"If you go through a whole play that way you will have a real conception of its inner life. Even when that life is still in the embryonic stage, it is vital. Moreover, you can speak for your character in your own person. This is of utmost importance as you develop your work systematically and in detail. Everything that you add from an inner source will find its rightful place. Therefore, you should bring yourself to the point of taking hold of a new role concretely, as if it were your own life. When you sense that real kinship to your part, you will be able to pour feelings into your inner creative state, which borders on the subconscious, and boldly begin the study of the play and its main theme.

"You will now realize what a long, arduous task it is to find a broad, deep, stirring super-objective and through line of action that will be capable of leading you to the threshold of the subconscious and carrying you off into its depths. Also you see now how important it is, during your search, to sense what the author of the play had in his mind and to find in yourself a responsive chord.

"How many themes must be cut back so that others will

grow! How many times must we aim and shoot before we hit the bull's eye!

"Every real artist should make it his object, while he is on the stage, to centre his entire creative concentration on just the super-objective and through line of action, in their broadest and deepest meaning. If they are right all the rest will be brought about subconsciously, miraculously, by nature. This will happen on condition that the actor recreates his work, each time he repeats his part, with sincerity, truth and directness. It is only on that condition that he will be able to free his art from mechanical and stereotyped acting, from 'tricks' and all forms of artificiality. If he accomplishes this he will have real people and real life all around him on the stage, and living art which has been purified from all debasing elements."

6

"Let us go still farther!" exclaimed the Director as he began the lesson. "Imagine some IDEAL ARTIST who has decided to devote himself to a single, large purpose in life: to elevate and entertain the public by a high form of art; to expound the hidden, spiritual beauties in the writings of poetic geniuses. He will give new renderings of already famous plays and parts, in ways calculated to bring out their more essential qualities. His whole life will be consecrated to this high cultural mission.

"Another type of artist may use his personal success to convey his own ideas and feelings to the masses. Great people may have a variety of high purposes.

"In their cases the super-objective of any one production will be merely a step in the fulfillment of an important life purpose, which we shall call a *supreme objective* and its execution a *supreme through line of action*.

"To illustrate what I mean I shall tell you of an incident from my own life.

"A long time ago, when our company was on tour in St. Petersburg, I was kept late in the theatre by an unsuccessful, badly prepared rehearsal. I was upset by the attitude of some of my colleagues. I was tired and angry as I left. Suddenly I found myself in a mass of people in the square before the theatre. Bonfires were blazing, people were sitting on campstools, on the snow half asleep, some were huddled in a kind of tent that protected them from the cold and wind. The extraordinary number of people—there were thousands of them—were waiting for morning and the box office to open.

"I was deeply stirred. To appreciate what these people were doing I had to ask myself: 'What event, what glorious prospect, what amazing phenomenon, what world-famous genius could induce me to shiver night after night out in the cold, especially when this sacrifice would not even give me the desired ticket but only a coupon entitling me to stand in line on the chance of obtaining a seat in the theatre?'

"I could not answer the question because I could not find any happening that could persuade me to risk my health, perhaps even my life, for its sake. Think what the theatre meant to those people! We should be deeply conscious of that. What an honour for us that we can bring such a high order of happiness to thousands of people. I was instantly seized with the desire to set a supreme goal for myself, the carrying out of which would constitute a supreme through line of action and in which all minor objectives would be absorbed.

"The danger would lie in letting one's attention centre for too long on some small, personal problem."

"Then what would happen?"

"The same thing that happens to a child when he ties a weight on the end of a string and winds it up on a stick. The more it winds the shorter the string becomes and the smaller the circle it describes. Finally it strikes the stick. But suppose another child pushes his stick into the orbit of the weight. Its momentum will cause it to wind its string on the second stick and the first child's game is ruined.

"We actors have a tendency to become sidetracked in the same way, and to put our energy into problems aside from our main purpose. That, of course, is dangerous and has a deteriorating influence on our work."

7

All during these recent lessons I had been rather dismayed at hearing so much reasoning about the subconscious. The subconscious is inspiration. How can you *reason* about it? I was even more shocked by being obliged to piece the subconscious together out of small bits and crumbs. So I went to the Director and spoke my mind.

"What makes you think," said he, "that the subconscious belongs altogether to inspiration? Without stopping to think, instantly, give me the name of some noun!"

Here he turned abruptly to Vanya who said, "A shaft."

"Why a shaft, why not a table, which is standing in front of you, or a chandelier, hanging overhead?"

"I don't know," answered Vanya.

"Neither do I," said Tortsov. "Moreover, I know that no one knows. Only your subconscious can tell why that particular object came into the foreground of your mind."

Here he put another question to Vanya: "What are you thinking about, and what do you feel?"

"I?" Vanya hesitated, then he ran his fingers through his hair, stood up abruptly and then sat down, rubbed his wrists on his knees, picked up a scrap of paper from the floor and folded it up, all this in preparation of his reply.

Tortsov laughed heartily.

"Let me see you repeat *consciously* every little movement you just made before you were ready to answer my question. Only your subconscious could solve the puzzle of why you went through all those motions."

Thereupon he turned back to me and said, "Did you notice how everything Vanya did was lacking in inspiration yet contained a great deal of subconsciousness? So, too, you will find it to some degree in the simplest act, desire, problem, feeling, thought, communication or adjustment. We live very close to it ordinarily. We find it in every step we take. Unfortunately we cannot adapt all of these moments of subconsciousness to our uses, and also there are fewer of them where we need them most, when we are on the stage. Just try to find any in a well-polished, ingrained, hackneyed, production. There will be nothing in it but hard and fast, established habits, conscious and mechanical."

"But mechanical habits are partly subconscious," insisted Grisha.

"Yes, but not the kind of subconsciousness we are discussing," replied Tortsov. "We need a creative, human, subconscious and the place to look for it above all is in a stirring objective and its through line of action. There consciousness and subconsciousness are subtly and marvelously blended. When an actor is completely absorbed by some profoundly moving objective, so that he throws his whole being passionately into its execution, he reaches a state that we call *inspiration*. In it almost everything he does is subconscious and he has no conscious realization of how he accomplishes his purpose.

"So you see, these periods of subconsciousness are scattered all through our lives. Our problem is to remove whatever interferes with them and to strengthen any elements that facilitate their functioning."

Our lesson was short today as the Director was appearing in a performance in the evening.

8

"Now let us have a check up," proposed the Director as he came into class today, for our last lesson.

"After nearly a year's work, each of you must have formed a definite conception of the dramatic, creative process. Let us try to compare that conception with the one you had when you came here.

"Maria, do you remember searching for a brooch in the folds of the curtain here because the continuance of your work in our school depended on your finding it? Can you recall how hard you tried, how you ran around and pretended to play despair, and how you enjoyed it? Would that kind of acting satisfy you now?"

Maria thought for a moment and then an amused smile broke over her face. Finally she shook her head, evidently entertained by the memory of her former naïve ways.

"You see, you laugh. And why? Because you used to play 'in general', trying to reach your goal by a direct onslaught. It is not surprising that all you accomplished was to give an external and wrong picture of the feelings of the person you were portraying.

"Now remember what you experienced when you played the scene with the foundling infant, and you found yourself rocking a dead baby. Then tell me, when you contrast your inner mood in that scene with your former exaggeration, whether you are satisfied with what you have learned here during this course."

Maria was thoughtful. Her expression was first serious and then sombre; there was a look of terror in her eyes for an instant, then she nodded her head affirmatively.

"Now you are no longer laughing," said Tortsov. "Indeed, the very memory of that scene has almost brought you to tears. Why? Because in creating that scene you followed an entirely different path. You did not make a direct assault on the feelings of your spectators. You planted the seeds and let them come to fruition. You followed the laws of creative nature.

"But you have to know how to induce that dramatic state. Technique alone cannot create an image that you can believe in and to which both you and your spectators can give yourselves up completely. So now you realize that creativeness is not a technical trick. It is not an external portrayal of images and passions as you used to think.

"*Our type of creativeness is the conception and birth of a new being—the person in the part. It is a natural act similar to the birth of a human being.*

"If you follow each thing that happens in an actor's soul during the period in which he is living into his part, you will admit that my comparison is right. Each dramatic and artistic image, created on the stage, is unique and cannot be repeated, just as in nature.

"As with human beings, there is an analogous, embryonic stage.

"In the creative process there is the father, the author of the play; the mother, the actor pregnant with the part; and the child, the role to be born.

"There is the early period when the actor first gets to know his part. Then they become more intimate, quarrel, are reconciled, marry and conceive.

"In all this the director helps the process along as a sort of matchmaker.

"Actors, in this period, are influenced by their parts, which affect their daily lives. Incidentally the period of gestation for a part is at least as long as that of a human being, and often considerably longer. If you analyse this process you will be convinced that laws regulate organic nature, whether she is creating a new phenomenon biologically or imaginatively.

"You can go astray only if you do not understand that truth; if you do not have confidence in nature; if you try to think up 'new principles', 'new bases', 'new art'. Nature's laws are binding on all, without exception, and woe to those who break them."